THE CHRISTIAN ECLECTIC READERS
AND STUDY GUIDE™

THE
ECLECTIC FOURTH READER

by

William H. McGuffey

Revised and Edited by

Charles and Betty Burger

WILLIAM B. EERDMANS PUBLISHING COMPANY
GRAND RAPIDS, MICHIGAN / CAMBRIDGE, U.K.

A McCaffrey Communications, Inc. Book

First published 1837
This edition published 1998 by
Wm. B. Eerdmans Publishing Co.
255 Jefferson Ave. S.E., Grand Rapids, Michigan 49503 /
P.O. Box 163, Cambridge CB3 9PU U.K.

Revisions copyright © 1998 by McCaffrey Communications, Inc.
A McCaffrey Communications, Inc. Book
All rights reserved

Printed in the United States of America

02 01 00 99 98   7 6 5 4 3 2 1

Set of five volumes, including study guide,
ISBN 0-8028-4480-4

CONTENTS

LESSON I

Remarkable Preservation — Prof. Wilson

RULE. Be careful to pronounce every syllable distinctly and not to join the words together. Nothing is more important to good reading than attention to this rule, and yet most young readers violate it. This rule is so important that the first eleven lessons will all be under it.

EXERCISES UNDER THE RULE. In the following exercises, difficult sounds have been introduced which are commonly spoken indistinctly or entirely omitted. Before reading the lesson, read the exercises over several times slowly and distinctly. The difficult sounds are italicized.

He was *incapable of* it. (Here take care not to join *ble* and *of*.)

He was *amiable, respectable, formidable, unbearable, intolerable, unmanageable, terrible*. (Here the sound *ble* must be fully sounded.)

He was *branded* as a traitor. Thou *prob'st* my wound. He was *stretched on* the floor. But *Ruth clave* unto her.

You have often asked me to describe to you on paper an event in my life which, at the distance of thirty years, I cannot look back to without horror. No words can give an adequate image of the miseries I suffered during that fearful night. I shall try, nevertheless, to give you something like a faint shadow of them, that from it your soul may conceive what I must have suffered.

I was, you know, on my voyage back to my native country after an absence of five years spent in unintermitting toil in a foreign land, to which I had been driven by a singular fatality. Our voyage had been most cheerful and prosperous, and on Christmas day we were within fifty leagues of port. Passengers and crew were all in the highest spirits, and the ship was alive with mirth and jollity.

The ship was sailing at the rate of seven knots an hour. A strong snowstorm blew, but steadily and without danger. The ship kept boldly on her course, close reefed and mistress of the storm. While leaning over the gunwale, admiring the water rushing by like a foaming cataract, by some unaccountable accident I lost my balance and in an instant fell overboard into the sea.

I remember a convulsive shuddering all over my body and a hurried leaping of my heart as I felt myself about to lose hold of the vessel. Afterwards I had a sensation of the most icy chillness from immersion in the waves, but I remember nothing resembling a fall or precipitation. When below the water, I think that a momentary belief rushed across my mind that the ship had suddenly sunk and that I was but one of a perishing crew. I imagined that I felt a hand with long fingers clutching at my legs. I made violent efforts to escape, dragging after me, as I thought, the body of some drowning wretch.

On rising to the surface, I recollected in a moment what had befallen me. I uttered a cry of horror which is in my ears to this day and often makes me shudder as if it were the mad shriek of another person in extremity of perilous agony. Often have I dreamed over again that dire moment, and the cry I utter in my sleep is said to be something more horrible than a human voice. No ship was to be seen. She was gone forever.

The little happy world to which, a moment before, I had belonged had been swept by, and I felt that God had flung me at once from the heart of joy, delight, and happiness into the uttermost abyss of mortal misery and despair. Yes! I felt that Almighty God had done this — that there was an act, a fearful act of Providence. Miserable worm that I was, I thought that the act was cruel, and a sort of wild, indefinite, objectless rage and wrath assailed me and took for awhile the place of that first shrieking terror. I gnashed my teeth and cursed myself and, with bitter tears and yells, blasphemed the name of God.

It is true, my friend, that I did so. God forgave that wickedness. The Being, whom I then cursed, was in His tender mercy not unmindful of me — of me, a poor, blind, miserable, mistaken worm. The waves dashed over me, struck me on the face, and howled at me; the winds yelled and the snow beat like drifting sand into my eyes — and the ship, the *ship* was *gone*. There I was left to struggle and buffet and gasp and sink and perish alone, unseen and unpitied by man and, as I thought, too, by the everlasting God.

I tried to penetrate the surrounding darkness with my glaring eyes, eyes that felt as if they were leaping from their sockets. I saw, as if by miraculous power, to a great distance through the night — but no ship — nothing but white-crested waves and the dismal noise of thunder.

I shouted, shrieked, and yelled, that I might be heard by the crew, till my voice was gone — and that, too, when I knew that there were none to hear me. At last I became utterly speechless, and when I tried to call aloud, there was nothing but a silent gasp and convulsion. All the while the waves came upon me like stunning blows reiterated and drove me along like a log of wood or a dead animal.

All this time I was not conscious of any act of swimming, but I soon found that I had instinctively been exerting all my power and skill; both were requisite to keep me alive in the tumultuous wake of the ship. Then something struck me harder than a wave. What it was I knew not, but I grasped it with a passionate violence, for the hope of salvation came suddenly over me. With a sudden transition from despair, I felt that I was rescued.

I had the same thought as if I had been suddenly heaved on shore by a wave. The crew had thrown overboard everything they thought could afford me the slightest chance of escape from death, and a hen coop had drifted towards me. At once all the stories I had ever read of mariners miraculously saved at sea rushed across my recollection. I had an object to cling to which I knew would enable me to prolong my existence.

I was no longer helpless on the cold weltering world of waters. The thought that my friends were thinking of me and doing all they could for me gave to me a wonderful courage. I may yet pass the night in the ship, I thought, and

I looked around eagerly to hear the rush of her prow or to see through the snowdrift the gleaming of her sails.

This was but a momentary gladness. The ship, I knew, could not be far off, but for any good she could do me, she might as well have been in the heart of the Atlantic Ocean. Ere she could have altered her course, I must have drifted a long way to leeward, and in that dim snowy night how was such a speck to be seen? I saw a flash of lightning, and then there was thunder. It was the ship firing a gun to let me know, if still alive, that she was lying somewhere nearby.

But wherefore? I was separated from her by a dire necessity — by many thousand fierce waves that would not let my shrieks be heard. Each succeeding gun was heard fainter and fainter till at last I cursed the sound that, scarcely heard above the hollow rumbling of the tempestuous sea, told me that the ship was farther and farther off, till she and her heartless crew had left me to my fate.

Why did they not send out all their boats to row round and round all that night through for the sake of one whom they pretended to love so well? I blamed, blessed, and cursed them by fits until every emotion of my soul was exhausted, as I clung in sullen despair to the wretched piece of wood that still kept me from eternity.

Everything was now seen in its absolute dreadful reality. I was a castaway — no hope of rescue. It was broad daylight and the storm had ceased, but clouds lay round the horizon and no land was to be seen. What dreadful clouds! some black as pitch and charged with thunder, others like cliffs of fire, and here and there all streaked over with blood. It was indeed a sullen, wrathful, and despairing sky.

The sun itself was a dull brazen orb, cold, dead, and beamless. I beheld three ships afar off, but all their heads were turned away from me. For whole hours they would adhere motionless to the sea while I drifted away from them, and then a rushing wind would spring up and carry them, one by one, into the darkness of the stormy distance. Many birds came close to me as if to flap me with their large spreading wings, screamed round and round me, and then flew away in their strength, beauty, and happiness.

I now felt myself indeed dying. A calm came over me. I prayed devoutly for forgiveness of my sins and for all my friends on earth. A ringing was in my ears, and I remember only the hollow fluctuations of the sea, with which I seemed to be blended, and a sinking down and down to an unfathomable depth, which I thought was Death, and into the kingdom of the eternal Future.

I awoke from insensibility and oblivion with a hideous, racking pain in my head and loins, and in a place of utter darkness. I heard a voice say, "Praise the Lord." My agony was dreadful and I cried aloud. Wan, glimmering, melancholy lights kept moving to and fro. I heard dismal whisperings, and now and then a pale silent ghost glided by. A hideous din was overhead and around me the fierce dashing of the waves. Was I in the land of spirits?

But, why strive to recount the mortal pain of my recovery, the soul-humbling gratitude that took possession of my being? I was lying in the cabin of a ship and kindly tended by a humane and skillful man. I had been picked up, apparently dead, and cold. The hand of God was there.

Adieu, my dear friend. It is now the hour of rest, and I hasten to fall down on my knees before the merciful Being who took pity upon me and who, at the intercession of our Redeemer, may, I hope, pardon all my sins.

QUESTIONS. 1. Narrate this story in your own words. 2. What were the professor's feelings when he first fell into the water? 3. What did he imagine was clutching at his heels? 4. How did he act upon rising to the surface? 5. How did he escape a watery grave?

SPELL AND DEFINE. 1. adequate 2. unintermitting 3. passengers 4. moonlight 5. gunwale (pronounced *gunnel*) 6. unaccountable 7. shuddering 8. immersion 9. precipitation 10. momentary 11. clutching 12. uttermost 13. shrieking 14. unmindful 15. surrounding 16. miraculous 17. instinctively 18. overboard 19. leeward 20. tempestuous 21. streaked 22. fluctuations 23. unfathomed

LESSON II

The Maniac — Anonymous

RULE. Be careful to pronounce every syllable distinctly and not to join the words together.

EXERCISES UNDER THE RULE. Read over several times.

The *ribs of death*. Can you *cry crackers, crime, cruelty, crutches?* The *orb'd moon*. It was the worst *act* of all *acts*. It is a *mixed government*. The *idle spindle*. Long *droves of cattle*. Their *deeds show* their feelings. The *length and breadth and height and depth of* the thing. It was *highly and holily* done.

A gentleman who had traveled in Europe relates that he one day visited the hospital of Berlin, where he saw a man whose exterior was very striking. His figure, tall and commanding, was bending with age, but more with sorrow. The few scattered hairs which remained on his temples were white, almost as the driven snow, and the deepest melancholy was depicted in his countenance.

On inquiring who he was and what brought him there, he startled, as if from sleep, and after looking round him, began with slow and measured steps to stride the hall, repeating in a low but audible voice, "Once one is two. Once one is two."

Now and then he would stop and remain for some minutes with his arms folded on his breast, as if in contemplation. Then, again resuming his walk, he would continue to repeat, "Once one is two. Once one is two." His story, as our traveler understood it, was as follows.

Conrad Lange, collector of the revenues of the city of Berlin, had long been known as a man whom nothing could divert from the paths of honesty. Scrupulously exact in all his dealings and assiduous in the discharge of his official duties, he had acquired the good will and esteem of all who knew him and the confidence of the minister of finance, whose duty it was to inspect the accounts of all officers connected with the revenue.

On casting up his accounts at the close of a particular year, he found a *deficit* of ten thousand ducats. Alarmed at this discovery, he went to the minister, presented his accounts, and informed him that he did not know how it had arisen and that he had been robbed by some person bent on his ruin.

Thinking it a duty to secure a person who might probably be a defaulter, the minister had him arrested and put his accounts into the hands of one of his secretaries for inspection. The secretary returned them the day after with the information that the deficiency arose from a miscalculation: in multiplying, Mr. Lange had said *once one is two* instead of *once one is one.*

The poor man was immediately released from confinement, his accounts returned, and the mistake pointed out. During his imprisonment, which lasted but two days, he had neither eaten, drunk, nor taken any repose — and when he appeared, his countenance was as pale as death. On receiving his accounts, he was a long time silent. Then suddenly awaking as if from a trance, he repeated, "Once one is two."

He appeared to be entirely insensible of his situation, would neither eat nor drink unless solicited, and took notice of nothing that passed around him. While repeating his accustomed phrase, if anyone corrected him by saying, "Once one is *one,*" he was recalled for a moment and said, "Ah, right, once one *is* one." Then resuming his walk, he continued to repeat, "Once one is two." He died shortly after the traveler left Berlin.

This affecting story, whether true or untrue, obviously abounds with lessons of instruction. Alas! How easily is the human mind thrown off its "balance," especially when it is stayed on *this world* only and has no experimental knowledge of the meaning of the injunction of Scripture, to cast all our cares upon Him who careth for us and who heareth even the young ravens when they cry.

QUESTIONS. 1. Sketch the circumstances here narrated. 2. How do you account for the unhinging of this man's mind? 3. Is it common that one idea keeps possession of a maniac's mind?

SPELL AND DEFINE. 1. hospital   2. commanding   3. melancholy
4. measured   5. contemplation   6. traveler   7. assiduous   8. finance
9. defaulter   10. secretaries   11. miscalculation   12. multiplying
13. imprisonment 14. solicited 15. experimental

LESSON III

Scene at the Sandwich Islands — Stewart

RULE. Be careful to pronounce every syllable distinctly and not to join the words together.

EXERCISES UNDER THE RULE. Read over several times.

They *reef'd* the topsails. No dangers *frighten* him. He *quenched* a flame. She *laughs* at him. *A frame of adamant. She begged pardon.* Thou *look'st from* thy throne in the clouds and *laugh'st* at the storm. The *glowworm* lights her lamp. The table *groans beneath* its burden. All clothed in *rags an infant* lay. The birds were all *fledg'd* in the nest.

At an early hour of the morning, even before we had taken our breakfast on board ship, a single islander here or there or a group of three or four, wrapped in their large mantles of various hues, might be seen winding their way among the groves fringing the bay on the east or descending from the hills and ravine on the north towards the chapel. By degrees their numbers increased until, in a short time, every path along the beach and over the uplands presented an almost uninterrupted procession of both sexes and every age, all pressing to the house of God.

So few canoes were round the ship yesterday and the landing place had been so little thronged as our boats passed to and fro, that one might have thought the district but thinly inhabited. Now, however, such multitudes were seen gathering from various directions that the exclamation, *"What crowds of people! What crowds of people!"* was heard from the quarterdeck to the forecastle.

Even to me it was a sight of surprise — surprise not at the magnitude of the population but that the object for which they were evidently assembling should bring together so great a multitude. And as my thoughts re-echoed the words, "What crowds of people!" remembrances and affections of deep power came over me, and the silent musings of my heart were, "What a change — what a happy change!"

At this very place, only four years ago, the known wishes and example of chiefs of high authority, the daily persuasion of teachers, added to motives of curiosity and novelty, could scarcely induce a hundred of the inhabitants to give an irregular, careless, and impatient attendance on the services of the sanctuary. But now,

> Like mountain torrents pouring to the main,
> From every glen a living stream came forth —
> From every hill, in crowds, they hastened down,
> To worship Him, who deigns, in humblest fane,
> On wildest shore, to meet th' upright in heart.

The scene, as looked on from our ship in the stillness of a brightly-beaming Sabbath morning, was well calculated, with its associations, to prepare the mind for strong impressions on a nearer view, when the conclusion of our own public worship should allow us to go on shore. Mr. Goodrich had apprised us that he had found it expedient to hold both the services of the Sabbath in the forepart of the day, that all might have the benefit of two sermons and still reach their abodes before nightfall. For,

> Numbers dwelt remote,
> And first must traverse many a weary mile,
> To reach the altar of the God they love.

It was arranged that on this occasion the second service would be postponed so the officers would be at liberty to leave the ship. It was near twelve o'clock when we went on shore — the captain and first lieutenant, the purser, surgeon, several of the midshipmen, and I. Though the services had commenced when we landed, large numbers were seen circling the doors without, but, as we afterwards found, only from the impracticability of obtaining places within.

The house was an immense structure capable of containing many thousands, every part of which was filled except for a small area in front of the pulpit where seats were reserved for us. We made our way in slow and tedious procession because of the difficulty of finding a spot to place even our footsteps without treading on limbs of the people, seated on their feet as closely, almost, as they could be stowed.

As we entered, Mr. Goodrich paused in his sermon until we were seated. I ascended the pulpit beside him, from which I had a full view of the congregation. The suspenseful attention of the people was only momentary, notwithstanding the novelty of the officers in their laced coats, cocked hats, and other appendages of naval uniform. I can scarcely describe the emotions experienced in glancing over the immense number, seated so thickly on the matted floor as to seem literally one mass of heads, covering an area of more than nine thousand square feet. The sight was most striking and soon became, not only to me but to some of my fellow officers, deeply affecting.

I have listened with delighted attention to some of the highest eloquence the pulpits of America and England of the present day can boast. I have seen tears of conviction and penitence flow freely under the sterner truths of the Word of God. But it was left for one at Hido, the most obscure corner of these distant islands, to excite the liveliest emotions ever experienced and leave the deepest impressions of the extent and unsearchable riches of the Gospel which I have ever known.

It seemed, even while I gazed, that the majesty of that Power might be seen rising and erecting to itself a throne, permanent and glorious, in the hearts of these but recently utterly-benighted and deeply-polluted people. When I compared them, as they had once been known to me and as they now appeared, the change seemed the result of a mandate scarcely less mighty in its power or speedy in its result than that exhibited when it was said, "Let there be light, and there was light"!

The depth of the impression arose from the irresistible conviction that the Spirit of God was there. It could have been nothing else. With the exception of the inferior chiefs who have charge of the district, their dependents, two or three native members of the church, and the mission family, scarcely one of the whole multitude was in other than the native dress, the simple garments of their primitive state.

In this respect and in the attitude of sitting, the assembly was purely pagan. But the breathless silence, the eager attention, the half-suppressed sigh, the tear, and the various feelings of sadness, peacefulness, and joyousness discoverable in the faces of many — all spoke the presence of an invisible but omnipotent Power — the Power which alone can melt and renew the heart of man, even as it alone first brought it into existence.

It was, in a word, a heathen congregation laying hold on the hopes of eternity — a heathen congregation fully sensible of the degradation of their original state, exulting in the first beams of truth and in the no uncertain dawning of the Sun of Righteousness, thirsting after knowledge even while they sweetly drank of the waters of life. Under the inspiring influence, by every look, they expressed the heartfelt truth: "Beautiful on the mountains are the feet of him that bringeth good tidings, that bringeth good tidings of good, that publisheth SALVATION!"

The simple appearance and yet Christian deportment of that obscure congregation, whom I had recently known only as a set of rude, licentious, and wild pagans, did more to rivet the conviction of the divine origin of the Bible and of the holy influences by which it is accompanied to the hearts of men than all the arguments, apologies, and defenses of Christianity I ever read.

An entire moral reformation has taken place. Instruction of every kind is eagerly and universally sought and, from many a humble dwelling, now

Is daily heard
The voice of prayer and praise to Jacob's God,
And many a heart in secret heaves the sigh,
To Him who hears, well pleased, the sigh contrite.

QUESTIONS. 1. Where are the Sandwich Islands? 2. What is the degree of population? 3. What change has taken place in the moral character of the population? In how long a time? 4. To what is this change to be attributed? 5. Give your own description of this.

SPELL AND DEFINE. 1. uninterrupted 2. procession 3. multitudes 4. remembrances 5. re-echoed 6. assembling 7. hundred 8. irregular 9. inhabitants 10. associations 11. apprised 12. nightfall 13. postponed 14. midshipmen 15. impracticability 16. congregation 17. appendages 18. worshiping

LESSON IV

Contrasted Soliloquies — Jane Taylor

RULE. Be careful to pronounce every syllable distinctly and not to join the words together.

EXERCISES UNDER THE RULE. Read over several times.

My *Uncle Toby* was *racked with* pain. *Racked with whirlwinds.* *Victory will weaken* the enemy. *Think'st thou* so meanly of me? On *the river Elbe*. We saw *the elk*. And he cried, *hold, hold, hold. Fall'n, fall'n, fall'n, fall'n, fall'n from* his high estate. There was no *help for* it. He *watch'd and wept.* He *felt and pray'd* for all. It was a *willfully false* account.

"Alas!" exclaimed a silver-headed sage, "how narrow is the utmost extent of human science! How circumscribed the sphere of intellectual exertion! I have spent my life in acquiring knowledge, but how little do I know! The farther I attempt to penetrate the secrets of nature the more I am bewildered and benighted. Beyond a certain limit all is but confusion or conjecture, so that the advantage of the learned over the ignorant consists greatly in having ascertained how little is to be known.

"It is true that I can measure the sun and compute the distances of the planets; I can calculate their periodic movements and even ascertain the laws by which they perform their sublime revolutions. But with regard to their construction and the beings which inhabit them, what do I know more than the clown?

"Delighting to examine the economy of nature in our own world, I have analyzed the elements and have given names to their component parts. And yet, should I not be as much at a loss to explain the burning of fire or to account for the liquid quality of water as the vulgar, who use and enjoy them without thought or examination?

"I remark that all bodies, unsupported, fall to the ground, and I am taught to account for this by the law of gravitation. But what have I gained here more than a term? Does it convey to my mind any idea of the nature of that mysterious and invisible chain which draws all things to a common center? I observe the effect, I give a name to the cause, but can I explain or comprehend it?

"Pursuing the track of the naturalist, I have learned to distinguish the *animal, vegetable,* and *mineral* kingdoms and to divide these into their distinct tribes and families. But can I tell, after all this toil, whence a single blade of grass derives its vitality? Could the most minute research enable me to discover the exquisite pencil that paints and fringes the flower of the field? Have I ever detected the secret that gives their brilliant dye to the ruby and the emerald, or the art that enamels the delicate shell?

"I observe the *instinct* of animals and speculate upon its various degrees of approximation to the reason of man. But, after all, I know as little of the cogitations of the brute as he does of mine. When I see a flight of birds overhead performing their evolutions or steering their course to some distant settlement, their signals and cries are as unintelligible to me as are the learned languages to the unlettered rustic. I understand as little of their policy and laws as they do of Blackstone's Commentaries.

"Leaving the material creation, my thoughts have often ascended to loftier subjects and indulged in *metaphysical* speculation. And here, while I easily perceive in myself the two distinct qualities of matter and mind, I am baffled in every attempt to comprehend their mutual dependence and mysterious connection. When my hand moves in obedience to my will, have I the most distant conception of the manner in which the volition is either communicated or understood? Thus, in the exercise of one of the most simple and ordinary actions, I am perplexed and confounded if I attempt to account for it.

"Again, how many years of my life were devoted to the acquisition of those languages by the means of which I might explore the records of remote ages and become familiar with the learning and literature of other times! What have I gathered from these but the mortifying fact that man has ever been struggling with his own impotence and vainly endeavoring to overleap the bounds which limit his anxious inquiries?

"Alas! then, what have I gained by my laborious research but a humbling conviction of my weakness and ignorance? How little has man, at his best estate, of which to boast! What folly in him to glory in his contracted power or to value himself upon his imperfect acquisitions!"

"Well," exclaimed a young lady just returned from school, "my education is at last finished! Indeed, it would be strange if, after five years' hard application, anything were left incomplete. Happily, *that* is all over now, and I have nothing to do but to exercise my various accomplishments.

"Let me see — as to *French,* I am complete mistress of that and speak it, if possible, with more fluency than English. *Italian* I can read with ease and pronounce very well, as well, at least, as any of my friends, and that is all one need wish for in Italian. *Music* I have learned until I am perfectly sick of it. But now that we have a grand piano, it will be delightful to play when we have company; I must still continue to practice a little. It is the only thing, I think, that I need now to improve myself in. Then there are my Italian songs! which everybody allows I sing with taste; since so few people can pretend to, I am particularly glad that I can.

"My *drawings* are universally admired — especially the shells and flowers, which are beautiful, certainly. Besides this, I have a decided taste in all kinds of fancy ornaments. And then my *dancing* and *waltzing* — in which our master himself owned that he could take me no farther — I have just the figure for it, certainly. It would be unpardonable if I did not excel.

"As to *common* things, *geography* and *history, poetry* and *philosophy* — thank my stars I have gotten through them all! so that I may consider myself not only perfectly accomplished but also thoroughly well informed. Well, to be sure, how much I have toiled through! The only wonder is that one head can contain it all!"

QUESTIONS. 1. What is the subject of this lesson? 2. What is meant by soliloquies? 3. What soliloquies are here contrasted? 4. What is the substance of the old man's soliloquy? 5. What is the substance of the young lady's? 6. Which reasons most correctly, the old man or the young lady? 7. What feeling is manifested by the old man in view of his attainments? 8. What by the young lady? 9. If we are truly wise, will we be vain?

SPELL AND DEFINE. 1. circumscribed 2. intellectual 3. penetrate 4. conjecture 5. ascertained 6. compute 7. revolutions 8. construction 9. economy 10. analyzed 11. component 12. gravitation 13. exquisite 14. animal 15. vegetable 16. mineral 17. vitality 18. enamels

19. instinct   20. approximation   21. cogitation   22. unintelligible
23. metaphysical 24. volition 25. incomplete 26. fluency 27. waltzing

LESSON V

On Letter Writing — Blackwood

RULE. Be careful to pronounce every syllable distinctly and not to join the words together.

EXERCISES UNDER THE RULE. Read over several times.

It was a species of *calx which* he showed me. The word *filch is* of doubtful derivation. If thou *fall'st*, thou *fall'st* a blessed martyr. *Health is indispensable* to the soldier. Those who lie *entombed in* the cemetery. The *attempt, and* not the deed, confounds us. But truth *and* liberty *and* virtue would fall with him. The *song began* from Jove. Do you mean *plain* or *playing?*

Epistolary as well as personal discourse is, according to the mode in which it is carried on, one of the pleasantest or most irksome things in the world. It is delightful to drop in on a friend without the solemn prelude of invitation and acceptance — to join a social circle where we may suffer our minds and hearts to relax and expand in the happy consciousness of perfect security from invidious remark and carping criticism. There we may give the reins to the sportiveness of innocent fancy or the enthusiasm of warm-hearted feeling, talking sense or nonsense (I pity people who *cannot* talk nonsense) without fear of being looked into icicles by the coldness of unimaginative people — those living pieces of clockwork who dare not themselves utter a word or lift up a little finger without first weighing the important point in the hair balance of propriety and good breeding.

It is equally delightful to let the pen talk freely and unpremeditatedly to one by whom we are sure of being understood. But a formal letter, like a ceremonious morning visit, is tedious alike to the writer and receiver. They are for the most part spun out with unmeaning phrases, trite observations, complimentary flourishes, and protestations of respect and attachment — not, however, deceitful, as they never deceive anybody. Oh, the misery of having to compose a set, proper, well worded, correctly pointed, polite, elegant epistle! — one that must have a beginning, a middle, and an end as methodically arranged and portioned out as the several parts of a sermon under three heads or the three gradations of shade in a schoolgirl's first landscape.

For my part, I would rather be set to beat hemp or weed in a turnip field than to write such a letter exactly every month or every fortnight at the precise point of time from the date of our correspondent's last letter, that he or she wrote after the reception of ours — as if one's thoughts bubbled up to the wellhead at regular periods, a pint at a time, to be bottled for immediate use. Thought! What has thought to do in such a correspondence? It murders thought, quenches fancy, wastes time, spoils paper, wears out goose quills. "I'd rather be a kitten and cry mew! than one of those same" prosing lettermongers.

Surely in this age of invention something may be struck out to obviate the necessity (if such necessity exists) of so degrading the human intellect. Why should not a sort of mute barrel organ be constructed on the plan of those that play sets of tunes and country dances, to indite a catalogue of polite epistles calculated for all the ceremonious observances of good breeding? Oh, the unspeakable relief (could such a machine be invented) of having only to *grind* an answer to one of one's "dear five hundred friends"!

Or, suppose there were to be an epistolary steam engine — aye, that's the thing — steam does everything nowadays. Dear Mr. Brunel, set about it, I beseech you, and achieve the most glorious of your undertakings. The block machine at Portsmouth would be nothing to it — *that* spares manual labor — *this* would relieve mental drudgery and thousands yet unborn.

But hold! I am not so sure the female sex in general may quite enter into my views of the subject. There are those who pique themselves on the elegant style of their letters or those fair scribblerinas just emancipated from boarding school restraints or the "dragonism" of their governess. They are just beginning to taste the refined enjoyments of sentimental, confidential, soul-breathing correspondence with some Angelina, Seraphina, or Laura Matilda inditing beautiful little notes with long-tailed letters upon vellum paper with pink margins, sealed with sweet mottoes and dainty devices, the whole deliciously perfumed with musk and attar of roses. These young ladies collect "copies of verses" and charades, keep albums, copy patterns, make bread seals, work little dogs upon footstools, and paint flowers without shadow. Oh! no, the epistolary steam engine will never come into vogue with those dear creatures. *They* must enjoy the "feast of reason and the flow of soul," and they must write — yes, and how they *do* write!

They are a genus of female scribes — unhappy innocents who groan in spirit at the dire necessity of having to hammer out one of those aforesaid terrible epistles. After they have, in due form, dated the gilt-edged sheet that lies outspread before them in appalling whiteness and felicitously achieved the graceful exordium, "My dear Mrs. P." or "My dear Lady V." or "My dear anything else," they then feel that they are *in for it* and must say something. Oh, that something that must come of nothing! Those bricks that must be made without straw! Those pages that must be filled with words! Yea, with words that must be sewed into sentences! Yea, with sentences that must *seem* to mean something, the whole to be tacked together, all neatly fitted and dovetailed so as to form one smooth, polished surface!

What were the labors of Hercules to such a task! The very thought of it puts me into a mental perspiration. From my inmost soul I compassionate the unfortunates now (at this very moment, perhaps) screwed up perpendicular in the seat of torture, having in the right hand a freshly nibbed patent pen dipped ever into the ink bottle, as if to hook up ideas, and under the outspread palm of the left hand a fair sheet of best Bath post (ready to receive thoughts yet unhatched), on which their eyes are riveted with a stare of disconsolate perplexity infinitely touching to a feeling mind.

I deeply sympathize in the miseries of such unhappy persons. Have I not groaned under similar horrors from the hour when I was first shut up (under lock and key, I believe) to indite a dutiful epistle to an honored aunt? I remember, as if it were yesterday, the moment when she who had enjoined the task entered to inspect the performance which, by her calculation, should have been fully completed. I remember how sheepishly I hung down my head when she snatched from before me the paper (on which I had made no further progress than, "My dear *ant,*"), angrily exclaiming: "What, child! Have you been shut up here three hours to call your aunt a pismire?"

From that hour of humiliation I have too often groaned under the endurance of similar penance, and I have learned from my own sufferings to compassionate those of my dear sisters in affliction. To such unhappy persons, then, I would fain offer a few hints (the fruit of long experience) which, if they have not already been suggested by their own observation, may prove serviceable in the hour of emergency. I address myself to *one* particular sufferer — there is something more confidential in that manner of communicating one's ideas; as Moore says, "Heart speaks to heart."

I say then, take always special care to write by candlelight, for not only is the apparently unimportant operation of snuffing the candle in itself a momentary relief to the depressing consciousness of mental vacuum, but not infrequently that trifling act or the brightening flame of the taper elicits, as it were, from the dull embers of fancy a sympathetic spark of fortunate conception. When such a one occurs, seize it quickly and dexterously but, at the same time, with such cautious prudence as not to huddle and contract in one short, paltry sentence that which, if ingeniously handled, may undulate gracefully and smoothly over a whole page.

For the more ready practice of this invaluable art of dilating, it will be expedient to stock your memory with a large assortment of those precious words of many syllables that fill whole lines at once, such as *incomprehensibly, amazingly, decidedly, solicitously, inconceivably, incontrovertibly.* To a distressed writer, an opportunity of using these is delightful. They run on with such delicious smoothness!

QUESTIONS. 1. Upon what does the pleasure of epistolary and social discourse depend? 2. What is meant by talking nonsense? 3. What is the intention of the writer of this piece?

SPELL AND DEFINE. 1. epistolary   2. invidious   3. enthusiasm
4. nonsense   5. unimaginative   6. wellhead   7. correspondent
8. lettermonger   9. invention   10. manual   11. scribblerinas
12. emancipated   13. genus   14. mental   15. compassionate
16. disconsolate 17. humiliation 18. elicits 19. communicating 20. dilate

LESSON VI

Ginevra — Rogers

RULE. Be careful to pronounce every syllable distinctly and not to join the words together.

EXERCISES UNDER THE RULE. Read over several times.

The *range of* the valleys is his. He was the *first ambassador sent.* *Swords and pens* were both employed. I do not *flinch from* the argument. He never *winced, for* it hurt him not. Do not *singe your* gown. *Pluck'd from* its native tree. *Nipped in* the bud. Thou *found'st me* poor and *keep'st me so.*

If ever you should come to Modena,
Stop at a palace near the Reggio Gate,

Dwelt in of old by one of the Donati.
Its noble gardens, terrace above terrace,
And rich in fountains, statues, cypresses,
Will long detain you — but, before you go,
Enter the house — forget it not, I pray you —
And look awhile upon a picture there.

'Tis of a lady in her earliest youth,
The last of that illustrious family;
Done by Zampieri — but by whom I care not.
He who observes it — ere he passes on,
Gazes his fill and comes and comes again,
That he may call it up when far away.

She sits, inclining forward as to speak,
Her lips half open, and her finger up,
As though she said, "Beware!" her vest of gold
Broidered with flowers and clasped from head to foot,
An emerald stone in every golden clasp;
And on her brow, fairer than alabaster,
A coronet of pearls.

But then her face,
So lovely, yet so arch, so full of mirth,
The overflowings of an innocent heart —
It haunts me still, though many a year has fled,
Like some wild melody!

Alone it hangs
Over a moldering heirloom; its companion,
An oaken chest half-eaten by the worm,
But richly carved by Antony of Trent
With Scripture stories from the life of Christ;
A chest that came from Venice and had held
The ducal robes of some old ancestors —
That by the way — it may be true or false.

But don't forget the picture, and you will not,
When you have heard the tale they told me there.

She was an only child — her name Ginevra,
The joy, the pride of an indulgent father;
And in her fifteenth year became a bride,
Marrying an only son, Francesco Doria,
Her playmate from her birth and her first love.

Just as she looks there, in her bridal dress,
She was all gentleness, all gaiety,
Her pranks the favorite theme of every tongue.
But now the day was come, the day, the hour;
Now, frowning, smiling for the hundredth time,
The nurse, that ancient lady, preached decorum;
And, in the luster of her youth, she gave
Her hand, with her heart in it, to Francesco.

Great was the joy, but at the nuptial feast,
When all sat down, the bride herself was wanting.
Nor was she to be found! Her father cried,
"'Tis but to make a trial of our love!"
And filled his glass to all, but his hand shook,
And soon from guest to guest the panic spread.

'Twas but that instant she had left Francesco,
Laughing and looking back and flying still,
Her ivory tooth imprinted on his finger.
But now, alas! she was not to be found;
Nor from that hour could anything be guessed,
But that she was not!

                              Weary of his life,
Francesco flew to Venice, and embarking,
Flung it away in battle with the Turk.
Donati lived — and long might you have seen
An old man wandering as in quest of something,

Something he could not find — he knew not what.
When he was gone, the house remained awhile,
Silent and tenantless — then went to strangers.

Full fifty years were past and all forgotten,
When on an idle day, a day of search
Mid the old lumber in the gallery,
That moldering chest was noticed, and 'twas said
By one as young, as thoughtless as Ginevra,
"Why not remove it from its lurking place?"
'Twas done as soon as said, but on the way
It burst, it fell; and lo! a skeleton
With here and there a pearl, an emerald stone,
A golden clasp, clasping a shred of gold.
All else had perished — save a wedding ring
And a small seal, her mother's legacy,
Engraved with a name, the name of both —
"Ginevra."

There, then, had she found a grave!
Within that chest had she concealed herself,
Fluttering with joy, the happiest of the happy;
When a spring lock, that lay in ambush there,
Fastened her down forever!

QUESTIONS. 1. Where is Modena? 2. Who was the painter of the picture? 3. Describe the attitude and dress. 4. What lies beneath the picture? 5. Relate the story which gives interest to the chest and picture.

SPELL AND DEFINE. 1. statues   2. terrace   3. cypresses
4. illustrious   5. broidered   6. emerald   7. overflowing   8. moldering
9. ancestors   10. heirloom   11. indulgent   12. ancient   13. nuptial
14. imprinted 15. embarking 16. engraved 17. ambush

LESSON VII

The Whale Ship — Prov. Lit. Journal

RULE. Be careful to pronounce every syllable distinctly and not to join the words together.

EXERCISES UNDER THE RULE. Read over several times.

We constructed *an arc* and began the problem. The *surf beat* heavily. *Arm! warriors, arm! Return to thy* dwelling, *all lovely return. Weave the warp* and *weave the woof.* Lend me *Smith's Thucydides.* Thou *tear'st* my heart asunder. I give my hand and *heart, too, to* this vote.

They who go down to the sea in ships pursue a perilous vocation and well deserve the prayers which are offered for them in the churches. It is a hard life — full of danger and of strange attraction. The seaman rarely abandons the glorious sea. It requires, however, a pretty firm spirit both to brave the ordinary dangers of the deep and to carry on war with its mightiest tenants. Yet it is a service readily entered upon and zealously followed, though indisputably the most laborious and most terrific of all human pursuits. Well might Burke speak glowingly of that hardy spirit of adventure, which had pursued this gigantic game from the constellations of the north to the frozen serpent of the south.

The most common accident to which whalers are exposed is that of being "stove," as they express it, by the huge animal before they can back out from their dangerous proximity. A slight tap of his tail is quite sufficient to shiver a common whaleboat to atoms. If this danger be escaped, the whale, with the harpoon in his hide, sinks beneath the sounding of the deep-sea lead. Not long will he stay at the bottom. He rises for air, and this is a signal for the renewal of the battle. The boat is drawn up, and the lance is buried in his giant body. Not safe is the game until it is fairly bagged. Often, in the moment of victory, the vanquished leviathan settles quietly down in the deep sea, and no tackle can draw him up. The curses of the exhausted seamen are "not loud, but deep."

On 28 May 1817, the *Royal Bounty,* an English ship, fell in with a great number of whales. There was neither ice nor land in sight. The boats were manned and sent in pursuit. After a chase of five hours, a harpooner, who had rowed out of sight of the ship, struck one of the whales. This was about four o'clock in the morning. The captain directed the course of the ship to the place where he had last seen the boats and at about eight o'clock got sight of the boat which displayed the signal for being fast. Soon after, another boat approached the first and struck a second harpoon.

By midday two more harpoons were struck, but such was the astonishing vigor of the whale that, although it constantly dragged through the water from four to six boats together with sixteen hundred fathoms of line, it pursued its flight nearly as fast as a boat could row. Whenever a boat passed beyond its tail, it would dive. All endeavors to lance it were, therefore, in vain. The crews of the loose boats then moored themselves to the fast boats. At eight o'clock in the evening a line was taken to the ship, with a view of retarding its flight, and topsails were lowered — but the harpoon "drew." In three hours another line was taken on board, which immediately snapped.

At four in the afternoon of the next day, thirty-six hours after the whale was struck, two of the fast lines were taken on board the ship. The wind blowing a moderately brisk breeze, the topgallant sails were taken in, the courses hauled up, and the topsails clewed down. In this situation she was towed directly to windward during an hour and a half, with the velocity of from one and a half to two knots. And then, though the whale must have been greatly exhausted, it beat the water with its fins and tail so tremendously that the sea around was in a continual foam; the most hardy seamen scarcely dared to approach it. At length, at about eight o'clock, after forty hours of incessant exertion, this formidable and astonishingly vigorous animal was killed.

The most strange and dreadful calamity that ever befell the wanderers of the sea, in any age, however, was that which happened in 1820 to the ship *Essex,* of Nantucket. Some of those who survived the terrible catastrophe are yet alive and bear their united testimony to the truth of the statements which one of them has published. It is a story which no man, for any conceivable purpose, would be likely to invent. The captain of the *Essex* is yet living upon his native island. It is a fact pregnant with meaning that, so vivid to this day is his recollection of the horrors which he witnessed, he is never heard to mention the subject, and nothing can induce him to speak of it. He has abandoned the sea forever. The story bears the marks of truth upon it. It may be briefly told.

The *Essex,* a sound and substantial ship, sailed for the Pacific Ocean on a whaling voyage from Nantucket on 12 August 1820. On 20 November, a shoal of whales was discovered. Three boats were manned and sent in pursuit. The mate's boat was struck by a whale, and he was obliged to return to the ship to repair the damage. While thus engaged, a sperm whale, eighty-five feet long, broke water about twenty rods from the ship, on her weather bow. He was going at the rate of three knots an hour, and the ship at the same rate, when he struck the bows of the vessel just forward of the chains.

The shock produced by the collision of two such masses of matter in motion may well be imagined. The ship shook like a leaf. The whale dove, passed under the vessel — grazed her keel — and appeared at the ship's length distant, lashing the sea with his fins and tail as if suffering the most horrible agony. He was evidently hurt by the collision and rendered frantic with rage. In a few minutes he seemed to recover himself and started, with great speed, directly across the bows of the vessel, to windward. Meantime, the hands on board discovered the vessel to be gradually settling down by the bows, and the pumps were to be rigged. While engaged in fixing the pumps, one of the men exclaimed, "Here he comes upon us again!"

The whale had turned at the distance of one hundred rods from the ship and was making for her with double his former speed. His pathway was white with foam. He struck her bow, and the blow shook every timber in the ship. Her bows were stove in. The whale dove under the vessel and disappeared. The vessel immediately filled, and the crew took to the boat that had returned. All this was transacted in the space of a few minutes. The other boats rowed up and when they came together — when a sense of their loneliness and helplessness came over them — no man had the power of utterance. They were in the midst of the "illimitable sea" — far, far from land — in open whaleboats, relying only on God for succor in this hour of their utmost need.

They gathered what they could from the wreck — the ship went down — and on 22 November they put away for the coast of South America, distant two thousand miles! How their hearts must have died within them as they looked at the prospect before and around them! After incredible hardships and sufferings, on 20 December they reached a low island. It was a mere sandbank, almost barren, which supplied them with nothing but water. On this island, desolate as it was, three of the men chose to remain rather than to commit themselves again to the uncertain chances of the sea.

On 27 December the three boats, with the remainder of the men, started in company from the island for Juan Fernandez, a distance of 2,500 miles! On 12 January the boats parted company in a gale. Then commenced a scene of suffering which cannot be contemplated without horror. The men died one after another. In the captain's boat, on 1 February, three only were living.

The mate's boat was taken up by the *Indian*, of London, on 19 February, *ninety-three days* from the time of the catastrophe, with three living men of that boat's crew. The captain's boat was taken up on 23 February by the *Dauphin* of Nantucket. The other boat was never heard from. The three men who were left on the island were saved by a ship which was sent for their deliverance. No wonder that the heart of that brave man recoils and shudders when this terrific scene is forced upon his recollection.

QUESTIONS. 1. What is the character of the seaman's profession (particularly of the whalers)? 2. What are the most common accidents to which whalers are liable? 3. How do they often lose their game when vanquished? 4. How long did it take to vanquish the whale first mentioned? 5. At what rate was he able to draw the ship through the water? 6. Can you give a sketch of what occurred to the ship *Essex* in 1820? 7. Narrate the adventures and fate of the crew after the destruction of their vessel.

SPELL AND DEFINE. 1. zealously 2. indisputably 3. glowingly 4. gigantic 5. constellations 6. proximity 7. vanquished 8. leviathan 9. latitude 10. longitude 11. approached 12. harpoon 13. fathoms 14. moored 15. retarding 16. moderately 17. topgallant 18. clewed 19. windward 20. exhausted 21. tremendously 22. incessant 23. formidable

LESSON VIII

The Winged Worshipers — Sprague
(Addressed to two swallows that flew into church during worship)

RULE. Be careful to pronounce every syllable distinctly and not to join the words together.

EXERCISES UNDER THE RULE. Read over several times.

We saw a *large dead fish floating*. And he *slew him*. Every *man's house is* his castle. This meteoric vapor is called *"will-o'-the-wisp." I thrust three thousand thistles through the thick of my thumb. Braid broad braids,* my *brave babes*. We never *swerved,* but lost our *swivel* gun.

Gay, guiltless pair,
What seek ye from the fields of heaven?
Ye have no need of prayer,
Ye have no sins to be forgiven.

Why perch ye here,
Where mortals to their Maker bend?
Can your pure spirits fear
The God ye never could offend?

Ye never knew
The crimes for which we come to weep.
Penance is not for you,
Bless'd wand'rers of the upper deep.

To you 'tis given
To wake sweet nature's untaught lays;
Beneath the arch of heaven
To chirp away a life of praise.

Then spread each wing,
Far, far above, o'er lakes and lands,
And join the choirs that sing
In yon blue dome not reared with hands.

Or if ye stay
To note the consecrated hour,
Teach me the airy way,
And let me try your envied power.

Above the crowd,
On upward wings could I but fly,
I'd bathe in yon bright cloud,
And seek the stars that gem the sky.

'Twere heaven indeed,
Through fields of trackless light to soar,

On nature's charms to feed,
And nature's own great God adore.

QUESTIONS. 1. On what occasion was this poem written? 2. We address letters to our friends. Was this addressed to the birds in the same sense? 3. Do you discover any beautiful expressions in this lesson? 4. Point them out.

SPELL AND DEFINE. 1. guiltless 2. perch 3. penance 4. untaught 5. choirs 6. consecrated 7. trackless

LESSON IX

Death at the Looking Glass — diary of a physician

RULE. Be careful to pronounce every syllable distinctly and not to join the words together.

EXERCISES UNDER THE RULE. Read over several times.

The bell *tinkles.* The man *truckles* to power. Thou *chuckl'dst* over thy gains too soon. It was *barb'd* and *bulb'd.* The *bulbs* are sprouting. The pert fairies and the dapper *elves.* Is this *delft* or *delftware?* The *costliest silks* are there. *Overwhelm'd with whirlwinds and tempestuous* fire.

"What can Charlotte be doing all this while?" inquired her mother. She listened. "I have not heard her moving for the last three quarters of an hour! I will call the maid and ask." She rang the bell, and the servant appeared.

"Betty, Miss Jones is not gone yet, is she? Go up to her room, Betty, and see if she wants anything, and tell her it is half past nine," said Mrs. Jones. The servant, accordingly, went upstairs and knocked at the bedroom door — once, twice, thrice — but received no answer. There was a dead silence, except when the wind shook the window. Could Miss Jones have fallen asleep? Oh, impossible!

She knocked again but as unsuccessfully as before. She became a little flustered and after a moment's pause opened the door and entered. There was Miss Jones sitting at the glass. "Why ma'am!" commenced Betty in a petulant tone, walking up to her, "here have I been knocking for these five minutes and — "

Betty staggered, horror struck, to the bed and uttering a loud shriek, alarmed Mrs. Jones, who instantly tottered upstairs almost palsied with fright. Miss Jones was dead!

I was there within a few minutes, for my house was not more than two streets distant. It was a stormy night in March, and the desolate aspect of things without — deserted streets, the dreary howling of the wind, the incessant pattering of the rain — contributed to cast a gloom over my mind. When connected with the awful event that had summoned me out, it deepened the horror of the spectacle I was doomed to witness.

On reaching the house, I found Mrs. Jones in violent hysterics, surrounded by several of her neighbors who had been called to her assistance. I repaired to the scene of death and beheld what I never shall forget.

The room was occupied by a white-curtained bed. There was but one window, and before it was a table on which stood a looking glass hung with a little white drapery. Various paraphernalia of the dressing table lay scattered about — pins, brooches, curling papers, ribbons, gloves, etc. —

An armchair was drawn to this table, and in it sat Miss Jones, stone dead. Her head rested upon her right hand, her elbow supported by the table, while her left hung down by her side, grasping a pair of curling irons. Each of her wrists was encircled by a showy gilt bracelet.

She was dressed in a white muslin frock with a little bordering of blonde. Her face was turned towards the glass, which by the light of the expiring candle reflected with frightful detail her clammy, fixed features daubed with rouge and carmine, the fallen lower jaw, and the eyes directed full into the glass with a cold stare that was appalling.

On examining the countenance more narrowly, I thought I detected the traces of a smirk of conceit and self-complacency which not even the palsying touch of death could wholly obliterate. The hair of the corpse, all smooth and glossy, was curled with elaborate precision; the skinny, sallow neck was encircled with a string of glistening pearls. The ghastly visage of death thus leering through the tinsel of fashion — the "vain show" of artificial joy — was a horrible mockery of the fooleries of life!

Indeed, it was a most humiliating and shocking spectacle. Poor creature! struck dead in the very act of sacrificing at the shrine of female vanity.

On examination of the body, we found that death had been occasioned by disease of the heart. Her life might have been protracted, possibly for years, had she but taken my advice and that of her mother.

I have seen many hundreds of corpses, some in the calm composure of natural death and others mangled and distorted by violence, but never have I seen so startling a satire upon human vanity, so repulsive, unsightly, and loathsome a spectacle as *a corpse dressed for a ball!*

QUESTIONS. 1. Narrate, in a few words, the story which you have been reading. 2. What was the true cause of this young lady's death? 3. Is it common for persons to die suddenly? 4. As no one knows the time of his death, how should all live? 5. What is the reason given in the Bible for obeying parents? 6. Is a ballroom a suitable place to prepare for death?

SPELL AND DEFINE. 1. impossible 2. unsuccessfully 3. petulant 4. shriek 5. palsied 6. desolate 7. incessant 8. hysterics 9. drapery 10. paraphernalia 11. encircled 12. obliterate 13. elaborate 14. precision 15. artificial 16. humiliating 17. protracted 18. corpse

LESSON X

Death of Absalom — 2 Samuel 18

RULE. Be careful to pronounce every syllable distinctly and not to join the words together.

EXERCISES UNDER THE RULE. Read over several times

He was *burn'd* in the hand. He *learned* the art of war in Spain. A song *bursts* from the groves. *Earth's ample* breast. The *busts of* Fox and Pitt were there. The *songs broke* the stillness of the night. A *rat ran over the roof of the house* with a *raw lump of liver in his mouth.*

1 And David numbered the people that were with him, and set captains of thousands and captains of hundreds over them.

2 And David sent forth a third part of the people under the hand of Joab, and a third part under the hand of Abishai the son of Zeruiah, Joab's brother, and a third part under the hand of Ittai the Gittite. And the king said unto the people, I will surely go forth with you myself also.

3 But the people answered, Thou shalt not go forth: for if we flee away, they will not care for us; neither if half of us die, will they care for us: but now thou art worth ten thousand of us: therefore now it is better that thou succor us out of the city.

4 And the king said unto them, What seemeth you best I will do. And the king stood by the gate side, and all the people came out by hundreds and by thousands.

5 And the king commanded Joab and Abishai and Ittai, saying, Deal gently for my sake with the young man, even with Absalom. And all the people heard when the king gave all the captains charge concerning Absalom.

6 So the people went out into the field against Israel: and the battle was in the wood of Ephraim;

7 Where the people of Israel were slain before the ser-

vants of David, and there was there a great slaughter that day of twenty thousand men.

8 For the battle was there scattered over the face of all the country: and the wood devoured more people that day than the sword devoured.

9 And Absalom met the servants of David. And Absalom rode upon a mule, and the mule went under the thick boughs of a great oak, and his head caught hold of the oak, and he was taken up between the heaven and the earth; and the mule that was under him went away.

10 And a certain man saw it, and told Joab, and said, Behold, I saw Absalom hanged in an oak.

11 And Joab said unto the man that told him, And, behold, thou sawest him, and why didst thou not smite him there to the ground? and I would have given thee ten shekels of silver, and a girdle.

12 And the man said unto Joab, Though I should receive a thousand shekels of silver in mine hand, yet would I not put forth mine hand against the king's son: for in our hearing the king charged thee and Abishai and Ittai, saying, Beware that none touch the young man Absalom.

13 Otherwise I should have wrought falsehood against mine own life: for there is no matter hid from the king, and thou thyself wouldest have set thyself against me.

14 Then said Joab, I may not tarry thus with thee. And he took three darts in his hand, and thrust them through the heart of Absalom, while he was yet alive in the midst of the oak.

15 And ten young men that bare Joab's armor compassed about and smote Absalom, and slew him.

16 And Joab blew the trumpet, and the people returned from pursuing after Israel: for Joab held back the people.

17 And they took Absalom, and cast him into a great pit in the wood, and laid a very great heap of stones upon him: and all Israel fled everyone to his tent.

18 Now Absalom in his lifetime had taken and reared up for himself a pillar, which is in the king's dale: for he said, I

have no son to keep my name in remembrance: and he called the pillar after his own name: and it is called unto this day, Absalom's place.

19 Then said Ahimaaz the son of Zadok, Let me now run, and bear the king tidings, how that the Lord hath avenged him of his enemies.

20 And Joab said unto him, Thou shalt not bear tidings this day, but thou shalt bear tidings another day: but this day thou shalt bear no tidings, because the king's son is dead.

21 Then said Joab to Cushi, Go tell the king what thou hast seen. And Cushi bowed himself unto Joab, and ran.

22 Then said Ahimaaz the son of Zadok yet again to Joab, But howsoever, let me, I pray thee, also run after Cushi. And Joab said, Wherefore wilt thou run, my son, seeing that thou hast no tidings ready?

23 But howsoever, said he, let me run. And he said unto him, Run. Then Ahimaaz ran by the way of the plain, and overran Cushi.

24 David sat between the two gates: and the watchman went up to the roof over the gate unto the wall, and lifted up his eyes, and looked, and behold a man running alone.

25 And the watchman cried, and told the king. And the king said, If he be alone, there is tidings in his mouth. And he came apace, and drew near.

26 And the watchman saw another man running: and the watchman called unto the porter, and said, Behold another man running alone. And the king said, He also bringeth tidings.

27 And the watchman said, Methinketh the running of the foremost is like the running of Ahimaaz the son of Zadok. And the king said, He is a good man, and cometh with good tidings.

28 And Ahimaaz called, and said unto the king, All is well. And he fell down to the earth upon his face before the king, and said, Blessed be the Lord thy God, which hath

delivered up the men that lifted up their hand against my lord the king.

29 And the king said, Is the young man Absalom safe? And Ahimaaz answered, When Joab sent the king's servant, and me thy servant, I saw a great tumult, but I knew not what it was.

30 The king said unto him, Turn aside, and stand here. And he turned aside, and stood still.

31 And, behold, Cushi came; and Cushi said, Tidings, my lord the king: for the Lord hath avenged thee this day of all them that rose up against thee.

32 And the king said unto Cushi, Is the young man Absalom safe? And Cushi answered, The enemies of my lord the king, and all that rise against thee to do thee hurt, be as that young man is.

33 And the king was much moved, and went up to the chamber over the gate, and wept: and as he went, thus he said, O my son Absalom! my son, my son Absalom! would God I had died for thee, O Absalom, my son, my son!

QUESTIONS. 1. What three officers did David appoint over the host? 2. Why did not David himself go forth to the battle? 3. What charge did David give to the three officers respecting Absalom? 4. What was the result of the battle? 5. What was the fate of Absalom? 6. What motives probably influenced Joab to such a course of cruelty? 7. What was the effect of the news of Absalom's death upon King David?

SPELL AND DEFINE. 1. thousands   2. succor   3. concerning 4. Ephraim   5. slaughter   6. shekels   7. otherwise   8. compassed 9. remembrance 10. Ahimaaz 11. watchman 12. methinketh 13. tumult 14. avenged

LESSON XI

Absalom — Willis

RULE. Be careful to pronounce every syllable distinctly and not to join the words together.

EXERCISES UNDER THE RULE. Read over several times.

Earth, that *entomb'st all* that my *heart holds* dear. *His attempts were* fruitless. *Hold off your hands, gentlemen.* The *sounds of horses' hoofs* were heard. What *want'st thou* here? It *was wrenched* by the hand of violence. Their *singed tops,* tho' bare, *still stand.* The *strength of* his *nostrils is* terrible. A gentle current *rippled by.* He *barb'd* the dart. How do you *like herbs* in your broth? Thou *barb'st* the dart that *wounds* thee. Thou *barb'd'st* the dart.

King David's limbs were weary. He had fled
From far Jerusalem, and now he stood,
With his faint people, for a little rest
Upon the shore of Jordan. The light wind
Of morn was stirring, and he bared his brow
To its refreshing breath, for he had worn
The mourner's covering, and he had not felt
That he could see his people until now.

They gathered round him on the fresh green bank
And spoke their kindly words, and as the sun
Rose up in heaven, he knelt among them there
And bowed his head upon his hands to pray.

Oh! when the heart is full — when bitter thoughts
Come crowding thickly up for utterance,
And the poor common words of courtesy
Are such a very mockery — how much
The bursting heart may pour itself in prayer!

He prayed for Israel; his voice went up
Strongly and fervently. He prayed for those
Whose love had been his shield, and his deep tones
Grew tremulous. But, oh! for Absalom —
For his estranged, misguided Absalom —
The proud, bright being who had burst away
In all his princely beauty, to defy

The heart that cherished him — for him he poured,
In agony that would not be controlled,
Strong supplication, and forgave him there
Before his God for his deep sinfulness.

The pall was settled. He who slept beneath
Was straightened for the grave, and as the folds
Sunk to the still proportions, they betrayed
The matchless symmetry of Absalom.

His hair was yet unshorn, and silken curls
Were floating round the tassels as they swayed,
glossy, in the admitted air.
His helm was at his feet; his banner, soiled
With trailing through Jerusalem, was laid,
Reversed, beside him, and the jeweled hilt,
Whose diamonds lit the passage of his blade,
Rested, like mockery, on his covered brow.

The soldiers of the king trod to and fro,
Clad in the garb of battle; their chief,
The mighty Joab, stood beside the bier
And gazed upon the dark pall steadfastly,
As if he feared the slumberer might stir.

A slow step startled him. He grasped his blade
As if a trumpet rang, but the bent form
Of David entered, and he gave command,
In a low tone, to his few followers,
Who left him with his dead. The king stood still
Till the last echo died. Then, throwing off
The sackcloth from his brow and laying back
The pall from the still features of his child,
He bowed his head upon him and broke forth
In the resistless eloquence of woe:

"Alas! my noble boy, that thou should'st die!
    Thou, who wert made so beautifully fair!
That Death should settle in thy glorious eye,
    And leave his stillness in this clustering hair!
How could he mark thee for the silent tomb,
        My proud boy, Absalom!

"Cold is thy brow, my son! and I am chill,
    As to my bosom I have tried to press thee.
How was I wont to feel my pulses thrill,
    Like a rich harp-string yearning to caress thee,
And hear thy sweet 'my father' from these dumb
        And cold lips, Absalom!

"The grave hath won thee. I shall hear the gush
    Of music and the voices of the young;
And life will pass me in the mantling blush,
    And the dark tresses to the soft winds flung,
But thou no more, with thy sweet voice, shalt come
        To meet me, Absalom!

"And, oh! when I am stricken, and my heart,
    Like a bruised reed, is waiting to be broken,
How will its love for thee, as I depart,
    Yearn for thine ear to drink its last deep token!
It were so sweet amid death's gathering gloom,
        To see thee, Absalom!

"And now, farewell! 'Tis hard to give thee up,
    With death so like a gentle slumber on thee —
And thy dark sin! — Oh! I could drink the cup,
    If from this woe its bitterness had won thee.
May God have called thee, like a wanderer, home,
        My erring Absalom!"

He covered up his face and bowed himself
A moment on his child; then, giving him

A look of melting tenderness, he clasped
His hand convulsively, as if in prayer.
And, as if a strength were given him of God
He rose up calmly and composed the pall
Firmly and decently and left him there,
As if his rest had been a breathing sleep.

QUESTIONS. 1. What had Absalom done to wring the heart of his father? 2. What was the manner of his death? 3. Specify some of the poetic beauties of this piece.

SPELL AND DEFINE. 1. mourners 2. bitter 3. courtesy 4. mockery 5. misguided 6. estranged 7. cherished 8. controlled 9. straightened 10. matchless 11. symmetry 12. tassels 13. reversed 14. jeweled 15. hilt 16. steadfastly 17. sackcloth 18. eloquence 19. mantling 20. convulsively

LESSON XII

A Forest Hymn — Bryant

RULE. Give a full and prolonged sound to the vowels, yet be careful not to alter their proper sounds.

This rule is intended to correct a very common fault which makes reading flat, inexpressive, and uninteresting. Some vowel sounds cannot be prolonged without altering the proper sound, while others may be lengthened to almost any extent without any appreciable alteration of sound. Let every pupil repeat these words, giving the vowel sound that is italicized a long, loud, and full sound that gradually diminishes in strength.

hail, all, the, isle, own, how, now, awe, show, do, ooze, eel

Then let them repeat these sentences several times, prolonging the vowel sounds that are italicized.

Hail holy light. We *praise thee, O Lord God. High* on a *throne* of *royal state.*

The reader will need to guard against a drawling style of reading, after these exercises.

The groves were God's first temples. Ere man learned
To hew the shaft, and lay the architrave,
And spread the roof above them — ere he framed
The lofty vault, to gather and roll back
The sound of anthems; in the darkling wood,
Amid the cool and silence, he knelt down,
And offered to the Mightiest solemn thanks
And supplication. For his simple heart
Might not resist the sacred influences
Which, from the stilly twilight of the place,
And from the gray old trunks that high in heaven
Mingled their mossy boughs, and from the sound
Of the invisible breath that swayed at once
All their green tops, stole over him, and bowed
His spirit with the thought of boundless power
And inaccessible majesty. Ah, why
Should we, in the world's riper years, neglect
God's ancient sanctuaries, and adore
Only among the crowd, and under roofs
That our frail hands have raised? Let me, at least,
Here, in the shadow of this aged wood,
Offer one hymn — thrice happy, if it find
Acceptance in His ear.

                              Father, thy hand
Hath reared these venerable columns, thou
Didst weave this verdant roof. Thou didst look down
Upon the naked earth, and, forthwith, rose
All these fair ranks of trees. They, in thy sun,
Budded, and shook their green leaves in thy breeze,
And shot towards heaven. The century-living crow
Whose birth was in their tops, grew old and died
Among their branches, till, at last, they stood,
As now they stand, massy, and tall, and dark,
Fit shrine for humble worshipper to hold
Communion with his Maker. These dim vaults,
These winding aisles, of human pomp or pride

Report not. No fantastic carvings show
The boast of our vain race to change the form
Of thy fair works. But thou art here — thou fill'st
The solitude. Thou art in the soft winds
That run along the summit of these trees
In music; thou art in the cooler breath
That from the inmost darkness of the place
Comes, scarcely felt; the barky trunks, the ground,
The fresh moist ground, are all instinct with thee.
Here is continual worship; — Nature, here,
In the tranquillity that thou dost love,
Enjoys thy presence. Noiselessly, around,
From perch to perch, the solitary bird
Passes; and yon clear spring, that, midst its herbs,
Wells softly forth and wandering steeps the roots
Of half the mighty forest, tells no tale
Of all the good it does. Thou hast not left
Thyself without a witness, in the shades,
Of thy perfections. Grandeur, strength, and grace
Are here to speak of thee. This mighty oak —
By whose immovable stem I stand and seem
Almost annihilated — not a prince,
In all the proud old world beyond the deep,
E'er wore his crown as loftily as he
Wears the green coronal of leaves with which
Thy hand had graced him. Nestled at his root
Is beauty, such as blooms not in the glare
Of the broad sun. That delicate forest flower,
With scented breath and look so like a smile,
Seems, as it issues from the shapeless mould,
An emanation of the indwelling Life.
A visible token of the upholding Love,
That are the soul of this great universe.

My heart is awed within me when I think
Of the great miracle that still goes on,
In silence, round me — the perpetual work

Of thy creation, finished, yet renewed
Forever. Written on thy works I read
The lesson of thy own eternity.
Lo! all grow old and die — but see again,
How on the faltering footsteps of decay
Youth presses — every gay and beautiful youth
In all its beautiful forms. These lofty trees
Wave not less proudly than their ancestors
Moulder beneath them. Oh, there is not lost
One of earth's charms: upon her bosom yet,
After the flight of untold centuries,
The freshness of her far beginning lies
And yet shall lie. Life mocks the idle hate
Of his arch-enemy Death — yea, seats himself
Upon the tyrant's throne — the sepulchre,
And of the triumphs of his ghastly foe
Makes his own nourishment. For he came forth
From thine own bosom, and shall have no end.

There have been holy men who hid themselves
Deep in the woody wilderness, and gave
Their lives to thought and prayer, till they outlived
The generation born with them, nor seemed
Less aged than the hoary trees and rocks
Around them; — and there have been holy men
Who deemed it were not well to pass life thus.
But let me often to these solitudes
Retire, and in thy presence reassure
My feeble virtue. Here its enemies,
The passions, at thy plainer footsteps shrink
And tremble and are still. O God! when thou
Dost scare the world with tempests, set on fire
The heavens with falling thunderbolts, or fill,
With all the waters of the firmament,
The swift dark whirlwind that uproots the woods
And drowns the villages; when, at thy call,
Uprises the great deep and throws himself

Upon the continent, and overwhelms
Its cities — who forgets not, at the sight
Of these tremendous tokens of thy power,
His pride, and lays his strifes and follies by?
Oh, from these sterner aspects of thy face
Spare me and mine, nor let us need the wrath
Of the mad unchained elements to teach
Who rules them. Be it ours to meditate,
In these calm shades, thy milder majesty,
And to the beautiful order of thy works
Learn to conform the order of our lives.

QUESTIONS. 1. What were the most ancient temples of worship? 2. What meditations become the forest scenes? 3. Of what kind of poetic measure is this piece?

SPELL AND DEFINE. 1. architrave   2. darkling   3. supplication 4. influences   5. twilight   6. invisible   7. inaccessible   8. sanctuaries 9. worshiper 10. instinct 11. tranquillity 12. immovable 13. annihilated 14. emanation   15. indwelling   16. upholding   17. sepulcher 18. thunderbolt 19. tremendous

LESSON XIII

On Elocution and Reading — N. A. Review

RULE. Give a full and prolonged sound to the vowels, yet be careful not to alter their proper sounds.

EXERCISES UNDER THE RULE. Prolong the vowel sounds that are italicized.

war, orb, flows, pure, down, aid, low, save
These are thy *glorious* works, *parent of good. Fairest* of *stars! last* in the *train* of *night.*

The business of training our youth in elocution must be commenced in childhood. The first school is the nursery.

There, at least, may be formed a distinct articulation, which is the first requisite for good speaking. How rarely is it found in perfection among our orators! Words, says one, referring to articulation, should "be delivered out from the lips as beautiful coins newly issued from the mint, deeply and accurately impressed, perfectly finished, neatly struck by the proper organs, distinct, in due succession, and of due weight." How rarely do we hear a speaker whose tongue, teeth, and lips do their office so perfectly, as in any wise, to answer to this beautiful description! The common faults in articulation, it should be remembered, take their rise from the very nursery. But let us refer to other particulars.

Grace in eloquence — in the pulpit, at the bar — cannot be separated from grace in the ordinary manners, in private life, in the social circle, in the family. It cannot well be superinduced upon all the other acquisitions of youth any more than that nameless but invaluable quality called good breeding. You may, therefore, begin the work of forming the orator with your child not merely by teaching him to declaim but, what is of more consequence, by observing and correcting his daily manners, motions, and attitudes.

When he comes into your apartment or presents you with something, a book or letter, in an awkward and blundering manner, you can say, "Return and enter this room again," or, "Present me that book in a different manner," or, "Put yourself into a different attitude." You can explain to him the difference between thrusting or pushing out his hand and arm in straight lines and at acute angles and moving them in flowing, circular lines and easy, graceful action. He will readily understand you. Nothing is more true than that "the motions of children are originally graceful," and it is by suffering them to be perverted that we lay the foundation for invincible awkwardness in later life.

We go, next, to the schools for children. It ought to be a leading object in these schools to teach the art of reading. It ought to occupy threefold more time than it does. The teachers of these schools should labor to improve *themselves*.

They should feel that to them, for a time, are committed the future orators of the land.

We would rather have a child, even of the other sex, return to us from school a first-rate reader than a first-rate performer on the piano. We should feel that we had a far better pledge for the intelligence and talent of our child. The accomplishment, in its perfection, would give more pleasure. The voice of song is not sweeter than the voice of eloquence, and there may be eloquent readers as well as eloquent speakers. We speak of *perfection* in this art, and it is something, we must say in defense of our preference, which we have never yet seen. Let the same pains be devoted to reading as are required to form an accomplished performer on an instrument; let us have — as the ancients had — the formers of the voice, the music masters of the *reading* voice; let us see years devoted to this accomplishment, and then we should be prepared to stand the comparison.

It is, indeed, a most intellectual accomplishment. So is music, too, in its perfection. We do by no means undervalue this noble and most delightful art, to which Socrates applied himself even in his old age. But one recommendation of the art of reading is that it requires a constant exercise of mind. It demands continual and close reflection and thought — the *finest* discrimination of thought. It involves, in its perfection, the whole art of criticism on language. A man may possess a fine genius without being a perfect reader, but he cannot be a perfect reader without genius.

QUESTIONS. 1. When must the business of training in elocution be commenced? 2. What excellent comparison is made use of in illustrating proper enunciation? 3. What is the relative importance of good reading? 4. How does the power of reading with perfection compare with the power of excellent musical performance?

SPELL AND DEFINE. 1. elocution   2. articulation   3. accurately
4. succession 5. description 6. particulars 7. eloquence 8. superinduced
9. acquisitions   10. invaluable   11. consequence   12. apartment
13. awkwardness   14. thrusting   15. invincible   16. committed

17. intelligence   18. accomplishment   19. instrument   20. comparison
21. intellectual 22. undervalue 23. recommendation 24. discrimination

LESSON XIV

Necessity of Education — Beecher

RULE. Give a full and prolonged sound to the vowels, yet be careful not to alter their proper sounds.

EXERCISES UNDER THE RULE. Prolong the vowel sounds that are italicized.

err, all, age, arm, old, our, eel, boy, isle
Our *Father,* who *art* in heaven. *Woe* unto *thee, Chorazin! Woe* unto *thee, Bethsaida!*

We must educate! We must educate! or we must perish by our own prosperity. If we do not, short will be our race from the cradle to the grave. If in our haste to be rich and mighty we outrun our literary and religious institutions, they will never overtake us — or only come up after the battle of liberty is fought and lost, as spoils to grace the victory and as resources of inexorable despotism for the perpetuity of our bondage.

What will become of the West if her prosperity rushes up to such a majesty of power while those great institutions linger which are necessary to form the mind, the conscience, and the heart of that vast world? It must not be permitted.

Yet what is done must be done quickly, for population will not wait, commerce will not cast anchor, manufactures will not shut off the steam nor shut down the gate, and agriculture, pushed by millions of freemen on their fertile soil, will not withhold her corrupting abundance.

Let no man in the East quiet himself and dream of liberty, whatever may become of the West. Our alliance of blood, political institutions, and common interests is such that we cannot stand aloof in the hour of her calamity, should it ever come. *Her* destiny is *our* destiny; the day that her gallant ship goes down, our little boat sinks in the vortex!

The motives which call on us to cooperate in this glorious work of consummating the institutions of the West, essential to the perpetuity of her greatness and glory, are neither few nor feeble nor obscure.

All in the West is on a great scale, and the minds and the views of the people correspond with these relative proportions. It is not parsimony which renders momentary aid necessary to the West, it is want of time and assimilation for the consciousness and wielding of her powers. And how cheaply can the aid be rendered for rearing immediately the first generation of her institutions! cheaper than we could rear the barracks to accommodate an army for the defense of our liberty, for a single campaign; cheaper than the taxations of crime and its punishment during the same period, in the absence of literary and evangelical influence.

Consider, also, that the mighty resources in the West are worse than useless without the supervening influence of the government of God.

To balance the temptation of such unrivaled abundance, the capacity of the West for self-destruction, without religious and moral culture, will be as terrific as her capacity for self-preservation, with it, will be glorious.

But all the moral energies of the government of God over men are indissolubly associated with "the ministry of reconciliation." The Sabbath and the preaching of the Gospel are Heaven's consecrated instruments for the efficacious administration of the government of mind in a happy, social state. By these only does the Sun of Righteousness arise with healing in His beams. Ignorance, vice, and superstition encamp around evangelical institutions, to rush in whenever their light and power is extinct.

The great experiment is now in the making, and from its extent and rapid filling up, is deciding in the West whether the perpetuity of our republican institutions can be reconciled with universal suffrage. Without the education of the head and heart of the nation, it cannot be. The question to be decided is, Can the nation, or the vast balance power of it, be so imbued with intelligence and virtue as to bring out, in laws and their administration, a perpetual self-preserving energy? We know that the work is a vast one and of great difficulty, yet we believe it can be done.

QUESTIONS. 1. Why is education so necessary in this country? 2. What will, without education, contribute to our downfall? 3. What can save the nation's liberties? 4. Can the nation continue free without the influence of religion? 5. Read and explain paragraph 3. 6. Why is abundance said to be "corrupting"? 7. Why should all cooperate in extending education? 8. Why are the teachers of religion called "the ministry of reconciliation"?

SPELL AND DEFINE. 1. educate   2. prosperity   3. resources
4. inexorable   5. despotism   6. perpetuity   7. conscience   8. permitted
9. population   10. commerce   11. manufactures   12. agriculture
13. corrupting   14. alliance   15. calamity   16. destiny   17. vortex
18. cooperate   19. consummating   20. essential   21. obscure
22. supervening   23. unrivaled   24. capacity   25. terrific   26. self-
preservation   27. indissolubly   28. reconciliation   29. consecrated
30. instruments   31. efficacious   32. superstition   33. evangelical
34. extinct 35. suffrage

LESSON XV

Necessity of Education — continued

RULE. Give a full and prolonged sound to the vowels, yet be careful not to alter their proper sounds.

EXERCISES UNDER THE RULE. Prolong the vowel sounds that are italicized.

know, free, they, dawn, now, bay, there, shore
Soothed with the *sound*, the *king* grew *vain*. *Roll* on, thou *deep* and *dark* blue ocean, *roll*.

I am aware that our ablest patriots are looking out on the deep, vexed with storms, with great forebodings, and failings of heart, for fear of the things that are coming upon us. I perceive a spirit of impatience rising and distrust in respect to the perpetuity of our republic, and I am sure that these fears are well founded and am glad that they exist. It is the star of hope in our dark horizon.

Fear is what we need, as the ship needs wind on a rocking sea after a storm, to prevent foundering. When our fear and our efforts shall correspond with our danger, the danger is past.

It is not the impossibility of self-preservation which threatens us, nor is it the unwillingness of the nation to pay the price of the preservation as she has paid the price of the purchase of our liberties — it is inattention and inconsideration, protracted until the crisis is past and the things which belong to our peace are hid from our eyes. Blessed be God that the tokens of a national waking up, the harbinger of God's mercy, are multiplying upon us!

We did not, in the darkest hour, believe that God had brought our fathers to this goodly land to lay the foundation of religious liberty, wrought such wonders in their preservation, and raised their descendants to such heights of civil and religious liberty only to reverse the analogy of His providence and abandon His work.

Though there now be clouds and the sea roaring and men's hearts failing, we believe there is light behind the cloud, that the imminence of our danger is intended, under the guidance of Heaven, to call forth and apply a holy, fraternal fellowship between the East and the West, which shall secure our preservation and make the prosperity of our nation durable as time and as abundant as the waves of the sea.

I would add, as a motive to immediate action, that if we do fail in our great experiment of self-government, our destruction will be as signal as the birthright abandoned, the mercies abused, and the provocation offered to beneficent Heaven. The descent of desolation will correspond with the past elevation. No punishments of Heaven are so severe as those for mercies abused; no instrumentality employed in their infliction is so dreadful as the wrath of man. No spasms are like the spasms of expiring liberty and no wailing such as her convulsions extort.

It took Rome three hundred years to die. Our death, if we perish, will be so much more terrific because our intelligence and free institutions have given to us more bone, sinew, and vitality. May God hide from me the day when the dying agonies of my country shall begin! Oh, thou beloved land, bound together by the ties of brotherhood and common interest and perils, live forever — one and undivided!

QUESTIONS. 1. Why should men regard the prospects of this nation with fear? 2. What can be the advantage of a spirit of fear? 3. Why may we trust that God will not abandon our nation to ruin? 4. What will ensure her destruction? 5. Suppose our nation were destroyed, how great would be the destruction? 6. What are the most dreadful punishments Heaven can inflict upon a nation? 7. How would our destruction compare with that of Rome?

SPELL   AND   DEFINE.   1. correspond   2. impossibility
3. inconsideration 4. harbinger 5. multiplying 6. analogy 7. birthright
8. instrumentality 9. spasm 10. institutions

LESSON XVI

Parrhasius — Willis

RULE. Give a full and distinct sound to the consonants in every syllable.

EXERCISES UNDER THE RULE. Pronounce the following words, protracting the sound of the consonant that is italicized. The object is to promote distinct enunciation.

b-ow, *d*-are, *f*-ame, *g*-ave, *h*-orse, *J*-ew, *k*-ite, *l*-ord, *m*-an, *n*-o, *p*-it, *q*-ueer, *r*-ow, *s*-ir, *t*-ake, *v*-ow, *w*-oe, *y*-e, *g*-one, *th*-ou, *th*-umb, *wh*-at, *wh*-oa, *ch*-urch

Parrhasius, a painter of Athens, bought one of those Olynthian captives which Philip of Macedon brought home to sell. When he had him at his house, he put him to death with extreme torture and torment, the better by his example to express the pains and passions of his Prometheus, which he was then about to paint.

Parrhasius stood, gazing forgetfully
Upon his canvass. There Prometheus lay,
Chained to the cold rocks of Mount Caucasus,
The vulture at his vitals and the links
Of the lame Lemnian festering in his flesh;
And, as the painter's mind felt through the dim,
Rapt mystery, and plucked the shadows wild
Forth with its reaching fancy, and with form
And color clad them, his fine, earnest eye
Flashed with a passionate fire, and the quick curl
Of his thin nostril, and his quivering lip,
Were like the winged god's breathing from his flight.

"Bring me the captive now!
My hand feels skillful, and the shadows lift
From my waked spirit airily and swift;
     And I could paint the bow
Upon the bended heavens — around me play
Colors of such divinity today.

"Ha! bind him on his back!
Look! as Prometheus in my picture here,
Quickly — or he faints! — stand with the cordial near!
     Now — bend him to the rack!
Press down the poisoned links into his flesh!
And tear agape that healing wound afresh!

"So — let him writhe! How long
Will he live thus? Quickly, my good pencil, now

What a fine agony works upon his brow!
Ha! grey-haired and so strong!
How fearfully he stifles that short moan!
Gods! if I could but paint a dying groan!

"'Pity' thee! So I do,
I pity the dumb victim at the altar.
But does the robed priest for his pity falter?
I'd rack thee, though I knew
A thousand lives were perishing in thine —
What were ten thousand to a fame like mine?

"Ah! there's a deathless name,
A spirit that the smothering vault shall spurn,
And, like a steadfast planet, mount and burn.
And though its crown of flame
Consumed my brain to ashes as it won me,
By all the fiery stars, I'd pluck it on me!

"Aye — though it bid me rifle
My heart's last fount for its insatiate thirst,
Though every life-strung nerve be maddened first —
Though it should bid me stifle
The yearning in my throat for my sweet child,
And taunt its mother till my brain went wild —

"All — I would do it all —
Sooner than die, like a dull worm, to rot;
Thrust foully in the earth to be forget.
O heavens — but I appall
Your heart, old man! — forgive — ha! on your lives
Let him not faint! Rack him till he revives!

"Vain — vain — give o'er. His eye
Glazes apace. He does not feel you now —
Stand back! I'll paint the death-dew on his brow!
Gods! if he do not die

But for one moment — one — till I eclipse
Conception with the scorn of those calm lips!

   "Shivering! Hark! He mutters
Brokenly now — that was a difficult breath —
Another? Wilt thou never come, oh, Death?
   Look! how his temple flutters!
Is his heart still? Aha! lift up his head!
He shudders — gasps — Jove help him — so he's
    dead."

How like a mountain devil in the heart
Rules this unreined ambition! Let it once
But play the monarch, and its haughty brow
Glows with a beauty that bewilders thought
And unthrones peace forever. Putting on
The very pomp of Lucifer, it turns
The heart to ashes, and with not a spring
Left in the desert for the spirit's lip,
We look upon our splendor and forget
The thirst of which we perish!

QUESTIONS. 1. Who was Philip of Macedon? 2. Can you relate the fable of Prometheus? 3. Who was the lame Lemnian? 4. What heathen deity is alluded to in line 12? 5. Why did the painter torture the old man? 6. Is such ambition justifiable? 7. What caused the fallen angels to rebel?

SPELL AND DEFINE. 1. festering 2. airily 3. stifles 4. smothering 5. yearning 6. apace 7. conception 8. unreined 9. unthrones

LESSON XVII

The Scriptures and the Savior — Rousseau

RULE. Give a full and distinct sound to the consonants in every syllable.

EXERCISES UNDER THE RULE. Pronounce the following words, sounding the last consonant very distinctly.

or-*b,* ai-*d,* i-*f,* Geor-*ge,* rich-*er,* a-*ll,* ai-*m,* ow-*n,* ti-*p,* wa-*r,* hi-*ss,* ha-*t,* gi-*ve,* a-*dd,* so-*ng,* brea-*th,* tru-*th,* pu-*sh,* bir-*ch*

The majesty of the Scriptures strikes me with astonishment, and the sanctity of the Gospel addresses itself to my heart. Look at the volumes of the philosophers with all their pomp, how contemptible do they appear in comparison to this! Is it possible that a book at once so simple and sublime can be the work of man?

Can He who is the subject of its history be Himself a mere man? Was His the tone of an enthusiast or of an ambitious sectary? What sweetness! What purity in His manners! What an affecting gracefulness in His instructions! What sublimity in His maxims! What profound wisdom in His discourses! What presence of mind, what sagacity and propriety in His answers! How great the command over His passions! Where is the man, where the philosopher who could so live, suffer, and die without weakness and without ostentation!

When Plato described his imaginary good man, covered with all the disgrace of crime yet worthy of all the rewards of virtue, he described exactly the character of Jesus Christ. The resemblance was so striking it could not be mistaken, and all the fathers of the church perceived it. What prepossessions, what blindness must it be to compare the son of Sophronius to the Son of Mary! What an immeasurable distance between them! Socrates, dying without pain and without ignominy, easily supported his character to the last. If his death, however easy, had not crowned his life, it might have been doubted whether Socrates, with all his wisdom, was anything more than a mere sophist.

He invented, it is said, the theory of moral science. Others, however, had before him put it in practice, and he had nothing to do but to tell what they had done and to reduce their examples to precept. Aristides had been just, before Socrates defined what justice was; Leonidas had died for his country before Socrates made it a duty to love one's country. Sparta had been temperate before Socrates eulogized sobriety; before he celebrated the praises of virtue, Greece had abounded in virtuous men.

But from whom of all His countrymen could Jesus have derived that sublime and pure morality, of which He only has given us both the precepts and example? In the midst of the most licentious fanaticism the voice of the sublimest wisdom was heard, the simplicity of the most heroic virtue crowned one of the humblest of all the multitude.

The death of Socrates, peaceably philosophizing with his friends, is the most pleasant that could be desired! That of Jesus, expiring in torments, outraged, reviled, and execrated by a whole nation, is the most horrible that could be feared. Socrates in receiving the cup of poison blessed the weeping executioner who presented it, but Jesus, in the midst of excruciating torture, prayed for His merciless tormentors.

Yes! if the life and death of Socrates were those of a sage, the life and death of Jesus were those of a God. Shall we say that the evangelical history is a mere fiction — it does not bear the stamp of fiction, but the contrary. The history of Socrates, which nobody doubts, is not as well attested as that of Jesus Christ. Such an assertion, in fact, only shifts the difficulty without removing it. It is more inconceivable that a number of persons should have agreed to fabricate this book than that one only should have furnished the subject of it.

The Jewish authors were incapable of the diction and strangers to the morality contained in the Gospel, the marks of whose truth are so striking, so perfectly inimitable that the inventor would be a more astonishing man than the hero.

QUESTIONS. 1. What was the character of Rousseau? 2. How could an infidel testify thus without renouncing his infidelity? 3. How does

Plato's character of what a good man ought to be correspond with what Christ was? 4. What differences can you mention between the life and death of Christ and that of Socrates? 5. In what country did Aristides, Leonidas, Plato, and Socrates live? 6. What is the character of each? 7. Is the history of Socrates any better attested than that of Christ? 8. Why is it inconceivable that the book is a fiction? 9. Suppose it an invention of man — which would be the most wonderful, the inventor or the hero?

SPELL AND DEFINE. 1. majesty 2. astonishment 3. philosophers 4. contemptible 5. comparison 6. enthusiast 7. sectary 8. gracefulness 9. discourses 10. sagacity 11. ostentation 12. imaginary 13. resemblance 14. prepossession   15. Sophronius   16. immeasurable   17. eulogized 18. outraged   19. execrated   20. executioner   21. excruciating 22. evangelical 23. inimitable

LESSON XVIII

Washington's Birthday — Webster

RULE. Take care not to let the voice grow weaker and weaker as you approach the end of a sentence.

The name of Washington is intimately blended with whatever belongs most essentially to the prosperity, liberty, free institutions, the renown of our country. That name was of power to rally a nation in the hour of thick-thronging public disasters and calamities; that name shone amid the storm of war, a beacon light to cheer and guide the country's friends; it flamed, too, like a meteor, to repel her foes.

That name, in the days of peace, was a lodestone attracting to itself a whole people's confidence, a whole people's love, and the whole world's respect; that name, descending with all time, spreading over the whole earth, and uttered in all the languages belonging to the tribes and races of men, will forever be pronounced with affectionate gratitude by everyone in whose breast there shall arise an aspiration for human rights and human liberty.

All experience evinces that human sentiments are strongly influenced by associations. The recurrence of anniversaries or of longer periods of time naturally freshens the recollection and deepens the impression of events with which they are historically connected. Renowned places, also, have a power to awaken feeling, which all acknowledge. No American can pass by the fields of Bunker Hill, Monmouth, or Camden as if they were ordinary spots on the earth's surface. Whoever visits them feels the sentiment of love of country kindling anew, as if the spirit that belonged to the transactions which have rendered these places distinguished still hovered around, with power to move and excite all who in future time may approach them.

But neither of these sources of emotion equals the power with which great moral examples affect the mind. When sublime virtues cease to be abstractions, when they become embodied in human character and exemplified in human conduct, we should be false to our own nature if we did not indulge in the spontaneous effusions of our gratitude and our admiration. A true lover of the virtue of patriotism delights to contemplate its purest models, and that love of country may be well suspected which affects to soar so high into the regions of sentiment as to be lost and absorbed in the abstract feeling and becomes too elevated or too refined to glow with fervor in the commendation or the love of individual benefactors. All this is unnatural.

It is as if one should be so enthusiastic a lover of poetry as to care nothing for Homer or Milton; so passionately attached to eloquence as to be indifferent to Cicero and Chatham; such a devotee to the arts, in such an ecstasy with the elements of beauty, proportion, and expression as to regard the masterpieces of Raphael and Michelangelo with coldness or contempt. We may be assured, gentlemen, that he who really loves the thing itself loves its finest exhibitions. A true friend of his country loves her friends and benefactors and thinks it no degradation to commend and commemorate them.

The voluntary outpouring of the public feeling made today, from the north to the south and from the east to the west, proves this sentiment to be both just and natural. In the cities and in the villages, in the public temples and in the family circles, among all ages and sexes, gladdened voices today bespeak grateful hearts and a freshened recollection of the virtues of the father of his country.

And it will be so, in all time to come, so long as public virtue is itself an object of regard. The ingenuous youth of America will hold up to themselves the bright model of Washington's example and study to be what they behold; they will contemplate his character till all its virtues spread out and display themselves to their delighted vision, as the earliest astronomers, the shepherds on the plains of Babylon, gazed at the stars till they saw them form into clusters and constellations, overpowering at length the eyes of the beholders with the blaze of a thousand lights.

QUESTIONS. 1. When is Washington's birthday? 2. In what year was he born? 3. In what year did he die? 4. What has Washington done for us — or in what way are we happier by his career? 5. What is the strength of associations connected with times and places compared with the strength of those connected with character? 6. How must the lover of virtue feel towards all virtuous men? 7. What will be the effect of Washington's character on future generations in America?

SPELL AND DEFINE. 1. intimately 2. blended 3. renown 4. beacon 5. meteor 6. lodestone 7. aspiration 8. sentiments 9. associations 10. recurrence 11. anniversaries 12. ordinary 13. abstractions 14. embodied 15. exemplified 16. spontaneous 17. effusions 18. admiration 19. patriotism 20. benefactors 21. enthusiastic 22. devotee 23. ecstasy 24. masterpieces 25. degradation 26. commemorate 27. voluntary 28. ingenuous 29. vision 30. constellations

LESSON XIX

Nature and Revelation — Psalm 19

RULE. Listen while the student reads, and then mention which syllables were pronounced wrong and which were omitted or indistinctly sounded.

1 The heavens declare the glory of God; and the firmament sheweth his handywork.

2 Day unto day uttereth speech, and night unto night sheweth knowledge.

3 There is no speech nor language, where their voice is not heard.

4 Their line is gone out through all the earth, and their words to the end of the world. In them hath he set a tabernacle for the sun,

5 Which is as a bridegroom coming out of his chamber, and rejoiceth as a strong man to run a race.

6 His going forth is from the end of the heaven, and his circuit unto the ends of it: and there is nothing hid from the heat thereof.

7 The law of the Lord is perfect, converting the soul: the testimony of the Lord is sure, making wise the simple.

8 The statutes of the Lord are right, rejoicing the heart: the commandment of the Lord is pure, enlightening the eyes.

9 The fear of the Lord is clean, enduring for ever: the judgments of the Lord are true and righteous altogether.

10 More to be desired are they than gold, yea, than much fine gold: sweeter also than honey and the honeycomb.

11 Moreover by them is thy servant warned: and in keeping of them there is great reward.

12 Who can understand his errors? cleanse thou me from secret faults.

13 Keep back thy servant also from presumptuous sins; let them not have dominion over me: then shall I be upright,

and I shall be innocent from the great transgression.

14 Let the words of my mouth, and the meditation of my heart, be acceptable in thy sight, O Lord, my strength, and my redeemer.

QUESTIONS. 1. What is the character of God as exhibited by the works of nature? 2. What is the character and influence of the law of God? 3. How can a man be kept from sin?

SPELL AND DEFINE. 1. firmament   2. language   3. tabernacle 4. bridegroom 5. circuit 6. testimony 7. commandment 8. enlightening 9. judgments   10. honeycomb   11. presumptuous   12. transgression 13. meditation 14. redeemer

LESSON XX

Niagara Falls — Howison

RULE. Sound the vowels correctly and very full.

EXERCISES UNDER THE RULE. Prolong the following vowel sounds that are italicized: *a*-we, *a*-ge, *a*-rm, *o*-ld, *o*-r, *ee*-l, *oo*-ze, bu-*oy*, *i*-sle.

These are the only vowel sounds that can be much prolonged without altering their proper sound.

The form of Niagara Falls is that of an irregular semicircle about three quarters of a mile in extent. This is divided into two distinct cascades by Goat Island, the extremity of which is perpendicular and in a line with the precipice over which the water is projected. The cataract on the Canadian side of the river is called the Horseshoe, or Great Falls, from its peculiar form, and that next to the United States, the American Falls.

Three extensive views of the falls may be obtained from three different places. In general, the first opportunity travelers have of seeing the cataract is from the high road, which at one point lies near the back of the river. This place, however, being considerably above the level of the falls and a good way beyond them, affords a view that is comparatively imperfect and unimposing.

The Table Rock, from which the falls of the Niagara may be contemplated in all their grandeur, lies on an exact level with the edge of the cataract on the Canadian side and indeed forms a part of the precipice over which the water rushes. It derives its name from the circumstance of its projecting beyond the cliffs that support it, like the leaf of a table. To gain this position, it is necessary to descend a steep bank and to follow a path that winds among shrubbery and trees, which entirely conceal from the eye the scene that awaits him who traverses it.

When near the termination of this road, a few steps carried me beyond all these obstructions, and a magnificent amphitheater of cataracts burst upon my view with appalling suddenness and majesty. However, in a moment the scene was concealed from my eyes by a dense cloud of spray which involved me so completely that I did not dare to extricate myself.

A mingled and thunder-like rushing filled my ears. I could see nothing, except when the wind made a chasm in the spray, and then tremendous cataracts seemed to encompass me on every side while, below, a raging and foamy gulf of undiscoverable extent lashed the rocks with its hissing waves and swallowed, under a horrible obscurity, the smoking floods that were precipitated into its bosom.

At first the sky was obscured by clouds, but after a few minutes the sun burst forth and the breeze, subsiding at the same time, permitted the spray to ascend perpendicularly. A host of pyramidal clouds rose majestically, one after another, from the abyss at the bottom of the falls, and each, when it had ascended a little above the edge of the cataract, displayed a beautiful rainbow which in a few moments was gradually transferred into the bosom of the cloud that immediately succeeded.

The spray of the Great Falls had extended itself through a wide space directly over me and, receiving the full influence of the sun, exhibited a luminous and magnificent rainbow which continued to overarch and irradiate the spot on which I stood, while I enthusiastically contemplated the indescribable scene.

Any person who has nerve enough may plunge his hand into the water of the Great Falls, after it is projected over the precipice, merely by lying down flat with his face beyond the edge of the Table Rock and stretching out his arm to its utmost extent. The experiment is truly a horrible one and such as I would not wish to repeat, for, even to this day, I feel a shuddering and recoiling sensation when I recollect having been in the posture above described.

The body of water which composes the middle part of the Great Falls is so immense that it descends nearly two-thirds of the space without being ruffled or broken. The solemn calmness with which it rolls over the edge of the precipice is finely contrasted with the perturbed appearance it assumes after having reached the gulf below. But the water towards each side of the falls is shattered the moment it drops over the rock and loses, as it descends in a great measure, the character of a fluid, being divided into pyramidal-shaped fragments, the bases of which are turned upwards.

The surface of the gulf below the cataract presents a very singular aspect, seeming, as it were, filled with an immense quantity of hoarfrost which is agitated by small and rapid undulation. The particles of water are dazzlingly white and do not apparently unite together, as might be supposed, but seem to continue for a time in a state of distinct comminution and to repel each other with a thrilling and shivering motion which cannot easily be described.

The road to the bottom of the falls presents many more difficulties than that which leads to the Table Rock. After leaving the Table Rock the traveler must proceed down the river nearly half a mile where he will come to a small chasm in the bank, in which there is a spiral staircase enclosed in a wooden building. By descending the stair, which is seventy or eighty feet in perpendicular height, he will find himself under the precipice, on the top of which he formerly walked. A high but sloping bank extends from its base to the edge of the river, and on the summit of this there is a narrow slippery path, covered with angular fragments of rock, which leads to the Great Falls.

The impending cliffs, hung with a profusion of trees and brushwood, overarch this road and seem to vibrate with the thunders of the cataract. In some places they rise abruptly to the height of one hundred feet and display, upon their surfaces, fossil shells and the organic remains of a former world, thus sublimely leading the mind to contemplate the convulsions which nature has undergone since the creation.

As the traveler advances, he is frightfully stunned by the appalling noise. Clouds of spray sometimes envelop him and suddenly check his faltering steps; rattlesnakes start from the cavities of the rocks; the scream of eagles soaring among the whirlwinds of eddying vapor which obscure the gulf of the cataract, at intervals announce that the raging waters have hurled some bewildered animal over the precipice. After scrambling among piles of huge rocks that obscure his way, the traveler gains the bottom of the falls, where the soul can be susceptible only of one emotion — that of uncontrollable terror.

It was not until I had, by frequent excursions to the falls, in some measure familiarized my mind with their sublimities, that I ventured to explore the recesses of the Great Cataract. The precipice over which it rolls is very much arched underneath, while the impetus which the water receives in its descent projects it far beyond the cliff. Thus, an immense Gothic arch is formed by the rock and the torrent. Twice I entered this cavern and twice I was obliged to retrace my steps, lest I should be suffocated by the blast of dense spray that whirled around me. However, the third time I succeeded in advancing about twenty-five yards.

Here darkness began to encircle me. On one side, the black cliff stretched itself into a gigantic arch far above my head, and on the other, the dense and hissing torrent formed an impenetrable sheet of foam with which I was drenched in a moment. The rocks were so slippery that I could hardly keep my feet or hold securely by them, while the horrid din made me think the precipices above were tumbling down in colossal fragments upon my head.

A little way below the Great Falls the river is, comparatively speaking, so tranquil that a ferryboat plies between the Canadian and American shores for the convenience of travelers. When I first crossed, the heaving flood tossed about the skiff with a violence that seemed very alarming, but as soon as we gained the middle of the river my attention was altogether engaged by the surpassing grandeur of the scene before me.

I was now in the area of a semicircle of cataracts more than three thousand feet in extent and floated on the surface of a gulf, raging, fathomless, and interminable. Majestic cliffs, splendid rainbows, lofty trees, and columns of spray were the gorgeous decorations of this theater of wonders, while a dazzling sun shed refulgent glories upon every part of the scene.

Surrounded with clouds of vapor and stunned into a state of confusion and terror by the hideous noise, I looked upwards to the height of 150 feet and saw vast floods — dense, awful, and stupendous — vehemently bursting over the precipice and rolling down as if the windows of heaven were opened to pour another deluge upon the earth. Loud sounds, resembling discharges of artillery or volcanic explosions, were now distinguishable amidst the watery tumult and added terrors to the abyss from which they issued. The sun, looking majestically through the ascending spray, was encircled by a radiant halo, while fragments of rainbows floated on every side and momentarily vanished, only to give place to a succession of others more brilliant.

Looking backwards I saw the Niagara River, again becoming calm and tranquil, rolling magnificently between the towering cliffs that rose on either side. A gentle breeze ruffled the waters, and beautiful birds fluttered around as if to welcome its egress from those clouds and its thunders and rainbows, which were the heralds of its precipitation into the abyss of the cataract.

QUESTIONS. 1. What is the form and height of Niagara Falls? 2. Is there more than one fall? 3. What divides it? 4. From what place may the falls be seen in all their grandeur? 5. Where is Table Rock, and why is it so named? 6. Is there much water? 7. How does it appear below the falls? 8. What effect is produced upon the mind by the union of all these sights and sounds?

SPELL AND DEFINE. 1. irregular   2. semicircle   3. extensive
4. unimposing   5. opportunity   6. contemplated   7. conceal   8. traverses
9. termination   10. amphitheater   11. appalling   12. chasm
13. tremendous   14. encompass   15. obscurity   16. pyramidal
17. gradually 18. luminous 19. irradiate 20. indescribable 21. sensation
22. perturbed 23. undulations 24. comminution 25. spiral 26. impending
27. vibrate   28. convulsion   29. conscious   30. uncontrollable
31. suffocated 32. impetus 33. colossal 34. tranquil 35. interminable
36. gorgeous 37. decoration 38. halo 39. egress 40. herald

LESSON XXI

Niagara Falls — U. S. Review

RULE. Let the pupil stand at a great distance from the teacher and then try to read so loudly and distinctly that the teacher may hear each syllable.

Tremendous torrent! for an instant hush
The terrors of thy voice, and cast aside
Those wide-involving shadows, that my eyes
May see the fearful beauty of thy face!
I am not all unworthy of thy sight;

For, from my very boyhood, have I loved,
Shunning the meaner track of common minds,
To look on nature in her loftier moods.
At the fierce rushing of the hurricane,
At the near bursting of the thunderbolt,
I have been touched with joy, and when the sea,
Lashed by the wind, hath rocked my bark and
    showed
Its yawning caves beneath me, I have loved
Its dangers and the wrath of elements.
But never yet the madness of the sea
Hath moved me as thy grandeur moves me now.

    Thou flowest on in quiet, till thy waves
Grow broken 'midst the rocks; thy current then
Shoots onward, like the irresistible course
Of destiny. Ah! terribly they rage —
The hoarse and rapid whirlpools there! My brain
Grows wild, my senses wander as I gaze
Upon the hurrying waters, and my sight
Vainly would follow, as toward the verge
Sweeps the wide torrent — waves innumerable
Meet there and madden — waves innumerable
Urge on and overtake the waves before,
And disappear in thunder and in foam.

    They reach — they leap the barrier; the abyss
Swallows, insatiable, the sinking waves.
A thousand rainbows arch them, and the woods
Are deafened with the roar. The violent shock
Shatters to vapor the descending sheets,
A cloudy whirlwind fills the gulf and heaves
The mighty pyramid of circling mist
To heaven. The solitary hunter, near,
Pauses with terror in the forest shades.

God of all truth! in other lands I've seen
Lying philosophers, blaspheming men,
Questioners of thy mysteries that draw
Their fellows deep into impiety;
And therefore doth my spirit seek thy face
In earth's majestic solitudes. Even here
My heart doth open all itself to thee.
In this immensity of loneliness
I feel thy hand upon me. To my ear
The eternal thunder of the cataract brings
Thy voice, and I am humbled as I hear.

Dread torrent! that with wonder and with fear
Dost overwhelm the soul of him that looks
Upon thee and dost bear it from itself,
Whence hast thou thy beginning? Who supplies,
Age after age, thy unexhausted springs?
What power hath ordered that, when all thy weight
Descends into the deep, the swollen waves
Rise not and roll to overwhelm the earth?

The Lord hath opened His omnipotent hand,
Covered thy face with clouds, and given His voice
To thy down-rushing waters; He hath girt
Thy terrible forehead with His radiant bow.
I see thy never-resting water run,
And I bethink me how the tide of time
Sweeps to eternity. So pass of man —
Pass, like a noonday dream — the blossoming days,
And he awakes to sorrow.

Hear, dread Niagara! my latest voice.
Yet a few years, and the cold earth shall close
Over the bones of him who sings thee now
Thus feelingly. Would that this my humble verse
Might be, like thee, immortal. I, meanwhile,
Cheerfully passing to the appointed rest,

Might raise my radiant forehead in the clouds
To listen to the echoes of my fame.

QUESTIONS. 1. What is the difference between this lesson and the last? 2. What is the difference between prose and poetry? 3. Do the lines in poetry always rhyme? 4. What is that poetry called which does not? 5. What kind of poetry is this lesson? 6. What is meant by feet in poetic composition? 7. Answer the questions proposed in the fifth paragraph. 8. How are Niagara Falls like time?

SPELL AND DEFINE. 1. unworthy   2. yawning   3. grandeur 4. irresistible   5. innumerable   6. insatiable   7. pyramid   8. philosophers 9. majestic   10. immensity   11. overwhelm   12. swollen   13. omnipotent 14. radiant   15. immortal

LESSON XXII

Character of Wilberforce — Anonymous

RULE. Let the student notice, as he reads, when the final consonant of any word is joined to the vowel of the next word.

The speeches of Mr. Wilberforce are among the very few good things now remaining in the British Parliament. His diction is elegant, rich, and spirited; his tones are so distinct and so melodious that the most hostile ear hangs on them delighted. His address is so insinuating that, if he talked nonsense, you would feel yourself obliged to hear him. I recollect when the House had been tired night after night with discussing the endless questions relating to Indian policy, when the commerce and finances and resources of our oriental empire had exhausted the lungs of all the speakers and the patience of all the auditors — at that period Mr. Wilberforce, with a just confidence in his powers, ventured to broach the subject of Hindu conversion.

He spoke three hours, but nobody seemed fatigued. All, indeed, were pleased, some with the ingenious artifices of his manner but most with the glowing language of his heart. Much as I differed from him in opinion, it was impossible not to be delighted with his eloquence. I felt disposed to agree with him, that much good must arise to the human mind by being engaged in a controversy which will exercise most of its faculties.

Mr. Wilberforce is now verging towards age [written in 1814 or 1815] and speaks but seldom. He, however, never speaks without exciting a wish that he would say more. He maintains, like Mr. Grattan, great respectability of character by disdaining to mix in the daily paltry squabbles of party; he is no hunter after place.

I confess, I always look with equal respect and pleasure on this eloquent veteran, lingering among his bustling but far inferior posterity. Well has he a right to linger on the spot where he achieved one of the greatest laurels that ever brightened in the wreath of fame, a laurel better than that of the hero, as it is not stained with blood or tears, better than that of the statesman who improves the civilization of his country, inasmuch as to create is better than to improve.

Here is the man whose labors abolished the slave trade, who at one blow struck away the barbarism of a hundred nations and elevated myriads of human beings, degraded to the brute, into all the dignified capacities of civilized man. To have done this is the most noble, as it is the most useful, work which any individual could accomplish.

QUESTIONS. 1. What were the characteristics of Wilberforce's style? 2. When was this piece written? 3. What anecdote is given concerning the "Hindu conversion"? 4. What great achievement has immortalized the name of Wilberforce?

SPELL AND DEFINE. 1. Parliament   2. elegant   3. insinuating 4. discussing   5. commerce   6. confidence   7. hackneyed   8. ingenious 9. impossible   10. respectability   11. squabbles   12. civilization 13. barbarism 14. accomplish

LESSON XXIII

Pleasure in Affliction — Akenside

RULE. Sound the vowels correctly and very full.

EXERCISES UNDER THE RULE. Prolong the following vowel sounds that are italicized: *a*-ge, *a*-we, *a*-rm, *o*-ld, *ou*-r, *ee*-l, *oo*-ze, bu-*oy*, *i*-sle.

Behold the ways

Of Heaven's eternal destiny to man,
Forever just, benevolent, and wise;
That Virtue's awful steps, howe'er pursued,
By vexing fortune and intrusive pain,
Should never be divided from her chaste,
Her fair attendant, pleasure. Need I urge
Thy tardy thought through all the various round
Of this existence, that thy softening soul
At length may learn what energy the hand
Of Virtue mingles in the bitter tide
Of passion, swelling with distress and pain,
To mitigate the sharp, with gracious drops
Of cordial pleasure? Ask the faithful youth,
Why the cold urn of her whom long he loved,
So often fills his arms; so often draws
His lonely footsteps at the silent hour,
To pay the mournful tribute of his tears?
Oh! he will tell thee that the wealth of worlds
Should ne'er seduce his bosom to forego
That sacred hour, when, stealing from the noise
Of care and envy, sweet remembrance soothes,
With Virtue's kindest looks, his aching breast,
And turns his tears to rapture. Ask the crowd
Which flies impatient from the village-walk
To climb the neighboring cliffs, when far below,
The cruel winds have hurled upon the coast

Some helpless bark; while sacred pity melts
The general eye, or terror's icy hand
Smites their distorted limbs and horrent hair;
While every mother closer to her breast
Catches her child, and pointing where the waves
Foam through the shattered vessel, shrieks aloud,
As one poor wretch that spreads his piteous arms
For succor, swallowed by the roaring surge;
As now another, dashed against the rock,
Drops lifeless down. O deemest thou indeed
No kind endearment here by nature given
To mutual terror and compassion's tears?
No sweetly melting softness, which attracts
O'er all that edge of pain, the social powers
To this, their proper action and their end?

QUESTIONS. 1. What is the subject of this lesson?   2. What two instances are there (lines 1–7) of the figure of speech called personification?   3. Lines 6 to 13 form one question. What is the sense of it in a few words?   4. What is the pleasure enjoyed by the youth bereaved of a friend, even in mourning at the grave?   5. What is the pleasure felt in viewing the horrors of a shipwreck?

SPELL AND DEFINE.   1. destiny   2. benevolent   3. intrusive   4. existence   5. softening   6. energy   7. mitigate   8. cordial   9. mournful   10. remembrance   11. rapture   12. neighboring   13. horrent   14. deemest   15. endearment   16. compassion

LESSON XXIV

Make Way for Liberty — Montgomery

RULE. In reading poetry, be careful not to join the final consonant of one word to the vowel of the next word.

EXAMPLE. Loud as His thunder shout His praise, and sound it lofty as His throne.

The following way of reading it shows the fault to be remedied by observing the rule: Lou das His thunder shout His praise, and soun dit lofty as His throne.

At the battle of Sempach (A.D. 1386) between the Swiss and Austrians, the latter, having obtained possession of a narrow pass in the mountains, formed a phalanx with pre-sented spears. Until this was broken, the Swiss could not hope to make a successful attack. At last, Arnold Winkelried, leaving the Swiss ranks, rushed upon the Austrian spears and, receiving in his body as many points as possible, made a breach in the line which resulted in the complete rout of the Austrian army.

"Make way for Liberty!" he cried;
Made way for Liberty, and died!

In arms the Austrian phalanx stood,
A living wall, a human wood!
A wall, where every conscious stone
Seemed to its kindred-thousands grown;
A rampart all assaults to bear,
Till time to dust their frames should wear;
A wood, like that enchanted grove,
In which with fiends Rinaldo strove,
Where every silent tree possessed
A spirit prisoned in his breast,
Which the first stroke of coming strife
Would startle into hideous life.
So dense, so still, the Austrians stood,
A living wall, a human wood!
Impregnable their front appears,
All horrent with projected spears,
Whose polished points before them shine,
From flank to flank, one brilliant line,
Bright as the breakers' splendors run
Along the billows, to the sun.

Opposed to these, a hovering band,
Contending for their native land:
Peasants, whose newfound strength had broke
From manly necks the ignoble yoke,
And forged their fetters into swords,
On equal terms to fight their lords;
And what insurgent rage had gained,
In many a mortal fray maintained.
Marshaled once more at freedom's call,
They came to conquer or to fall,
Where he who conquered, he who fell,
Was deemed a dead, or living Tell!
Such virtue had that patriot breathed,
So to the soil his soul bequeathed,
That wheresoe'er his arrows flew,
Heroes in his own likeness grew,
And warriors sprang from every sod
Which his awakening footsteps trod.

And now the work of life and death
Hung on the passing of a breath;
The fire of conflict burned within;
The battle trembled to begin.
Yet while the Austrians held their ground,
Point for attack was nowhere found;
Where'er the impatient Switzers gazed,
The unbroken line of lances blazed;
That line 'twere suicide to meet,
And perish at their tyrants' feet —
How could they rest within their graves,
And leave their homes, the homes of slaves?
Would they not feel their children tread
With clanking chains above their head?

It must not be, this day, this hour,
Annihilates the oppressor's power;
All Switzerland is in the field,

She will not fly, she cannot yield —
She must not fall; her better fate
Here gives her an immortal date.
Few were the numbers she could boast;
But every freeman was a host
And felt as though himself were he,
On whose sole arm hung victory.

It did depend on *one* indeed;
Behold him — Arnold Winkelried!
There sounds not to the trump of fame
The echo of a nobler name.
Unmarked he stood amid the throng,
In rumination deep and long,
Till you might see with sudden grace,
The very thought come over his face;
And by the motion of his form,
Anticipate the bursting storm;
And by the uplifting of his brow
Tell where the bolt would strike, and how.

But 'twas no sooner thought than done;
The field was in a moment won:
"Make way for Liberty!" he cried,
Then ran, with arms extended wide,
As if his dearest friend to clasp,
Ten spears he swept within his grasp.
"Make way for Liberty!" he cried,
Their keen points met from side to side;
He bowed among them like a tree,
And thus made way for Liberty.
Swift to the breach his comrades fly;
"Make way for Liberty!" they cry,
And through the Austrian phalanx dart,
As rushed the spears through Arnold's heart;
While instantaneous as his fall,
Rout, ruin, panic, scattered all.

An earthquake could not overthrow
A city with a surer blow.

Thus Switzerland again was free;
Thus Death made way for Liberty!

QUESTIONS. 1. When, and between whom, did the battle of Lempach take place?   2. How were the Austrians drawn up?   3. What was the necessity for the self-sacrifice of Winkelried?   4. What was the result? 5. Who was Rinaldo?   6. How many spears did Winkelried receive in his body?   7. Is war justifiable?

SPELL AND DEFINE. 1. phalanx   2. rampart   3. impregnable 4. horrent   5. breakers   6. peasants   7. insurgent   8. rumination 9. instantaneous

LESSON XXV

Speech of Logan, Chief of the Mingoes — Jefferson

RULE. Sound the vowels correctly and very full.

EXERCISES UNDER THE RULE. Prolong the following vowel sounds that are italicized: *a*-ge, *a*-we, *a*-rm, *o*-ld, *o*-ur, *ee*-l, bu-*oy*, *i*-sle.

I may challenge the whole of the orations of Demosthenes and Cicero and, indeed, of any more eminent orators, if Europe or the world has furnished more eminent, to produce a single passage superior to the speech of Logan, a Mingo chief, delivered to Lord Dunmore when he was governor of Virginia. As a testimony of Indian talents in this line, I beg leave to introduce it by first stating the incidents necessary for understanding it.

In the spring of the year 1774, a robbery was committed by some Indians upon certain land adventurers on the Ohio River. The whites in that quarter, according to their custom, undertook to punish this outrage in a summary way. Captain Michael Cresap and one Daniel Greathouse, leading on these parties, surprised, at different times, traveling and hunting parties of the Indians, who had their women and children with them, and murdered many. Among these were unfortunately the family of Logan, a chief celebrated in peace and war and long distinguished as the friend of the whites.

This unworthy return provoked his vengeance. He, accordingly, signalized himself in the war which ensued. In the autumn of the same year a decisive battle was fought at the mouth of the Great Kenhawa between the collected forces of the Shawnees, the Mingoes, and the Delawares and a detachment of the Virginia militia. The Indians were defeated and sued for peace. Logan, however, disdained to be seen among the suppliants. But, lest the sincerity of a treaty from which so distinguished a chief absented himself should be distrusted, he sent, by a messenger, the following speech to be delivered to Lord Dunmore.

"I appeal to any white man to say, if ever he entered Logan's cabin hungry and he gave him not meat, if ever he came cold and naked and he clothed him not. During the course of the last long and bloody war, Logan remained idle in his cabin, an advocate for peace. Such was my love for the whites that my countrymen pointed as they passed and said, 'Logan is the friend of the white men.' I had even thought to live with you but for the injuries of one man. Colonel Cresap, last spring, in cold blood and unprovoked, murdered all the relatives of Logan, not sparing even my women and children. There runs not a drop of my blood in the veins of any living creature. This called on me for revenge. I have sought it. I have killed many. I have fully glutted my vengeance. For my country, I rejoice at the beams of peace but do not harbor a thought that mine is the joy of fear. Logan never felt fear. He will not turn on his heel to save his life. Who is there to mourn for Logan? Not one."

QUESTIONS. 1. Who was Demosthenes? 2. Cicero? 3. When was Dunmore governor of Virginia? 4. Who undertook to punish the Indians? 5. Whose family was killed? 6. Where was a decisive battle fought? 7. Where does the Kenhawa rise? 8. Did Logan appear among the suppliants?

SPELL AND DEFINE. 1. challenge   2. outrage   3. summary 4. signalized 5. detachment 6. glutted 7. harbor

LESSON XXVI

The Alhambra by Moonlight — Irving

RULE. When two or more consonants come together, let the pupil be careful to sound every one distinctly.

EXERCISES UNDER THE RULE. He clenched his *fists*. He *lifts* his awful form. He makes his *payments*. Thou *smoothed'st* his rugged path. The *president's speech*.

I have given a picture of my apartment on my first taking possession of it. A few evenings have produced a thorough change in the scene and in my feelings. The moon, which then was invisible, has gradually gained upon the nights and now rolls in full splendor above the towers, pouring a flood of tempered light into every court and hall. The garden beneath my window is gently lighted up; the orange and citron trees are tipped with silver; the fountain sparkles in the moonbeams; even the blush of the rose is faintly visible.

I have sat for hours at my window, inhaling the sweetness of the garden and musing on the checkered features of those whose history is dimly shadowed out in the elegant memorials around. Sometimes I have issued forth at midnight when everything was quiet and have wandered over the whole building. Who can do justice to a moonlit night in such a climate and in such a place! The temperature of an Andalusian midnight in summer is perfectly ethereal. We seem lifted up into a purer atmosphere; there is a serenity of soul, a buoyancy of spirits, an elasticity of frame that render mere *existence* enjoyment. The effect of moonlight, too, on the Alhambra, has something like enchantment. Every rent and chasm of time, every moldering tint and weather stain disappears; the marble resumes its original whiteness; the long colonnades brighten in the moonbeams; the halls are illuminated with a softened radiance until the whole edifice reminds one of the enchanted palace of an Arabian tale.

At such a time, I have ascended to the little pavilion called the queen's toilette to enjoy its varied and extensive prospect. To the right, the snowy summits of the Sierra Nevada would gleam, like silver clouds, against the darker firmament, and all the outlines of the mountain would be softened, yet delicately defined. My delight, however, would be to lean over the parapet of the Tocador and gaze down upon Granada, spread out like a map below me, all buried in deep repose and its white palaces and convents sleeping, as it were, in the moonshine.

Sometimes I would hear the faint sounds of castanets from some party of dancers lingering in the Alameda; at other times, I have heard the dubious tones of a guitar and the notes of a single voice rising from some solitary street and have pictured to myself some youthful cavalier serenading his lady's window, a gallant custom of former days but now sadly on the decline except in the remote towns and villages of Spain.

Such are the scenes that have detained me for many an hour, loitering about the courts and balconies of the castle, enjoying that mixture of reverie and sensation which steal away existence in a southern climate — and it has been almost morning before I have retired to my bed and been lulled to sleep by the falling waters of the fountain of Lindaraxa.

QUESTIONS. 1. What and where is the Alhambra?   2. What are castanets? 3. What is the natural instrument of the Spaniards? 4. Where is Andalusia?

SPELL AND DEFINE. 1. apartment   2. splendor   3. inhaling
4. checkered 5. memorials 6. enchantment 7. colonnades 8. buoyancy
9. pavilion   10. varied   11. firmament   12. palaces   13. castanets
14. cavalier 15. serenading 16. reverie 17. Lindaraxa

LESSON XXVII

Portrait of a Patriarch—Addison

RULE. Be careful to read the *last words* of every sentence with a slow
and full tone.

I cannot forbear making an extract of several passages
which I have always read with great delight in the book of
Job. It is the account which that holy man gives of his
behavior in the days of his prosperity and, if considered only
as a human composition, is a finer picture of a charitable
and good-natured man than is to be met with in any other
author.

"Oh that I were as in months past, as in the days when
God preserved me; when his candle shined upon my head,
and when by his light I walked through darkness;... when
the Almighty was yet with me, when my children were about
me; when I washed my steps with butter, and the rock
poured me out rivers of oil....

"When the ear heard me, then it blessed me; and when
the eye saw me, it gave witness to me: because I delivered
the poor that cried, and the fatherless, and him that had
none to help him. The blessing of him that was ready to
perish came upon me: and I caused the widow's heart to sing
for joy.... I was eyes to the blind, and feet was I to the lame.
I was a father to the poor: and the cause which I knew not I
searched out....

"Did not I weep for him that was in trouble? was not my
soul grieved for the poor?... Let me be weighed in an even
balance that God may know mine integrity... If I did despise

the cause of my manservant or of my maidservant, when
they contended with me; what then shall I do when God
riseth up? and when he visiteth, what shall I answer him?
Did not he that made me in the womb make him? and did
not one fashion us in the womb?

"If I have withheld the poor from their desire, or have
caused the eyes of the widow to fail; or have eaten my morsel
myself alone, and the fatherless hath not eaten thereof;... if
I have seen any perish for want of clothing, or any poor
without covering; if his loins have not blessed me, and if he
were not warmed with the fleece of my sheep; if I have lifted
up my hand against the fatherless, when I saw my help in
the gate: then let mine arm fall from my shoulder blade, and
mine arm be broken from the bone....

"If I rejoiced at the destruction of him that hated me, or
lifted up myself when evil found him; (Neither have I suffered my mouth to sin by wishing a curse to his soul.) if the
men of my tabernacle said not, Oh that we had of his flesh!
we cannot be satisfied. The stranger did not lodge in the
street: but I opened my doors to the traveler.... If my land cry
against me, or that the furrows likewise thereof complain; if
I have eaten the fruits thereof without money, or have
caused the owners thereof to lose their life: let thistles grow
instead of wheat, and cockle instead of barley."

QUESTIONS. 1. What character is here described?   2. What is a
patriarch? 3. Considered merely as an uninspired composition, how does
this compare with all others?

SPELL AND DEFINE. 1. composition   2. charitable   3. Almighty
4. fatherless 5. weighed 6. shoulder blade 7. destruction 8. cockle

LESSON XXVIII

An End of All Perfection—Mrs. Sigourney

RULE. Pronounce the vowels fully and give them the proper sound.

EXERCISES UNDER THE RULE. Sound the following vowels long and full: *e*-rr, *a*-ll, *o*-r, *a*-ge, *e*-dge, *a*-rm, *a*-t, *o*-ld, *ou*-r, *ee*-l, *i*-t, *oo*-ze, p-*u*-ll, b-*oy*, *i*-sle.

I have seen man in the glory of his days and the pride of his strength. He was built like the tall cedar that lifts its head above the forest trees, like the strong oak that strikes its root deeply into the earth. He feared no danger; he felt no sickness; he wondered that any should groan or sigh at pain. His mind was vigorous like his body; he was perplexed at no intricacy; he was daunted at no difficulty. Into hidden things he searched, and what was crooked he made straight.

He went forth fearlessly upon the face of the mighty deep; he surveyed the nations of the earth; he measured the distances of the stars and called them by their names; he gloried in the extent of his knowledge, in the vigor of his understanding, and strove to search even into what the Almighty had concealed. When I looked on him I said, "What a piece of work is man! how noble in reason! how infinite in faculties! in form and moving how express and admirable! in action how like an angel! in apprehension how like a god!"

I returned — his look was no more lofty nor his step proud. His broken frame was like some ruined tower, his hairs were white and scattered, and his eye gazed vacantly upon what was passing around him. The vigor of his intellect was wasted, and of all that he had gained by study, nothing remained. He feared when there was no danger, and when there was no sorrow he wept. His memory was decayed and treacherous and showed him only broken images of the glory that was departed.

His house was to him like a strange land, and his friends were counted as his enemies. He thought himself strong and healthful while his foot tottered on the verge of the grave. He said of his son, "He is my brother," of his daughter, "I know her not," and he inquired what was his own name. One who supported his last steps and ministered to his many wants said to me, as I looked on the melancholy scene, "Let thine heart receive instruction, for thou hast seen an end of all earthly perfection."

I have seen a beautiful female treading the first stages of youth and entering joyfully into the pleasures of life. The glance of her eye was variable and sweet, and on her cheek trembled something like the first blush of the morning; her lips moved, and there was harmony; when she floated in the dance, her light form, like the aspen, seemed to move with every breeze. I returned, but she was not in the dance; I sought her in the gay circle of her companions, but I found her not.

Her eye sparkled not there — the music of her voice was silent — she rejoiced on earth no more. I saw a train, sable and slow-paced, which bore sadly to an open grave what once was animated and beautiful. They paused as they approached, and a voice broke the awful silence: "Mingle ashes with ashes and dust with its original dust. To the earth whence it was taken, consign we the body of our sister." They covered her with the damp soil and the clods of the valley, and the worms crowded into her silent abode. Yet one sad mourner lingered, to cast himself upon the grave, and as he wept he said, "There is no beauty or grace or loveliness that continueth in man, for this is the end of all his glory and perfection."

I have seen an infant with a fair brow and a frame like polished ivory. His limbs were pliant in his sports; he rejoiced, and again he wept. But whether his glowing cheek dimpled with smiles or his blue eyes were brilliant with tears, still I said to my heart, "He is beautiful." He was like the first pure blossom which some cherished plant had shot forth, whose cup is filled with a dewdrop and whose head reclines upon its parent stem.

I again saw this child when the lamp of reason first dawned in his mind. His soul was gentle and peaceful, his eyes sparkled with joy as he looked round on this good and pleasant world. He ran swiftly in the ways of knowledge; he bowed his ear to instruction; he stood like a lamb before his teachers. He was not proud or envious or stubborn, and he had never heard of the vices and vanities of the world. When I looked upon him, I remembered that our Savior had said, "Except ye become as little children, ye cannot enter into the kingdom of heaven."

Then the scene was changed, and I saw a man whom the world called honorable, and many waited for his smile. They pointed out the fields that were his and talked of the silver and gold that he had gathered; they admired the stateliness of his domes and extolled the honor of his family. And his heart answered secretly, "By my wisdom have I gotten all this." So he returned no thanks to God, neither did he fear or serve Him.

As I passed along, I heard the complaints of the laborers who had reaped down his fields and the cries of the poor whose covering he had taken away. But the sound of feasting and revelry was in his apartments, and the unfed beggar came tottering from his door. He considered not that the cries of the oppressed were continually entering into the ears of the Most High. When I knew that this man was once the teachable child that I had loved, the beautiful infant that I had gazed upon with delight, I said in my bitterness, "I have seen an end of all perfection," and I laid my mouth in the dust.

QUESTIONS. 1. What changes pass upon the proudest forms — and the most undaunted intellects — from the lapse of time? 2. What takes the place of childhood and manhood? 3. What becomes of vanity, as time flies past? 4. What becomes of the docility and loveliness of childhood?

SPELL AND DEFINE. 1. perplexed   2. intricacy   3. fearlessly 4. understanding 5. apprehension 6. vacantly 7. intellect 8. treacherous 9. joyfully   10. returned   11. continued   12. envious   13. stubborn 14. honorable 15. extolled 16. complaints 17. apartments 18. tottering 19. perfection

LESSON XXIX

A Rest for the Weary — Montgomery

RULE. When anything very solemn or devotional is to be read, there should be a full, solemn tone of voice. The piece should be read slowly, and long pauses should be made at the commas.

There is a calm for those who weep,
A rest for weary pilgrims found,
They softly lie and sweetly sleep,
Low in the ground.

The storm that wrecks the wint'ry sky
No more disturbs their deep repose,
Than summer evening's latest sigh
That shuts the rose.

I long to lay this painful head
And aching heart beneath the soil,
To slumber in that dreamless bed
From all my toil.

For misery stole me at my birth
And cast me helpless on the wild.
I perish; O my mother, Earth,
Take home thy child.

On thy dear lap these limbs reclined,
Shall gently molder into thee;
Nor leave one wretched trace behind,
Resembling me.

Hark! A strange sound affrights me
My pulse, my brain runs wild, I rave;
Ah! who art thou whose voice I hear?
I am the Grave!

The Grave, that never spake before,
Hath found at length a tongue to chide.
O listen! I will speak no more;
Be silent, Pride.

Art thou a wretch, of hope forlorn,
The victim of consuming care?
Is thy distracted conscience torn
By fell despair?

Do foul misdeeds of former times
Wring with remorse thy guilty breast?
And ghosts of unforgiven crimes
Murder thy rest?

Lash'd by the furies of the mind,
From wrath and vengeance would'st thou flee?
Ah! think not, hope not, fool, to find
A friend in me.

By all the terrors of the tomb,
Beyond the power of tongue to tell,
By the dread secrets of my womb,
By death and hell,

I charge thee live! repent and pray;
In dust thine infamy deplore;
There yet is mercy; go thy way
And sin no more.

Whate'er thy lot, whoe'er thou be,
Confess thy folly, kiss the rod,
And in thy chastening sorrows see
The hand of God.

A bruised reed He will not break;
Afflictions all His children feel,

He wounds them for His mercy's sake,
He wounds to heal!

Humbled beneath His mighty hand,
Prostrate His Providence adore.
Tis done! arise! He bids thee stand,
To fall no more.

Now traveler in the vale of tears!
To realms of everlasting light
Through time's dark wilderness of years,
Pursue thy flight.

There is a calm for those that weep,
A rest for weary pilgrims found.
And while the moldering ashes sleep
Low in the ground;

The soul, of origin divine,
God's glorious image, freed from clay,
In heaven's eternal sphere shall shine
A star of day!

The sun is but a spark of fire,
A transient meteor in the sky,
The soul, immortal as its sire,
Shall never die.

QUESTIONS. 1. Who is represented as speaking in the eighth verse and onward? 2. What is a figure of speech? 3. What is that figure of speech called which represents the grave or any inanimate object as speaking? 4. With what sentiments should thoughts of death inspire us? 5. Why is death ever desirable? 6. To what will it introduce us? 7. Is it wise to make no preparation for death? 8. Should not our eternal welfare be our chief concern in the world?

SPELL AND DEFINE. 1. pilgrims 2. dreamless 3. reclined 4. molder 5. resembling 6. affrights 7. chide 8. forlorn 9. victim 10. consuming 11. conscience 12. remorse 13. vengeance 14. terrors 15. infamy

16. deplore   17. chastening   18. afflictions   19. prostrate   20. adore
21. realms   22. everlasting   23. wilderness   24. pursue   25. origin
26. eternal   27. sphere   28. transient   29. meteor

LESSON XXX

Character of Mr. Brougham — Anonymous

RULE. Let the pupil notice, as he reads, where a comma is not marked by a proper pause.

Brougham is a thunderbolt. He may come in the dark, he may come at random, his path may be in the viewless and graspless air — but still give him something solid, let him come in contact with the earth, and, be it beautiful or barren, it feels the power of his terrible visitation.

You see not, or rather you heed not, the agent which works. But, just as when the archgiant of physical destroyers rends his way, you see the kingdoms of nature yielding at his approach and the mightiest of their productions brushed aside as though they were dust or torn as though they were gossamer.

While he raises his voice in the house, while he builds firmly and broadly the bases of his propositions and snatches from every science a beam to enlarge and strengthen his work, and while he indignantly beats down and tramples upon all that has been reared by his antagonist, you feel as if the wind of annihilation were in his hand and the power of destruction in his possession.

There cannot be a greater treat than to hear Brougham upon one of those questions which give scope for the mighty swell of his mind and which permit him to launch the bolts of that tremendous sarcasm for which he has not now, and perhaps never had, an equal in the House. When his display is a reply, you see his long and lathy figure drawn aside from others and coiled up within itself like a snake and his eyes glancing from under the slouched hat, as fiery and as fatal as those of the basilisk; you mark the twin sisters of irony and contempt playing about the tense and compressed line of his mouth.

Up rises the orator, slowly and clumsily, his body swung into an attitude which is none of the most graceful. His long and sallow visage seems lengthened and deepened in its hue. His eyes, his nose, and mouth seem huddled together as if, while he presses every illustration into his speech, he were at the same time condensing all his senses into one. There is a lowering sublimity in his brows, which one seldom sees equaled. The obliquity of the light shows the organization of the upper and lateral parts of his forehead, proud and palpable as the hills of his native north. His left hand is extended with the palm, prepared as an anvil upon which he is ever and anon to hammer, with the forefinger of his right as the preparation to that full swing which is to give life to every muscle and motion to every limb.

He speaks! In the most powerful and sustained and, at the same time, the most close, clear, and logical manner does he demolish the castle which his opponent had built for himself. You hear the sounds, you see the flash, you look for the castle, and it is not. Stone after stone, turret after turret, battlement after battlement, and wing after wing are melted away and nothing left save the sure foundation upon which the orator himself may build.

There are no political bowels in him. He gives no quarter, and no sooner has he razed the fort than he turns to torture the garrison. It is now that his mock solemnity is something more terrible then the satire of Canning, the glow of Burdett, or the glory of Mackintosh.

His features (which are always grave) assume the very depth of solemnity, and his voice (which is always solemn) falls into that under soprano (that visionary tone between speech and whisper), which men employ when they speak of their own graves and coffins. You would imagine it not audible and yet its lowest syllable runs through the House like wildfire. You would think it meant only for the ear of him who is the subject of it, yet it comes immediately and powerfully and without the possibility of being forgotten to everyone within the walls.

You would think it the fond admonition of a sainted father to the errors of a beloved son, yet it has in reality more of that feeling which the Devil is said to exercise when he acts as the accuser of the brethren. You may push aside the bright thing which raises a laugh; you may find a cover from the wit which ambles to you on antithesis or quotation. But against the home reproof of Brougham there is no defense, its course is so firm that you cannot dash it aside.

QUESTIONS. 1. To what is Brougham compared? 2. What is the marked attribute of his style? 3. His personal appearance? 4. His manner, voice, gestures, and so forth?

SPELL AND DEFINE. 1. thunderbolt 2. viewless 3. archgiant
4. mightiest 5. productions 6. gossamer 7. propositions 8. strengthen
9. indignantly   10. antagonist   11. annihilation   12. tremendous
13. sarcasm 14. slouched 15. basilisk 16. compressed 17. lengthened
18. huddled   19. illustration   20. organization   21. battlement
22. visionary 23. immediately 24. antithesis

LESSON XXXI

Elevated Character of Woman — Carter

RULE. Be careful to speak such little words as *of, the, a, in, from* very distinctly and yet not to hold so long on them as on the other more important words.

The influence of the female character is now felt and acknowledged in all the relations of life. I speak not now of those distinguished women who instruct their age through the public press nor of those whose devout strains we take upon our lips when we worship, but of a much larger class of those whose influence is felt in the relations of neighbor, friend, daughter, wife, mother.

Who waits at the couch of the sick to administer tender charities while life lingers or to perform the last acts of kindness when death comes? Where shall we look for those examples of friendship that most adorn our nature, those abiding friendships which trust even when betrayed and survive all changes of fortune? Where shall we find the brightest illustrations of filial piety? Have you ever seen a daughter, herself perhaps timid and helpless, watching the decline of an aged parent and holding out with heroic fortitude to anticipate his wishes, to administer to his wants, and to sustain his tottering steps to the very borders of the grave?

But in no relation does woman exercise so deep an influence, both immediately and prospectively, as in that of Mother. To her is committed the immortal treasure of the infant mind. Upon her devolves the care of the first stages of that course of discipline which is to form of a being, perhaps the most frail and helpless in the world, the fearless ruler of animated creation and the devout adorer of its great Creator.

Her smiles call into exercise the first affections that spring up in our hearts. She cherishes and expands the earliest germs of our intellects. She breathes over us her deepest devotions. She lifts our little hands and teaches our little tongues to lisp in prayer. She watches over us like a guardian angel and protects us through all our helpless years when we know not of her cares and her anxieties on our account. She follows us into the world of men and lives in us and blesses us when she lives not otherwise upon the earth.

What constitutes the center of every home? Whither do our thoughts turn when our feet are weary with wandering and our hearts sick with disappointments? Where shall the truant and forgetful husband go for sympathy unalloyed and without design but to the bosom of her who is ever ready and waiting to share in his adversity or his prosperity? If there be a tribunal where the sins and the follies of a froward child may hope for pardon and forgiveness this side of heaven, that tribunal is the heart of a fond and devoted mother.

Finally, her influence is felt deeply in religion. "If Christianity should be compelled to flee from the mansions of the great, the academies of philosophers, the halls of legislators, or the throng of busy men, we should find her last and purest retreat with woman at the fireside. Her last altar would be the female heart; her last audience would be the children gathered round the knees of the mother; her last sacrifice, the secret prayer escaping in silence from her lips and heard, perhaps, only at the throne of God."

QUESTIONS. 1. What is the influence of female character? 2. What traits of this influence are mentioned in paragraphs 1 and 2? 3. What is the principal sphere of woman's influence? 4. How is her influence, in respect to religion, compared with that of man?

SPELL AND DEFINE. 1. distinguished 2. neighbor 3. daughter 4. administer 5. betrayed 6. illustrations 7. exercise 8. immediately 9. prospectively 10. germs 11. guardian 12. truant 13. disappointments 14. froward 15. academies 16. philosophers

LESSON XXXII

The Passions — Collins

RULE. When reading poetry that rhymes, there should be a very slight pause after the words that are similar in sound, though the sense may not require it.

EXAMPLE. Sweet it is, at eve to rest
On the flowery meadow's breast.

Here a slight pause should be made after the word *rest,* which would not be made if it were prose instead of poetry.

When Music, heavenly maid, was young,
While yet in early Greece she sung,
The Passions oft, to hear her shell,
Thronged around her magic cell,
Exulting, trembling, raging, fainting,
Possessed beyond the Muse's painting;
By turns they felt the glowing mind
Disturbed, delighted, raised, refined;

Till once, 'tis said, when all were fired,
Filled with fury, rapt, inspired,
From the supporting myrtles round
They snatched her instruments of sound,
And as they oft had heard apart
Sweet lessons of her forceful art,
Each, for madness ruled the hour,
Would prove his own expressive power.

First Fear his hand, its skill to try,
    Amid the chords bewildered laid,
And back recoiled, he knew not why,
    E'en at the sound himself had made.

Next Anger rushed: his eyes, on fire,
    In lightnings owned his secret stings;
In one rude clash he struck the lyre,
    And swept with hurried hand the strings.

With woeful measures wan Despair —
    Low sullen sounds — his grief beguiled,
A solemn, strange, and mingled air;
    'Twas sad by fits, by starts 'twas wild.

But thou, O Hope, with eyes so fair,
    What was thy delightful measure?
    Still it whispered promised pleasure,
    And bade the lovely scenes at distance hail!

Still would her touch the strain prolong,
    And from the rocks, the woods, the vale,
She called on Echo still through all the song;
    And, where her sweetest theme she chose,
    A soft responsive voice was heard at every close,
And Hope, enchanted, smiled, and waved her golden
    hair.

And longer had she sung — but with a frown
    Revenge impatient rose.
He threw his bloodstained sword in thunder down,
    And with a withering look
    The war-denouncing trumpet took,
And blew a blast so loud and dread,
    Were ne'er prophetic sounds so full of woe.
    And ever and anon he beat
    The doubling drum with furious heat;

And though sometimes each dreary pause between,
    Dejected Pity at his side
    Her soul-subduing voice applied,
    Yet still he kept his wild unaltered mien,
While each strained ball of sight seemed bursting from
    his head.

Thy numbers, Jealousy, to nought were fixed,
    Sad proof of thy distressful state;
Of differing themes the veering song was mixed,
    And now it courted Love, now raving called on Hate.

With eyes upraised, as one inspired,
Pale Melancholy sat retired,
And from her wild sequestered seat,
In notes by distance made more sweet,
Poured through the mellow horn her pensive soul:
    And dashing soft from rocks around,
    Bubbling runnels joined the sound;

Through glades and glooms the mingled measure stole,
Or o'er some haunted stream, with fond delay,
    Round an holy calm diffusing,
    Love of peace and lonely musing,
In hollow murmurs died away.

But oh how altered was its sprightlier tone,
When Cheerfulness, a nymph of healthiest hue,
    Her bow across her shoulder flung,
    Her buskins gemmed with morning dew,
Blew an inspiring air, that dale and thicket rung,
    The hunter's call to Faun and Dryad known.
  The oak-crowned Sisters, and their chaste-eyed
    Queen,
  Satyrs and sylvan boys were seen,
  Peeping from forth their alleys green;
  Brown Exercise rejoiced to hear,
    And Sport leaped up, and seized his beechen
    spear.

Last came Joy's ecstatic trial,
He, with viny crown advancing,
    First to the lively pipe his hand addressed,
But soon he saw the brisk awakening viol,
    Whose sweet entrancing voice he loved the
    best.
    They would have thought who heard the
    strain,
    They saw in Tempe's vale her native maids,
Amidst the festal sounding shades,
To some unwearied minstrel dancing,
    While, as his flying fingers kissed the strings,
Love framed with Mirth a gay fantastic round,
Loose were her tresses seen, her zone unbound,
    And he amidst his frolic play,
    As if he would the charming air repay,
    Shook thousand odors from his dewy wings.

QUESTIONS. 1. What is that figure of speech by which passions, etc., are addressed as animated beings? 2. What is meant by "shell" in line 3? 3. What is this ode intended to illustrate? 4. Who were the Fauns and Dryads? 5. What do you know of Tempe's vale?

SPELL AND DEFINE. 1. passions 2. expressive 3. recoiled 4. beguiled 5. enchanted 6. revenge 7. sequestered 8. nymph 9. ecstatic 10. entrancing 11. tresses 12. festal 13. fantastic

LESSON XXXIII

Modes of Writing — Montgomery

RULE. Avoid reading in a monotonous way, as if you were not interested and do not understand what you read.

That the art of writing was practiced in Egypt before the emancipation of the Israelites appears almost certain from their frequent and familiar mention of this mode of keeping memorials. When the people had provoked the Lord to wrath by making and worshiping the golden calf, Moses, interceding in their behalf, says, "Yet now, if thou wilt forgive their sin — ; and if not, blot me, I pray thee, out of thy book which thou hast written. And the Lord said unto Moses, Whosoever hath sinned against me, him will I blot out of my book."

The allusion here is to a table of genealogy, the muster roll of an army, a register of citizenship, or even to those books of chronicles which were kept by order of ancient oriental princes, detailing the events of their reigns for reference and remembrance.

Besides, such a mode of publishing important documents is alluded to not merely as nothing new but as if even the common people were practically acquainted with it. "And thou shalt bind them [the statutes and testimonies of the Lord] as a sign upon thine hand, and they shall be as frontlets between thine eyes. And thou shalt write them upon the posts of thy house, and on thy gates." There are various parallel passages which no caviling of commentators can convert from plain meaning into paradox.

Not only the Egyptians and Hebrews possessed this invaluable knowledge at the time of which we speak (from fourteen to seventeen hundred years before Christ). We have direct and incidental testimony, both in sacred and profane history, that the Phoenicians, Arabians, and Chaldeans were instructed in the same. The book of Job lays the scene and the season of his affliction about this era and in the north of Arabia.

That extraordinary composition — extraordinary indeed, whether it be regarded as a historical, dramatic, or poetic performance — contains more curious and minute information concerning the manners and customs, the literature and philosophy, the state of arts and sciences during the patriarchal ages than can be collected in scattered hints from all later works put together.

In reference to the art and the materials of writing then in use, we meet with the following sublime and affecting apostrophe: "Oh that my words were now written! oh that they were printed [impressed or traced out] in a book! That they were graven with an iron pen and lead in the rock for ever!"

The latter aspiration probably alludes to the very ancient practice of hewing characters into the faces of vast rocks as eternal memorials of persons and events. It is said by travelers whose testimony seems worthy of credence, that various fragments of such inscriptions, now utterly indecipherable, may be seen to this day in the wilderness of Arabia Petrea — monuments at once of the grasp and the limitation of the mental power of man, thus making the hardest substances in nature the depositories of his thoughts and yet betrayed in his ambitious expectation of so perpetuating them.

The slow influences of the elements have been incessantly, though insensibly, obliterating what the chisel had plowed into the solid marble, till at length nothing remains but a mockery of skeleton letters. These are so unlike their pristine forms, so unable to explain their own meaning that you might as well seek among the human relics in a charnel vault the resemblances of the once living personages — or invoke the dead bones to tell their own history — as question these dumb rocks concerning the records engraved on them.

The passage just quoted shows the state of alphabetical writing in the age of Job, and according to the best commentators, he describes three modes of exercising it: "O that my words were now written — traced out in characters — in a book composed of palm leaves, or on a roll of linen! O that they were engraved with a pen of iron on tablets of lead or indented in the solid rock to endure to the end of time!"

Arguing against the perverse sophistry of his friends that he *must* have been secretly a wicked man *because* such awful calamities, which they construed into divine judgments, had befallen him, so fast does he hold his integrity that not only with passing words, liable to be forgotten as soon as uttered, does he maintain it, but by every mode that could give his expressions publicity and ensure them perpetuity, he longs that his confidence in God to vindicate him might be recorded, whatever might be the issue of those evils to himself, even though he were brought down by them to death and corruption, descending not only with sorrow but with ignominy to the grave. For saith he: "I know that my Redeemer liveth, and that he shall stand at the latter day upon the earth: And though after my skin worms destroy this body, yet in my flesh shall I see God: Whom I shall see for myself, and mine eyes shall behold, and not another; though my reins be consumed within me."

Had these words of the patriarch been indeed "engraved with a pen of iron on the rock forever," without some more certain medium of transmission to posterity, they would have been unknown at this day or only speaking in the desert with the voice of silence, which no eye could interpret, no mind could hear.

But, being inscribed on materials as frail as the leaves in my hand yet capable of infinitely multiplied transcription, they can never be lost. For though the giant characters enchased in everlasting flint would ere now have been worn down by the perpetual foot of time, yet committed with feeble ink to perishable paper liable "to be crushed before the moth" or destroyed by the touch of fire or water, the good man's hope can never fail, even on earth. It was "a hope full of immortality," and still through all ages and in all lands, while the sun and moon endure, it shall be said by people of every kindred and nation and in every tongue spoken under heaven, "I know that my Redeemer liveth."

QUESTIONS. 1. How early does it seem that the art of writing was practiced in Egypt? 2. How does it appear? 3. What is alluded to in the verse quoted in the first paragraph? 4. How many years before Christ was this? 5. What other nations besides the Jews and Egyptians possessed this knowledge? 6. What is said of the book of Job? 7. What ancient practice is referred to in the quotation in the sixth paragraph? 8. Are there any remains of such inscriptions known? 9. What was the state of alphabetic writing at the time of Job? 10. What is the comparative durability of written documents and monumental inscriptions?

SPELL AND DEFINE. 1. emancipation 2. memorials 3. allusion 4. genealogy 5. chronicles 6. citizenship 7. oriental 8. documents 9. practically 10. acquainted 11. testimonies 12. frontlets 13. caviling 14. commentators 15. paradox 16. extraordinary 17. composition 18. dramatic 19. philosophy 20. patriarchal 21. apostrophe 22. aspiration 23. credence 24. fragments 25. indecipherable 26. wilderness 27. depositories 28. perpetuating 29. incessantly 30. obliterating 31. sophistry

LESSON XXXIV

Joyous Devotion — Psalm 148

RULE. Do not read poetry with a drawling singsong tone.

Praise ye the Lord.
Praise ye the Lord from the heavens:
Praise him in the heights.
Praise ye him, all his angels:
Praise ye him, all his hosts.
Praise ye him, sun and moon:
Praise him, all ye stars of light.
Praise him, ye heavens of heavens,
And ye waters that be above the heavens.
Let them praise the name of the Lord:
For he commanded, and they were created.
He hath also stablished them forever and ever:
He hath made a decree which shall not pass.

Praise the Lord from the earth,
Ye dragons, and all deeps:
Fire, and hail; snow, and vapor;
Stormy wind fulfilling his word:
Mountains, and all hills;
Fruitful trees, and all cedars:
Beasts, and all cattle;
Creeping things, and flying fowl:
Kings of the earth, and all people;
Princes, and all judges of the earth:
Both young men, and maidens;
Old men, and children:
Let them praise the name of the Lord:
For his name alone is excellent;
His glory is above the earth and heaven.
He also exalteth the horn of his people,
The praise of all his saints;
Even of the children of Israel, a people near unto him.
Praise ye the Lord.

QUESTIONS. 1. What is meant by calling upon things inanimate and upon beasts to praise God? 2. What reason is assigned why God should be universally praised?

SPELL AND DEFINE. 1. heavens   2. commanded   3. dragons
4. fulfilling 5. mountains 6. exalteth

LESSON XXXV

A Night Scene in Turkey — Byron

RULE. In reading poetry, be careful to avoid that sort of singsong tone
which is made by marking too strongly with the voice the accented
syllables.

EXAMPLE. Sweet *is* the *work,* my *God* my *King,*
           To *praise* thy *name,* give *thanks* and *sing.*

Read the above example, accenting the italicized words, and the fault
which is to be avoided will be perceived.

'Twas midnight: on the mountains brown
The cold round moon shone brightly down;
Blue rolled the ocean, blue the sky
Spread like an ocean hung on high,
Bespangled with those isles of light,
So wildly, spiritually bright;
Who ever gazed upon them shining,
And turned to earth without repining,
Nor wished for wings to fly away,
And mix with their eternal ray?
The waves on either shore lay there
Calm, clear, and azure as the air,
And scarce their foam the pebbles shook,
But murmured meekly as the brook.
The winds were pillowed on the waves,
The banners drooped along their staves,
And as they fell, around them furling,
Above them shone the crescent curling;
And that deep silence was unbroke
Save when the watch his signal spoke,

Save when the steed neighed oft and shrill,
And echo answered from the hill,
And the wide hum of that wild host
Rustled like leaves from coast to coast,
As rose the muezzin's voice in air
In midnight call to wonted prayer.
It rose, that chaunted, mournful strain,
Like some lone spirit's o'er the plain;
'Twas musical, but sadly sweet,
Such as when winds and harp strings meet;
And take a long, unmeasured tone,
To mortal minstrelsy unknown.
It seemed to those within the wall,
A cry prophetic of their fall;
It struck even the besieger's ear
With something ominous and drear,
An undefined and sudden thrill,
Which makes the heart a moment still;
Then beat with quicker pulse, ashamed
Of that strange sense its silence framed;
Such as a sudden passing bell
Wakes, though but for a stranger's knell.

QUESTIONS. 1. In this lesson there are many similes. Can you select them? 2. Select a metaphor and point out the difference between it and the simile. 3. What Muhammadan custom is referred to in lines 25 and 26?

SPELL AND DEFINE. 1. midnight   2. bespangled   3. spiritually
4. repining   5. azure   6. murmured   7. furling   8. muezzins   9. mournful
10. musical   11. unmeasured   12. minstrelsy   13. prophetic   14. besieger
15. ominous   16. undefined

LESSON XXXVI

Criminality of Dueling — Nott

RULE. Be careful not to dwell long on the little words like *at, on, in, by, the, a, and* — and yet take care to pronounce them distinctly.

Hamilton yielded to the force of an imperious custom, and yielding, he sacrificed a life in which all had an interest. He is lost — lost to his country, lost to his family, lost to us. For this rash act, because he disclaimed it and was penitent, I forgive him. But there are those whom I cannot forgive. I mean not his antagonist, over whose erring steps, if there be tears in heaven, a pious mother looks down and weeps.

If he be capable of feeling, he suffers already all that humanity can suffer. Suffers, and wherever he may fly will suffer, with the poignant recollection of having taken the life of one who was too magnanimous in return to attempt his own. If he had known this, it must have paralyzed his arm while he pointed, at so incorruptible a bosom, the instrument of death. If he know this now, his heart, if it be not adamant, must soften — if it be not ice, it must melt. But on this article I forbear. Stained with blood as he is, if he be penitent, I forgive him — and if he be not, before these altars, where all of us appear as suppliants, I wish not to excite your vengeance but rather, in behalf of an object rendered wretched and pitiable by crime, to wake your prayers.

But I have said, and I repeat it, there are those whom I cannot forgive. I cannot forgive that minister at the altar who has hitherto forborne to remonstrate on this subject. I cannot forgive that public prosecutor who, entrusted with the duty of avenging his country's wrongs, has seen these wrongs and taken no measures to avenge them. I cannot forgive that judge upon the bench or that governor in the chair of state who has lightly passed over such offenses. I cannot forgive the public in whose opinion the duelist finds a sanctuary. I cannot forgive you, my brethren, who until this late hour have been silent whilst successive murders were committed.

No, I cannot forgive you, that you have not in common with the freemen of this state raised your voice to the powers that be and loudly and explicitly demanded an execution of your laws — demanded this in a manner which, if it did not reach the ear of government, would at least have reached the heavens and have pleaded your excuse before the God that filleth them. In His presence, as I stand, I should not feel myself innocent of the blood that crieth against us had I been silent. But I have not been silent. Many of you who hear me are my witnesses. The walls of yonder temple, where I have heretofore addressed you, are my witnesses, how freely I have spoken on this subject in the presence both of those who have violated the laws and of those whose indispensable duty it is to see the laws executed on those who violate them.

I enjoy another opportunity and would to God that I might be permitted to approach for once the last scene of death, would to God that I could there assemble on the one side the disconsolate mother with her seven fatherless children and on the other those who administer the justice of my country. Could I do this, I would point them to these sad objects. I would entreat them, by the agonies of bereaved fondness, to listen to the widow's heartfelt groans, to mark the orphan's sighs and tears. Having done this, I would uncover the breathless corpse of Hamilton; I would lift from his gaping wound his bloody mantle; I would hold it up to heaven before them, and I would ask, in the name of God, whether at the sight of it they felt no compunction. Ye who have hearts of pity, ye who have experienced the anguish of dissolving friendship, who have wept and still weep over the moldering ruins of departed kindred, ye can enter into this reflection.

O thou disconsolate widow! robbed, so cruelly robbed and in so short a time, both of a husband and a son! What must be the plenitude of thy suffering! Could we approach thee, gladly would we drop the tear of sympathy and pour into thy bleeding bosom the balm of consolation! But how could we comfort her whom God hath not comforted! To His throne let us lift up our voice and weep. O God! if Thou art still the widow's husband and the father of the fatherless — if in the fullness of Thy goodness there be yet mercy in store for miserable mortals, pity, O pity this afflicted mother and grant that her hapless orphans may find a friend, a benefactor, a father in Thee!

QUESTIONS. 1. To what imperious custom did Hamilton yield? 2. Why does the writer forgive him? 3. What is the duty of the minister, of the public prosecutor, of the judge, of the governor, of the public — in reference to dueling?

SPELL AND DEFINE. 1. imperious   2. disclaimed   3. antagonist 4. poignant   5. magnanimous   6. paralyzed   7. incorruptible   8. vengeance 9. forborne   10. prosecutor   11. sanctuary   12. successive   13. explicitly 14. indispensable   15. opportunity   16. disconsolate   17. compunction

LESSON XXXVII

Character of Napoleon Bonaparte — Phillips

RULE. When several consonants come together, give the full sound to each of them.

EXAMPLE. Pronounce the following words, sounding fully the consonants that are italicized: or-*b'd,* pro-*b'd'st,* trou-*bl'd'st,* trou-*bles,* trou-*bl'st,* ri*bs,* rob-*b'st,* han-*dl'd,* fon-*dl'st,* brea-*dths,* lau-*gh'st.*

He is fallen! We may now pause before that splendid prodigy which towered amongst us like some ancient ruin, whose frown terrified the glance its magnificence attracted.

Grand, gloomy, and peculiar, he sat upon the throne a sceptered hermit wrapped in the solitude of his own originality. A mind, bold, independent, and decisive; a will, despotic in its dictates; an energy that distanced expedition and a conscience pliable to every touch of interest marked the outline of this extraordinary character — the most extraordinary, perhaps, that in the annals of this world ever rose or reigned or fell. Flung into life in the midst of a revolution that quickened every energy of a people who acknowledge no superior, he commenced his course, a stranger by birth and a scholar by charity! With no friend but his sword and no fortune but his talents, he rushed in the list where rank, wealth, and genius had arrayed themselves, and competition fled from him as from the glance of destiny.

He knew no motive but interest, acknowledged no criterion but success, worshiped no God but ambition, and with an eastern devotion he knelt at the shrine of his idolatry. Subsidiary to this, there was no creed that he did not profess, there was no opinion that he did not promulgate; in the hope of a dynasty, he upheld the crescent; for the sake of a divorce, he bowed before the cross. The orphan of St. Louis, he became the adopted child of the republic, and with a parricidal ingratitude, on the ruins both of the throne and tribune, he reared the throne of his despotism. A professed Catholic, he imprisoned the pope; a pretended patriot, he impoverished the country; in the name of Brutus, he grasped without remorse and wore without shame the diadem of the Caesars!

Through this pantomime of policy, Fortune played the clown to his caprices. At his touch, crowns crumbled, beggars reigned, systems vanished, the wildest theories took the color of his whim, and all that was venerable and all that was novel changed places with the rapidity of a drama. Even apparent defeat assumed the appearance of victory — his flight from Egypt confirmed his destiny and ruin itself only elevated him to empire.

But if his fortune were great, his genius was transcendent. Decision flashed upon his councils, and it was the same to decide and to perform. To inferior intellects his combinations appeared perfectly impossible, his plans perfectly impracticable, but in his hands simplicity marked their development and success vindicated their adoption. His person partook the character of his mind — if the one never yielded in the cabinet, the other never bent in the field. Nature had no obstacle that he did not surmount, space no opposition he did not spurn; whether amid Alpine rocks, Arabian sands, or polar snows, he seemed proof against peril and empowered with ubiquity!

The whole continent trembled at beholding the audacity of his designs and the miracle of their execution. Skepticism bowed to the prodigies of his performance; romance assumed the air of history. Nor was there aught too incredible for belief or too fanciful for expectation when the world saw a subaltern of Corsica waving his imperial flag over her most ancient capitals. All the visions of antiquity became commonplaces in his contemplation; kings were his people, nations were his outposts. He disposed of courts and crowns and camps and churches and cabinets as if they were titular dignitaries of the chessboard! Amid all these changes, he stood immutable as adamant.

It mattered little whether in the field or in the drawing room, with the mob or the levee, wearing the Jacobin's bonnet or the iron crown, banishing a Braganza or espousing a Hapsburg, dictating peace on a raft to the czar of Russia or contemplating defeat at Waterloo, he was still the same military despot!

In this astonishing combination, his affectations of literature must not be omitted. The jailer of the press, he affected the patronage of letters; the proscriber of books, he encouraged philosophy; the persecutor of authors and the murderer of printers, he yet pretended to the protection of learning! The silencer of de Staël and the denouncer of

Kotzebue, he was the friend of David and sent his academic prize to the philosopher of England.

Such a medley of contradictions and at the same time such an individual consistency were never united in the same character. A royalist, a republican and an emperor, a Muhammadan, a Catholic and a patron of the synagogue, a subaltern and a sovereign, a traitor and a tyrant, a Christian and an infidel — he was, through all his vicissitudes, the same stern, impatient, inflexible original; the same mysterious, incomprehensible self; the man without a model and without a shadow.

QUESTIONS. 1. Read about Napoleon in an encyclopedia if you are unfamiliar with his life. 2. Why is Napoleon called the subaltern of Corsica? 3. Who were the Jacobins? 4. What is meant by "banishing a Braganza" and "espousing a Hapsburg"? 5. Who was de Staël? 6. Kotzebue? 7. David? 8. Look up questions 3-7 in an encyclopedia if you do not know the answers.

SPELL AND DEFINE. 1. dynasty   2. crescent   3. promulgate 4. parricidal   5. diadem   6. pantomime   7. development   8. ubiquity 9. prodigies 10. synagogue

LESSON XXXVIII

The Field of Waterloo — Lady Morgan

RULE. Pronounce the consonant sounds very distinctly.

EXAMPLE. Prolong the consonant sounds that are italicized in the following words: or-*b*, ai-*d*, a-*ll*, ar-*m*, ow-*n*, so-*ng*, wa-*r*, sa-*ve*, ama-*ze*.

It struck my imagination much while standing on the last field fought by Bonaparte, that the battle of Waterloo should have been fought on a Sunday. What a different scene did the Scotch Grays and English infantry present from that which, at that very hour, was exhibited by their relatives, when over England and Scotland each church bell had drawn together its worshipers! While many a mother's heart was sending up a prayer for her son's preservation, perhaps that son was gasping in agony. Yet, even at such a period, the lessons of his early days might give him consolation, and the maternal prayer might prepare the heart to support maternal anguish.

It is Christianity alone which is of universal application, both as a stimulant and a lenitive, throughout the varied heritage which falls to the lot of man. Yet we know that many thousands rushed into this fight, even of those who had been instructed in our religious principles, without leisure for one serious thought, and that some officers were killed in their ball dress! They made the leap into the gulf which divides the two worlds — the present from the immutable state — without one parting prayer or one note of preparation.

As I looked over this field, now green with growing grain, I could mark with my eye the spots where the most desperate carnage had been. The bodies had been heaped together and scarcely more than covered. So enriched is the soil that, in these spots, the grain never ripens. It grows rank and green to the end of harvest. This touching memorial, which endures when the thousand groans have expired and when the stain of human blood has faded from the ground, still seems to cry to Heaven that there is awful guilt somewhere and a terrific reckoning for those who caused destruction which the earth could not conceal. These hillocks of superabundant vegetation, as the wind rustled through the grain, seemed the most affecting monuments which nature could devise and gave a melancholy animation to this plain of death.

When we attempt to measure the mass of suffering which was here inflicted and to number the individuals that fell, considering each who suffered as our fellowman, we are overwhelmed with the agonizing calculation and retire from the field which has been the scene of our reflections with the simple, concentrated feeling — these armies once lived, breathed, and felt like us, and the time is at hand when we shall be like them.

QUESTIONS. (To answer questions 1–4, read about Waterloo in an encyclopedia.) 1. Between what powers was the battle of Waterloo fought? 2. On what day? 3. Who were the commanders in chief? 4. Which gained the battle? 5. How did Lady Morgan distinguish those spots where the most desperate carnage had been? 6. What feeling does the sight of the battlefield inspire?

SPELL AND DEFINE. 1. imagination   2. maternal   3. anguish 4. immutable 5. carnage 6. superabundant 7. vegetation 8. agonizing

LESSON XXXIX

The Splendor of War — Chalmers

RULE. When several consonants come together, give the full sound to each of them.

EXAMPLE. Pronounce the following words, sounding fully the consonants that are italicized: or-*b'd*, pro-*b'd'st*, trou-*bl'd'st*, trou-*bles*, trou-*bl'st*, ri*bs*, rob-*b'st*, han-*dl'd*, fon-*dl'st*, brea-*dths*, lau-*gh'st*.

The first great obstacle to the extinction of war is the way in which the heart of man is carried off from its barbarities and its horrors by the splendor of its deceitful accompaniments. There is a feeling of the sublime in contemplating the shock of armies just as there is in contemplating the devouring energy of a tempest. This so elevates and engrosses the whole man that his eye is blind to the tears of bereaved parents, and his ear is deaf to the piteous moan of the dying and the shriek of their desolated families.

There is a gracefulness in the picture of a youthful warrior burning for distinction on the field, and lured by this generous aspiration to the deepest of the animated throng, the opposing sons of valor struggle for a remembrance and a name. This side of the picture is so much the exclusive object of our regard, as to disguise from our view the mangled carcasses of the fallen and the writhing agonies of the hundreds and the hundreds more who have been laid on the cold ground and left to languish and to die.

There no eye pities them. No sister is there to weep over them. There no gentle hand is present to ease the dying posture or bind up the wounds which, in the maddening fury of the combat, had been given and received by the children of one common father. There death spreads its pale ensigns over every countenance, and when night comes on and darkness gathers around them, how many a despairing wretch must take up with the bloody field as the untented bed of his last sufferings, without one friend to bear the message of tenderness to his distant home, without one companion to close his eyes.

I avow it. On every side of me I see causes at work which go to spread a most delusive coloring over war, to remove its shocking barbarities to the background of our contemplations altogether. I see it in the history which tells me of the superb appearance of the troops and the brilliancy of their successive charges. I see it in the poetry which lends the magic of its numbers to the narrative of blood and transports its many admirers as, by its images and its figures and its nodding plumes of chivalry, it throws its treacherous embellishments over a scene of legalized slaughter.

I see it in the music which represents the progress of the battle and where, after being inspired by the trumpet notes of preparation, the whole beauty and tenderness of a drawing room are seen to bend over the sentimental entertainment. I do not hear the utterance of a single sigh to interrupt the death tones of the thickening contest and the moans of the wounded men as they fade away upon the ear and sink into lifeless silence.

All, all goes to prove what strange and half-sighted creatures we are. Were it not so, war could never have been seen in any other aspect than that of unmingled hatefulness, and I can look to nothing but to the progress of Christian sentiment upon earth to arrest the strong current of its popular and prevailing partiality for war.

Then only will an imperious sense of duty lay the check of severe principle on all the subordinate tastes and faculties of our nature. Then will glory be reduced to its right estimate, and the wakeful benevolence of the Gospel, chasing away every spell, will be devoted to simple but sublime enterprises for the good of the species.

QUESTIONS. 1. What is the cause of war? 2. Should all men endeavor to prevent war? 3. Why? 4. What is the first great obstacle to the extinction of war? 5. How do history, poetry, and music tend to keep alive the spirit of war? 6. Will it be finally extinguished? 7. How do you know? 8. How will it be done?

SPELL AND DEFINE. 1. obstacle   2. extinction   3. barbarities
4. accompaniments   5. contemplating   6. devouring   7. engrosses
8. gracefulness   9. remembrance   10. carcasses   11. languish
12. maddening 13. combat 14. untented 15. background 16. treacherous
17. embellishments   18. legalized   19. sentimental   20. thickening
21. subordinate 22. benevolence 23. species

LESSON XL

The Best of Classics — Grimke

RULE. Take care not to let the voice grow weaker and weaker as you approach the end of a sentence.

There is a classic, the best the world has ever seen, the noblest that has ever honored and dignified the language of mortals. If we look into its antiquity, we discover a title to our veneration, unrivaled in the history of literature. If we have respect to its evidences, they are found in the testimony of miracle and prophecy; in the ministry of man, of nature, and of angels, yea, even of "God, manifest in the flesh," of "God blessed forever."

If we consider its authenticity, no other pages have survived the lapse of time that can be compared with it. If we examine its authority, for it speaks as never man spoke, we discover that it came from Heaven, in vision and prophecy, under the sanction of Him who is Creator of all things and the Giver of every good and perfect gift.

If we reflect on its truths, they are lovely and spotless, sublime and holy as God Himself, unchangeable as His nature, durable as His righteous dominion, and versatile as the moral condition of mankind. If we regard the value of its treasures, we must estimate them not like the relics of classic antiquity, by the perishable glory and beauty, virtue and happiness of this world, but by the enduring perfection and supreme felicity of an eternal kingdom.

If we inquire, who are the men that have recorded its truths, vindicated its rights, and illustrated the excellence of its scheme? From the depth of ages and from the living world, from the populous continent and the isles of the sea comes forth the answer: the patriarch and the prophet, the evangelist and the martyr.

If we look abroad through the world of men, the victims of folly or vice, the prey of cruelty, of injustice, and inquire what are its benefits even in this temporal state, the great and the humble, the rich and the poor, the powerful and the weak, the learned and the ignorant reply as with one voice that humility and resignation, purity, order and peace, faith, hope, and charity are its blessings upon earth.

And if, raising our eyes from time to eternity, from the world of mortals to the world of just men made perfect, from the visible creation (marvelous, beautiful, and glorious as it is) to the invisible creation of angels and seraphs, from the footstool of God to the throne of God Himself, we ask, What are the blessings that flow from this single volume? Let the question be answered by the pen of the evangelist, the harp of the prophet, and the records of the Book of Life.

Such is the best of classics the world has ever admired; such, the noblest that man has ever adopted as a guide.

QUESTIONS. 1. What is the antiquity of the Bible? 2. Specify some of the reasons for considering the Bible the best of classics. 3. How does it differ from other classics of antiquity?

SPELL AND DEFINE. 1. classic   2. antiquity   3. testimony 4. literature 5. authenticity 6. authority 7. unchangeable 8. dominion 9. versatile 10. illustrated 11. excellence 12. patriarch 13. resignation 14. marvelous 15. beautiful 16. evangelist

LESSON XLI

The New Song — Revelation 5:9–13

RULE. Pronounce the consonant sounds very distinctly.

EXAMPLE. Prolong the consonant sounds that are italicized: *b*-old, *d*-eign, *f*-ather, *g*-ather, *j*-oy, *l*-ight, *m*-an, *n*-o, *q*-ueer, p-*r*-ay, *v*-ale, *w*-oe, *y*-ours, *z*-one, *h*-ang.

And they sung a new song, saying, Thou art worthy to take the book, and to open the seals thereof:

For thou wast slain, and hast redeemed us to God by thy blood out of every kindred, and tongue, and people, and nation; and hast made us unto our God kings and priests: and we shall reign on the earth.

And I beheld, and I heard the voice of many angels round about the throne, and the beasts, and the elders: and the number of them was ten thousand times ten thousand, and thousands of thousands; saying with a loud voice, Worthy is the Lamb that was slain to receive power, and riches, and wisdom, and strength, and honor, and glory, and blessing.

And every creature which is in heaven, and on the earth, and under the earth, and such as are in the sea, and all that are in them, heard I saying, Blessing, and honor, and glory, and power, be unto him that sitteth upon the throne, and unto the Lamb forever and ever.

QUESTIONS. 1. Where is the Book of Revelation found? 2. Who wrote it? 3. What is the character and style of this extract? 4. Is it poetic? 5. Wherein? 6. Who is meant by the "Lamb" in the third paragraph? 7. In what does Christ resemble a lamb?

SPELL AND DEFINE. 1. worthy 2. redeemed 3. kindred 4. elders 5. receive 6. thousand

LESSON XLII

The Deluge — Genesis 7

RULE. Pronounce the vowels fully and give them the proper sound.

EXERCISES UNDER THE RULE. Sound the following vowels long and full: e-rr, a-ll, o-r, a-ge, e-dge, a-rm, a-t, o-ld, ou-r, ee-l, i-t, oo-ze, p-u-ll, b-oy, i-sle

And the Lord said unto Noah, Come thou and all thy house into the ark; for thee have I seen righteous before me in this generation. Of every clean beast thou shalt take to thee by sevens, the male and his female: and of beasts that are not clean by two, the male and his female.

Of fowls also of the air by sevens, the male and the female; to keep seed alive upon the face of all the earth. For yet seven days, and I will cause it to rain upon the earth forty days and forty nights; and every living substance that I have made will I destroy from off the face of the earth.

And Noah did according unto all that the Lord commanded him. And Noah was six hundred years old when the flood of waters was upon the earth.

Noah went in, and his sons, and his wife, and his sons' wives with him, into the ark, because of the waters of the flood. Of clean beasts, and of beasts that are not clean, and of fowls, and of every thing that creepeth upon the earth, there went in two and two unto Noah into the ark, the male and the female, as God had commanded Noah. And it came to pass after seven days, that the waters of the flood were upon the earth.

In the six hundredth year of Noah's life, in the second month, the seventeenth day of the month, the same day were all the fountains of the great deep broken up, and the windows of heaven were opened. And the rain was upon the earth forty days and forty nights.

In the selfsame day entered Noah, and Shem, and Ham, and Japheth, the sons of Noah, and Noah's wife, and the three wives of his sons with them, into the ark; They, and every beast after his kind, and all the cattle after their kind, and every creeping thing that creepeth upon the earth after his kind, and every fowl after his kind, every bird of every sort.

And they went in unto Noah into the ark, two and two of all flesh, wherein is the breath of life. And they that went in, went in male and female of all flesh, as God had commanded him: and the Lord shut him in.

And the flood was forty days upon the earth; and the waters increased, and bare up the ark, and it was lifted up above the earth. And the waters prevailed, and were increased greatly upon the earth; and the ark went upon the face of the waters. And the waters prevailed exceedingly upon the earth; and all the high hills, that were under the whole heaven, were covered.

Fifteen cubits upward did the waters prevail; and the mountains were covered. And all flesh died that moved upon the earth, both of fowl, and of cattle, and of beast, and of every creeping thing that creepeth upon the earth, and every man: All in whose nostrils was the breath of life, of all that was in the dry land, died.

And every living substance was destroyed which was upon the face of the ground, both man, and cattle, and the creeping things, and the fowl of the heaven; and they were destroyed from the earth: and Noah only remained alive, and they that were with him in the ark. And the waters prevailed upon the earth a hundred and fifty days.

QUESTIONS. 1. From what part of the Bible is this lesson taken? 2. How long has it been since the Flood? 3. Why did God send a flood on the earth? 4. Who were saved? 5. Why did God preserve Noah and his family? 6. What were preserved with them? 7. What is the distinction between clean and unclean beasts? 8. How many of each class entered the ark? 9. How old was Noah when the Flood came? 10. How long did it continue? 11. How high did the waters rise? 12. What evidence is there in nature of there having been a flood? 13. What does this confirm?

SPELL AND DEFINE. 1. righteous   2. substance   3. fountains 4. increased 5. prevailed 6. exceedingly 7. cubits 8. nostrils 9. destroyed 10. remained

LESSON XLIII

A Hebrew Tale — Mrs. Sigourney

RULE. Avoid reading in a faint and low tone.

Twilight was deepening with a tinge of eve,
As toward his home in Israel's sheltered vales
A stately rabbi drew. His camels spied
Afar the palm trees' lofty heads, that decked
The dear, domestic fountain — and in speed
Pressed, with broad foot, the smooth and dewy glade.
The holy man his peaceful threshold passed
With hasting step. The evening meal was spread,
And she, who from life's morn his heart had shared,
Breathed her fond welcome. Bowing o'er the board,
The blessing of his fathers' God he sought;
Ruler of earth and sea. Then raising high
The sparkling wine-cup, "Call my sons," he bade,
"And let me bless them ere their hour of rest."

The observant mother spake with gentle voice
Somewhat of soft excuse, that they were wont
To linger long amid the prophet's school,
Learning the holy law their father loved.

His sweet repast with sweet discourse was blent,
Of journeying and return. "Wouldst thou hadst seen
With me, the golden morning break to light
Yon mountain summits, whose blue, waving line
Scarce meets thine eye, where chirp of joyous birds,
And breath of fragrant shrubs, and spicy gales,
And sigh of waving boughs, stirred in the soul
Warm orisons. Yet most I wished thee near
Amid the temple's pomp, when the high priest,
Clad in his robe pontifical, invoked
The God of Abraham, while from lute and harp,
Cymbal, and trump, and psaltery, and glad breath
Of tuneful Levite — and the mighty shout
Of all our people like the swelling sea,
Loud hallelujahs burst. When next I seek
Blest Zion's glorious hill, our beauteous boys
Must bear me company. Their early prayers
Will rise as incense. Thy reluctant love
No longer must withhold them — the new toil
Will give them sweeter sleep, and touch their cheek
With brighter crimson. Mid their raven curls
My hand I'll lay, and dedicate them there,
Even in those hallowed courts, to Israel's God,
Two spotless lambs, well pleasing in His sight.
But yet, methinks, thou'rt paler grown, my love!
And the pure sapphire of thine eye looks dim,
As though 'twere washed with tears."

Faintly she smiled,
"One doubt, my lord, I fain would have thee solve.
Gems of rich luster and of countless cost
Were to my keeping trusted. Now, alas!

They are demanded. Must they be restored?
Or may I not a little longer gaze
Upon their dazzling hues?" His eye grew stern,
And on his lip there lurked a sudden curl
Of indignation. "Doth *my wife* propose
Such doubt? as if a master might not claim
His own again." — "Nay, Rabbi, come behold
These priceless jewels ere I yield them back."
So to their spousal chamber with soft hand
Her lord she led. There, on a snow-white couch,
Lay his two sons, pale, *pale and motionless,*
Like fair twin-lilies, which some grazing kid
In wantonness had cropped. "My sons! my sons!
Light of my eyes!" the astonished father cried,
"My teachers in the law — whose guileless hearts
And prompt obedience warned me oft to be
More perfect with my God!" —

                                        To earth he fell,
Like Lebanon's rent cedar, while his breast
Heaved with such groans as when the laboring soul
Breaks from its clay companion's close embrace.
The mourning mother turned away and wept,
Till the first storm of passionate grief was still.
Then, pressing to his ear her faded lip,
She sighed in tone of tremulous tenderness,
"Thou didst instruct me, Rabbi, how to yield
The summoned jewels — See! the Lord did give,
The Lord hath taken away."

                                        "Yea!" said the sire,
"And blessed be His name. Even for thy sake
Thrice blessed be Jehovah." Long he pressed
On those cold, beautiful brows his quivering lip,
While from his eye the burning anguish rolled;
Then, kneeling low, those chastened spirits poured
Their mighty homage forth to God.

QUESTIONS. 1. What is a rabbi? 2. What was the character of this rabbi? 3. Where had he been journeying? 4. How do you know he had been at Jerusalem? 5. Where is Jerusalem? 6. How often did the Jews go up to Jerusalem for religious purposes? 7. What had happened during the rabbi's absence? 8. What had been the character of his sons? 9. How did his wife prepare him to hear of their death? 10. What is the best support in time of trouble and affliction?

SPELL AND DEFINE. 1. twilight 2. threshold 3. observant 4. orison 5. pontifical 6. cymbal 7. psaltery 8. hallelujah 9. beauteous 10. incense 11. reluctant 12. dedicate 13. hallowed

LESSON XLIV

External Appearance of England — A. H. Everett

RULE. Mention every syllable that is pronounced wrong as the student reads.

Whatever may be the extent of the distress in England or the difficulty of finding any remedies for it which shall be at once practicable and sufficient, it is certain that the symptoms of decline have not displayed themselves on the surface. No country in Europe, either at the present day or at any preceding period of ancient or of modern times, ever exhibited so strongly the outward marks of general industry, wealth, and prosperity.

The misery that exists, whatever it may be, retires from public view. The traveler sees no traces of it except in the beggars (which are not more numerous than they are on the continent), in the courts of justice, and in the newspapers. On the contrary, the impressions he receives from the objects that meet his view are almost uniformly agreeable.

He is pleased with the attention paid to his personal accommodation as a traveler, with the excellent roads, and the conveniences of the public carriages and inns. The country everywhere exhibits the appearance of high cultivation or else of wild and picturesque beauty. Even the unimproved lands are disposed with taste and skill so as to embellish the landscape very highly, if they do not contribute, as they might, to the substantial comfort of the people.

From every eminence, extensive parks and grounds spreading far and wide over hill and vale, interspersed with dark woods and variegated with bright waters, unroll themselves before the eye like enchanting gardens. While the elegant constructions of the modern proprietors fill the mind with images of ease and luxury, the moldering ruins that remain of former ages, of the castles and churches of their feudal ancestors, increase the interest of the picture by contrast and associate with it poetic and affecting recollections of other times and manners.

Every village seems to be the chosen residence of industry and her handmaids, neatness and comfort. In the various parts of the island, her operations present themselves under the most amusing and agreeable variety of forms. Sometimes her votaries are mounting to the skies in manufactories of innumerable stories in height and sometimes diving in mines into the bowels of the earth or dragging up drowned treasures from the bottom of the sea. At one time the ornamented grounds of a wealthy proprietor seem to realize the fabled Elysium, and again, as you pass in the evening through some village engaged in the iron manufacture, where a thousand forges are feeding at once their dark-red fires and clouding the air with their volumes of smoke, you might think yourself, for a moment, a little too near some drearier residence.

The aspect of the cities is as various as that of the country. Oxford, in the silent, solemn grandeur of its numerous collegiate palaces with their massy stone walls and vast interior quadrangles, seems like the deserted capital of some departed race of giants. This is the splendid sepulchre where science, like the Roman Tarpeia, lies buried under the weight of gold that rewarded her ancient services and where copious libations of the richest port and Madeira are daily poured out to her memory.

At Liverpool, on the contrary, all is bustle, brick, and business. Everything breathes of modern times, everybody is occupied with the concerns of the present moment excepting one elegant scholar, who unites a singular resemblance to the Roman face and dignified person of our Washington with the magnificent spirit and intellectual accomplishments of his own Italian hero.

At every change in the landscape you fall upon monuments of some new race of men among the number that have in their turn inhabited these islands. The mysterious monument of Stonehenge, standing remote and alone upon a bare and boundless heath, as much unconnected with the events of past ages as it is with the uses of the present, carries you back beyond all historical records into the obscurity of a wholly unknown period.

Perhaps the druids raised it, but by what machinery could these half-barbarians have wrought and moved such immense masses of rock? By what fatality is it that, in every part of the globe, the most durable impressions that have been made upon its surface were the work of races now entirely extinct? Who were the builders of the pyramids and the massy monuments of Egypt and India? Who constructed the Cyclopean walls of Italy and Greece or elevated the innumerable and inexplicable mounds which are seen in every part of Europe, Asia, and America? Who built the ancient forts upon the Ohio, on whose ruins the third growth of trees is now more than four hundred years old? All these constructions have existed through the whole period within the memory of man and will continue when all the architecture of the present generation, with its high civilization and improved machinery, shall have crumbled into dust. Stonehenge will remain unchanged when the banks of the Thames shall be as bare as Salisbury heath.

The Romans had something of the spirit of these primitive builders, and they left everywhere distinct traces of their passage. Half the castles in Great Britain were founded, according to tradition, by Julius Caesar, and abundant vestiges remain throughout the island of their walls, forts, and military roads. Most of their castles have, however, been built upon and augmented at a later period and belong, with more propriety, to the brilliant period of Gothic architecture. Thus the keep of Warwick dates from the time of Caesar, while the castle itself, with its lofty battlements, extensive walls, and large enclosures, bears witness to the age when every Norman chief was a military despot within his own barony.

To this period appertains the principal part of the magnificent Gothic monuments, castles, cathedrals, abbeys, priories, and churches in various stages of preservation and of ruin. Some, like Warwick and Alnwick castles, like Salisbury Cathedral and Westminster Abbey, retain all their original perfection. Others, like Kenilworth and Canterbury, are little more than a rude mass of earth and rubbish. Others, again, reveal the intermediate stages of decay, borrowing a sort of charm from their very ruin and putting on their dark-green robes of ivy to conceal the ravages of time, as if the luxuriant bounty of nature were purposely throwing a veil over the frailty and feebleness of art.

What a beautiful and brilliant vision was this Gothic architecture, shining out as it did from the deepest darkness of feudal barbarism! And here again, by what fatality has it happened that the moderns, with all their civilization and improved taste, have been as utterly unsuccessful in rivaling the divine simplicity of the Greeks as the rude grandeur of the Cyclopeans and ancient Egyptians?

Since the revival of arts in Europe, the builders have confined themselves wholly to a graceless and unsuccessful imitation of ancient models. Strange, that the only new architectural conception of any value, subsequent to the time of Phidias, should have been struck out at the worst period of society that has since occurred!

Sometimes the moderns, in their laborious poverty of invention, heap up small materials in large masses and think that St. Peter's or St. Paul's will be as much more sublime than the Parthenon as they are larger. At other times, they condescend to a servile imitation of the wild and native graces of the Gothic, as the Chinese, in their ignorance of perspective, can still copy, line by line and point by point, a European picture. But the Norman castles and churches, with all their richness and sublimity, fell with the power of their owners at the rise of the commonwealth.

The Independents were levelers of substance as well as form, and the material traces they left of their existence are the ruins of what their predecessors had built. They, too, had an architecture, but it was not in wood or stone. It was enough for them to lay the foundation of the nobler fabric of civil liberty. The effects of the only change in society that has since occurred are seen in the cultivated fields, the populous and thriving cities, the busy ports, and the general prosperous appearance of the country.

QUESTIONS. 1. What is the appearance of England, as to prosperity? 2. What is the appearance of things in respect to industry, neatness, etc.? 3. What is said of the cities? 4. Stonehenge? 5. How old is the "keep" and castle of Warwick? 6. Who were the Independents, and what did they do?

SPELL AND DEFINE. 1. symptoms   2. exhibited   3. prosperity
4. uniformly   5. accommodation   6. ceremonies   7. picturesque
8. enchanted   9. interspersed   10. feudal   11. recollections
12. innumerable   13. manufactories   14. ornamented   15. forges
16. quadrangles   17. intellectual   18. accomplishments   19. Stonehenge
20. architecture

LESSON XLV

Vision of a Spirit — Job 4

RULE. In reading poetry that does not rhyme, there should not be any pause at the end of a line terminating with an unimportant word, unless the sense requires it.

EXAMPLE. Ye who have anxiously and fondly watched
          Beside a fading friend, unconscious that
          The cheeks' bright crimson, lovely to the view,
          Like nightshade, with unwholesome beauty bloomed.

In this example there must be a slight pause at the end of the first line but none at all at the end of the second.

Then Eliphaz the Temanite answered and said,
If we assay to commune with thee, wilt thou be
      grieved?
But who can withhold himself from speaking?
Behold, thou hast instructed many,
And thou hast strengthened the weak hands.
Thy words have upholden him that was falling,
And thou hast strengthened the feeble knees.
But now it is come upon thee, and thou faintest;
It toucheth thee, and thou art troubled.
Is not this thy fear, thy confidence,
Thy hope, and the uprightness of thy ways?
Remember, I pray thee, who ever perished, being in-
      nocent?
Or where were the righteous cut off?
Even as I have seen, they that plow iniquity
And sow wickedness, reap the same.
By the blast of God they perish,
And by the breath of his nostrils are they consumed.
The roaring of the lion, and the voice of the fierce
      lion,

And the teeth of the young lions, are broken.
The old lion perisheth for lack of prey,
And the stout lion's whelps are scattered abroad.

Now a thing was secretly brought to me,
And mine ear received a little thereof.
In thoughts from the visions of the night,
When deep sleep falleth on men,
Fear came upon me, and trembling,
Which made all my bones to shake.
Then a spirit passed before my face;
The hair of my flesh stood up:
It stood still, but I could not discern the form thereof:
An image was before mine eyes,
There was silence, and I heard a voice, saying,
Shall mortal man be more just than God?
Shall a man be more pure than his Maker?
Behold, he put no trust in his servants;
And his angels he charged with folly:
How much less in them that dwell in houses of clay,
Whose foundation is in the dust,
Which are crushed before the moth?
They are destroyed from morning to evening:
They perish for ever without any regarding it.
Doth not their excellency which is in them go away?
They die, even without wisdom.

QUESTIONS. 1. Who was Eliphaz? 2. What is his argument against Job? 3. Is he trying to prove that Job must have committed some heinous crime? Does he prove it?

SPELL AND DEFINE. 1. commune 2. instructed 3. strengthened 4. upholden 5. uprightness 6. wickedness 7. trembling 8. foundation 9. excellency

LESSON XLVI

Character of the Puritan Fathers of New England —
Greenwood

RULE. Where two or more consonants come together, let the pupil be careful to sound every one distinctly.

EXERCISES UNDER THE RULE. Thou *shed'st* a sunshine on his head. The brown *forests. Hop'st* thou for *gifts* like these? Or ever thou *had'st* formed the earth. I have received *presents.*

One of the most prominent features which distinguished our forefathers was their determined resistance to oppression. They seemed born and brought up for the high and special purpose of showing to the world that the civil and religious rights of man, the rights of self-government, of conscience, and independent thought are not merely things to be talked of and woven into theories but to be adopted with the whole strength and ardor of the mind, felt in the profoundest recesses of the heart, carried out into the general life, and made the foundation of practical usefulness, visible beauty, and true nobility.

Liberty, with them, was an object of too serious desire and stern resolve to be personified, allegorized, and enshrined. They made no goddess of it as the ancients did — they had neither time nor inclination for such trifling; they felt that liberty was the simple birthright of every human creature. They called it so, claimed it as such, and reverenced and held it fast as the unalienable gift of the Creator, which was not to be surrendered to power nor sold for wages.

It was theirs, as men; without it, they did not esteem themselves men. More than any other privilege or possession, it was essential to their happiness, for it was essential to their original nature. Therefore they preferred it above wealth and ease and country, and that they might enjoy and exercise it fully, they forsook houses and lands and kindred, their homes, their native soil, and their fathers' graves.

They left all these. They left England, which, whatever it might have been called, was not to them a land of freedom. They launched forth on the pathless ocean, the wide, fathomless ocean, soiled not by the earth beneath and bounded, all round and above, only by heaven. It seemed to them like that better and sublimer freedom of which their country knew not but of which they had the conception and image in their hearts. After a toilsome and painful voyage, they came to a hard and wintry country, desolate, unguarded, and boundless. The fathomless silence interrupted not the ascent of their prayers, there being no eyes to watch, no ears to hearken, no tongues to speak. Here again there was an answer to their inmost desire, and they were satisfied and gave thanks to God that they were free, and the desert smiled.

I am telling an old tale, but it is one which need be told when we speak of those men. It is to their credit that they transmitted their principles to their children and that, peopled by such a race, our country was allowed peace. So long as its inhabitants were unmolested by the mother country in the exercise of their important rights, they submitted to the form of English government, but when those rights were invaded, they spurned even the form.

This act was the Revolution, the principles of which were not the suddenly acquired property of a few individuals. They were abroad in the land in the ages before. They had always been taught, having descended from father to son, down from those primitive days when the pilgrim, established in his simple dwelling and seated at his blazing fire piled high from the forest which shaded his door, repeated to his listening children the story of his wrongs and of his resistance and bade them rejoice that, though the wild winds and the wild beasts were howling without, they had nothing to fear from great men's oppression.

So it was at the beginning of the Revolution. Every

settler's hearth was a school of independence. The scholars were apt, and the lessons sunk deeply. Thus it came that our country was always free; it could not be other than free.

As deeply seated as was the principle of liberty and resistance to arbitrary power in the breasts of the Puritans, it was not more so than their piety and sense of religious obligation. They were emphatically a people whose God was the Lord. Their form of government was as strictly theocratic (if direct communication be excepted) as was that of the Jews, insomuch that it would be difficult to say where there was any civil authority among them entirely distinct from ecclesiastical jurisdiction.

Whenever a few of them settled a town, they immediately gathered themselves into a church. Their elders were magistrates and their code of laws was the Pentateuch. These were forms, it is true, but forms which faithfully indicated principles and feelings, for no people could have adopted such forms who were not thoroughly imbued with the Spirit and bent on the practice of religion.

God was their King, and they regarded Him as truly and literally so, as if He had dwelt in a visible palace in the midst of their state. They were His devoted, resolute, humble subjects. They undertook nothing which they did not beg of Him to prosper; they accomplished nothing without rendering to Him the praise; they suffered nothing without carrying up their sorrows to His throne; they ate nothing which they did not implore Him to bless.

Their piety was not merely external. It was sincere. It had the proof of a good tree, in bearing good fruit; it produced and sustained a strict morality. Their tenacious purity of manners and speech obtained for them, in the mother country, their name of Puritans, which though given in derision, was as honorable an appellation as was ever bestowed by man on man.

That there were hypocrites among them is not to be doubted, but they were rare. The men who voluntarily exiled themselves to an unknown coast and endured there every toil and hardship for conscience' sake, that they might serve God in their own manner, were not likely to set conscience at defiance and make the services of God a mockery. They were not likely to be, neither were they, hypocrites. I do not know that it would be arrogating too much for them to say that, on the extended surface of the globe, there was not a single community of men to be compared with them in the respects of deep religious impressions and an exact performance of moral duty.

QUESTIONS. 1. What was one of the prominent traits of character of our forefathers? 2. How did they regard liberty? 3. What was their conduct in support of liberty? 4. From whence were derived the principles of the Revolution? 5. How were their systems of government formed? 6. What was the character of their piety? 7. As a community, how will they bear comparison for moral worth with all other communities past or present?

SPELL AND DEFINE. 1. prominent 2. distinguished 3. determined 4. self-government   5. personified   6. allegorized   7. enshrined 8. birthright 9. unalienable 10. surrendered 11. essential 12. fathomless 13. transmitted   14. unmolested   15. spontaneously   16. independence 17. communication   18. ecclesiastical   19. jurisdiction   20. theocratic 21. immediately   22. magistrates   23. Pentateuch   24. honorable 25. hypocrites

LESSON XLVII

Character of the Puritan Fathers of New England — continued

RULE. When two or more consonants come together, be careful to sound every one distinctly.

EXERCISES UNDER THE RULE. Thou *waft'st* the flying ships. Thou *acknowledgests* thy crime. Thou *list'nests* to my tale. It *exists somewhere.* Thou *knewest* that I was a hard man.

What I would especially inculcate is that, estimating as impartially as we are able the virtues and defects of our forefathers' character, we should endeavor to imitate the first and avoid the last.

Were they tenderly jealous of their inborn rights and resolved to maintain them in spite of the oppressor? And shall we ever be insensible to their value and part with the vigilance which should watch and the courage which should defend them? Rather let the ashes of our fathers, which have been cold so long, warm and quicken in their graves and return embodied to the surface and drive away their degenerate sons from the soil which their toils and sufferings purchased! Rather let the beasts of the wilderness come back to a wilderness and couch for prey in our desolate gardens and bring forth their young in our markets and howl nightly to the moon amidst the grass-grown ruins of our prostrate cities! Rather let the red sons of the forest reclaim their pleasant hunting grounds and rekindle their council fires which once threw their glare upon the eastern water and roam over our hills and plains without crossing a single track of the white man!

I am no advocate for war. I abominate its spirit and its cruelties. But to me there appears a wide and essential difference between resistance and aggression. It is aggression, it is the love of arbitrary domination, it is the insane thirst for what the world has too long and too indiscriminately called glory which lights up the flames of war and devastation.

Without aggression on the one side, no resistance would be roused on the other, and there would be no war. If all aggression were met by determined resistance then, too, there would be no war, for the spirit of aggression would be humbled and repressed. I would that it might be the universal principle of our countrymen and the determination of our rulers never to offer the slightest injury, never to commit the least outrage, though it were to obtain territory or fame or any selfish advantage.

In this respect I would that the example which was sometimes set by our forefathers might be altogether forsaken. But let us never forsake their better example of stern resistance; let us cherish and perpetuate their lofty sentiments of freedom; let us tread the soil which they planted for us as free as they did — or lie down at once beside them.

> The land we from our fathers had in trust
> We to our children will transmit, or die.
> This is our maxim, this our piety,
> And God and nature say that it is just.
> That which we *would* perform in arms, we must!
> We read the dictate in the infant's eye,
> In the wife's smile, and in the placid sky,
> And at our feet, amid the silent dust
> Of them that were before us.

Our fathers were pious, eminently so. Let us then forever venerate and imitate this part of their character. When the children of the Pilgrims forget that Being who was the Pilgrim's Guide and Deliverer; when the descendants of the Puritans cease to acknowledge, obey, and love that Being for whose service the Puritans forsook all that men chiefly love, enduring scorn and reproach, exile and poverty, and finding at last a superabundant reward; when the sons of a religious and holy ancestry fall away from its high communion and join themselves to the assemblies of the profane — they have stained the luster of their parentage. They have forfeited the dear blessings of their inheritance, and they deserve to be cast out from this fair land without even a wilderness for their refuge. No! Let us still keep the ark of God in the midst of us. Let us adopt the prayer of the wise monarch of Israel: "The Lord our God be with us, as he was with our fathers: let him not leave us, nor forsake us: that he may incline our heats unto him, to walk in all his ways, and to keep his commandments, and his statutes, and his judgments, which he commanded our fathers."

But our fathers were too rigidly austere. It may be thought that, even granting this to be their fault, we are so rapidly advancing toward an opposite extreme that anything like a caution against it is out of season and superfluous. Yet, I see not why the notice of every fault should not be accompanied with a corresponding caution.

That we are in danger of falling into one excess is a reason why we should be most anxiously on our guard at the place of exposure, but it is no reason why another excess should not be reprobated and pointed out with the finger of warning. The difficulty is, and the desire and effort should be, between these as well as all other extremes, to steer an equal course and preserve a safe medium.

I acknowledge that luxury and the blandishments of prosperity and wealth are greatly to be feared. If our softnesses, indulgences, and foreign fashions must inevitably accomplish our seduction and lead us away from the simplicity, honesty, sobriety, purity, and manly independence of our forefathers, most readily and fervently would I exclaim: Welcome back to the pure old times of the Puritans! Welcome back to the strict observances of their strictest days! Welcome, thrice welcome to all their severity, all their gloom! for infinitely better would be hard doctrines and dark brows, Jewish sabbaths, strait garments, formal manners, and a harsh guardianship than dissoluteness and effeminacy, than empty pleasures and shameless debauchery, than lolling ease and pampered pride and fluttering vanity, than unprincipled, faithless, corrupted rulers and a people unworthy of a more exalted government.

But is it necessary that we must be either gloomy or corrupt, either formal or profane, either extravagant in strictness or extravagant in dissipation and levity? Can we not so order our habits and so fix our principles as not to suffer the luxuries of our days to choke and strangle with their rankness the simple morality of our fathers' days, nor permit a reverence for their stiff and inappropriate formalities and austerities to overshadow and repress our innocent comforts and delights?

Let us attempt, at least, to maintain ourselves in so desirable a medium. Let us endeavor to preserve whatever was excellent in the manners and lives of the Puritans, while we forsake what was inconsistent or unreasonable. Then we shall hardly fail to be wiser and happier, and even better, than they were.

QUESTIONS. 1. What should be especially inculcated in regard to the virtues and the defects of our forefathers' character? 2. How ought we to regard our rights? 3. Is this a spirit of war? 4. Did our fathers never fail in this respect? 5. How shall we regard their piety? 6. What shall we say of their austere and rigid severity? 7. What course ought we to pursue?

SPELL AND DEFINE. 1. inculcate   2. degenerate   3. abominate   4. aggression   5. indiscriminately   6. countrymen   7. superabundant   8. superfluous   9. reprobated   10. indulgences   11. inevitably   12. accomplish   13. guardianship   14. debauchery   15. unprincipled   16. extravagant   17. inappropriate   18. endeavor   19. excellent

LESSON XLVIII

Decisive Integrity — Wirt

RULE. Be careful to speak such little words as *the, of, a, in, from, at, by* very distinctly and yet not to dwell on them as long as on other more important words.

The man who is so conscious of the rectitude of his intentions as to be willing to open his bosom to the inspection of the world, is in possession of one of the strongest pillars of a decided character. The course of such a man will be firm and steady because he has nothing to fear from the world and is sure of the approbation and support of Heaven. In contrast, he who is conscious of secret and dark designs which, if known, would blast him, is perpetually shrinking and dodging from public observation and is afraid of all around and, much more, of all above him.

Such a man may, indeed, pursue his iniquitous plans steadily; he may waste himself to a skeleton in the guilty pursuit, but it is impossible that he can pursue them with the same health-inspiring confidence and exulting alacrity with him who feels, at every step, that he is in the pursuit of honest ends, by honest means. The clear unclouded brow, the open countenance, the brilliant eye which can look an honest man steadfastly yet courteously in the face, the healthfully beating heart and the firm elastic step belong to him whose bosom is free from guile and who knows that all his motives and purposes are pure and right.

Why should such a man falter in his course? He may be slandered, he may be deserted by the world, but he has that within which will keep him erect and enable him to move onward in his course, with his eyes fixed on Heaven, which he knows will not desert him.

Let your first step, then, in that discipline which is to give you decision of character be the heroic determination to be honest men and to preserve this character through every vicissitude of fortune and in every relation which connects you with society. I do not use this phrase, "honest men," in the narrow sense merely of meeting your pecuniary engagements and paying your debts, for this the common pride of gentlemen will constrain you to do. I use it in its larger sense of discharging all your duties, both public and private, both open and secret, with the most scrupulous, heaven-attesting integrity; in that sense which drives from the bosom all little, dark, crooked, sordid, debasing considerations of self and substitutes in their place a bolder, loftier, and nobler spirit — one that will dispose you to consider yourselves as born not so much for yourselves as for your country and your fellow creatures and which will lead you to act on every occasion sincerely, justly, generously, magnanimously.

There is a morality on a larger scale, perfectly consistent with a just attention to your own affairs, which it would be the height of folly to neglect — a generous expansion, a proud elevation, and conscious greatness of character which is the best preparation for a decided course in every situation into which you can be thrown. It is to this high and noble tone of character that I would have you to aspire.

I would not have you to resemble those weak and meager streamlets which lose their direction at every petty impediment that presents itself and stop, turn back, creep around, and search out every little channel through which they may wind their feeble and sickly course. Nor yet would I have you resemble the headlong torrent that carries havoc in its mad career.

But I would have you like the ocean, that noblest emblem of majestic decision which, in the calmest hour, still heaves its resistless might of waters to the shore, filling the heavens day and night with the echoes of its sublime declaration of independence and tossing and sporting on its bed with an imperial consciousness of strength that laughs at opposition. It is this depth, weight, power, and purity of character that I would have you resemble, and I would have you, like the waters of the ocean, to become the purer by your own action.

QUESTIONS. 1. What is the effect of conscious rectitude upon a man? 2. The effect of the want of it? 3. What then should be the first step in the attainment of a decisive character? 4. In what two senses may we be considered "honest men"? 5. With what beautiful metaphorical comparison does this piece terminate?

SPELL AND DEFINE. 1. rectitude   2. approbation   3. perpetually
4. shrinking   5. observation   6. iniquitous   7. health   8. inspiring
9. countenance   10. courteously   11. discipline   12. determination
13. vicissitude   14. pecuniary   15. engagements   16. scrupulous
17. heaven-attesting   18. considerations   19. magnanimously
20. consistent   21. streamlets   22. impediment   23. independence
24. consciousness

LESSON XLIX

On the Being of a God — Young

RULE. When anything very solemn or devotional is to be read, there should be a full, solemn tone of voice, the piece should be read slowly, and long pauses should be made at the commas.

Retire; the world shut out; thy thoughts call home;
Imagination's airy wing repress;
Lock up thy senses; let no passion stir;
Wake all to Reason, let her reign alone.
Then in thy soul's deep silence and the depth
Of nature's silence, midnight, thus inquire,
As I have done, and shall inquire no more.
In nature's channel thus the questions run:
What am I? and from whence? I nothing know,
But that I am, and since I am, conclude
Something eternal: had there e'er been nought,
Nought still had been — eternal there must be.
But what eternal? Why not human race?
And Adam's ancestors without an end?
That's hard to be conceived, since every link
Of that long-chained succession is so frail:
Can every part depend, and not the whole?
Yet grant it true, new difficulties rise;
I'm still quite out at sea, nor see the shore.
Whence earth, and these bright orbs? Eternal too?
Grant matter was eternal, still these orbs
Would want some other father; much design
Is seen in all their motions, all their makes;
Design implies intelligence and art
That can't be from themselves or man; that art
Man scarce can comprehend, could man bestow;
And nothing greater yet allow'd than man.
Who, motion, foreign to the smallest grain,

Shot through vast masses of enormous weight?
Who bid brute matter's restive lump assume
Such various forms, and gave it wings to fly?
Has matter innate motion? Then each atom,
Asserting its indisputable right
To dance, would form a universe of dust.
Has matter none? Then whence those glorious forms
And boundless flights, from shapeless and reposed?
Has matter more than motion? Has it thought,
Judgment and genius? Is it deeply learned
In mathematics? Has it framed such laws,
Which but to guess, a Newton made immortal?
If so, how each sage atom laughs at me,
Who think a clod inferior to a man!
If art to form, and counsel to conduct,
Resides not in each block, a Godhead reigns.
Grant then invisible eternal mind.
That granted, all is solved, but granting that
Draw I not o'er me a still darker cloud?
Grant I not that which I can ne'er conceive?
A Being without origin or end!
Hail human liberty! there is no God!
Yet why on either scheme that knot subsists;
Subsist it must, in God, or human race.
If in the last, how many knots beside,
Indissoluble all? Why choose it there,
Where chosen still subsist ten thousand more?
Reject it, where that chosen all the rest
Dispersed leave reason's whole horizon clear?
This is not Reason's dictate, Reason says
Choose with the side where one grain turns the scale.
What vast preponderance is here: Can Reason
With louder voice exclaim, "Believe a God"?
And Reason heard is the sole mark of man.
What things impossible must man think true,
On any other system! and how strange
To disbelieve through mere credulity?

If in this chain Lorenzo finds no flaw,
Let it forever bind him to belief.
And where the link in which a flaw he finds?
Such a God there is, that God how great!

QUESTIONS. 1. What question is discussed in this piece? 2. What inquiry is proposed in lines 9–14? 3. How is that inquiry answered in lines 15–18? 4. Suppose matter to be eternal, what is still the evidence of a designing God? 5. What is meant by the question, "Has matter innate motion?" 6. What would follow from such a supposition? 7. Can you state the conclusion of the argument?

SPELL AND DEFINE. 1. retire   2. imagination   3. repress
4. conclude   5. eternal   6. succession   7. design   8. intelligence
9. comprehend   10. allowed   11. foreign   12. enormous   13. restive
14. innate   15. asserting   16. indisputable   17. universe   18. reposed
19. judgment 20. mathematics 21. inferior 22. subsists 23. indissoluble
24. dispersed 25. dictate 26. preponderance 27. disbelieve 28. credulity

LESSON L

The Steamboat on Trial — Abbott

RULE. Be careful not to join the last part of one word to the beginning of the next word.

The Bible everywhere conveys the idea that this life is not our home, but a state of probation, that is, of *trial and discipline,* which is intended to prepare us for another. In order that all, even the youngest of my readers, may understand what is meant by this, I shall illustrate it by some familiar examples drawn from the actual business of life.

When a large steamboat is built, with the intention of having her employed upon the waters of a great river, she must be *proved* before put to service. Before trial, it is somewhat doubtful whether she will succeed. In the first place, it is not absolutely certain whether her machinery will work at all. There may be some flaw in the iron or an imperfection in some part of the workmanship which will prevent the motion of her wheels. Or if this is not the case, the power of the machinery may not be sufficient to propel her through the water with such force as to overcome the current. Or she may, when brought to encounter the rapids at some narrow passage in the stream, not be able to force her way against their resistance.

The engineer, therefore, resolves to try her in all these respects, that her security and her power may be properly *proved* before she is entrusted with her valuable cargo of human lives. He cautiously builds a fire under her boiler, watches with eager interest the rising of the steam gauge, and scrutinizes every part of the machinery as it gradually comes under the control of the tremendous power which he is apprehensively applying.

With what interest does he observe the first stroke of the ponderous piston! When, at length, the fastenings of the boat are let go and the motion is communicated to the wheels and the mighty mass slowly moves away from the wharf, how deep and eager an interest does he feel in all her movements and in every indication he can discover of her future success!

The engine, however, works imperfectly, as each one must on its first trial. The object in this experiment is not to gratify idle curiosity by seeing that she will move but to discover and remedy every little imperfection and to remove every obstacle which prevents greater success. For this purpose, you will see our engineer examining, most minutely and most attentively, every part of her complicated machinery. The crowd on the wharf may be simply gazing on her majestic progress as she moves off from the shore, but the engineer is within, looking with faithful examination into all the minutiae of the motion.

He scrutinizes the action of every lever and the friction of every joint; here he oils a bearing, there he tightens a nut; one part of the machinery has too much play, and he confines it — another too much friction, and he loosens it; now he stops the engine, now reverses her motion, and again sends the boat forward in her course. He discovers, perhaps, some great improvement of which she is susceptible, and when he returns to the wharf and has extinguished her fire, he orders from the machine shop the necessary alteration.

The next day he puts his boat to the trial again, and she glides over the water more smoothly and swiftly than before. The jar which he had noticed is gone and the friction reduced; the beams play more smoothly and the alteration which he has made produces a more equable motion in the shaft or gives greater effect to the stroke of the paddles upon the water.

When at length her motion is such as to satisfy him upon the smooth surface of the river, he turns her course, we will imagine, toward the rapids to see how she will sustain a greater trial. As he increases her steam to give her power to overcome the new force with which she has to contend, he watches with eager interest her boiler, inspects the gauge and the safety valves, and from her movements under the increased pressure of her steam, he receives suggestions for further improvements or for precautions which will insure greater safety.

These he executes, and thus he perhaps goes on for many days or even weeks, trying and examining, for the purpose of improvement, every working of that mighty power to which he knows hundreds of lives are soon to be entrusted. This now is probation — *trial for the sake of improvement.* What are its results? Why, after this course has been thoroughly and faithfully pursued, this floating palace receives upon her broad deck and in her carpeted and curtained cabins her four or five hundred passengers who pour along, in one long procession of happy groups, over the bridge of planks — father and son, mother and children, young husband and wife, all with implicit confidence, trusting themselves and their dearest interests to her power.

See her as she sails away — how beautiful and yet how powerful are all her motions! That beam glides up and down gently and smoothly in its grooves, and yet gentle as it seems, hundreds of horses could not hold it still. There is no apparent violence, but every movement is with irresistible power. How graceful is her form and yet how mighty is the momentum with which she presses on her way.

Loaded with life, and herself the very symbol of life and power, she seems something ethereal — unreal, which, ere we look again, will have vanished away. Though she has within her bosom a furnace glowing with furious fires and a reservoir of death — the elements of most dreadful ruin and conflagration, of destruction the most complete and agony the most unutterable, and though her strength is equal to the united energy of two thousand men, she restrains it all.

She was constructed by genius and has been *tried* and improved by fidelity and skill. One man governs and controls her, stops her and sets her in motion, turns her this way and that as easily and certainly as the child guides the gentle lamb. She walks over the 160 miles of her route without rest and without fatigue. Yet the passengers, who have slept in safety in their berths, with destruction by water without and by fire within, defended only by a plank from the one and by a sheet of copper from the other, land at the appointed time in safety.

My reader, you have within you susceptibilities and powers of which you have little present conception, energies which are hereafter to operate in producing fullness of enjoyment or horrors of suffering of which you now can form scarcely a conjecture. You are now on *trial*. God wishes you to prepare yourself for safe and happy action. He wishes you to look within, to examine the complicated movements of your heart, to detect what is wrong, to modify what needs change, and to rectify every irregular motion.

You go out to try your moral powers upon the stream of active life and then return to retirement to improve what is right and remedy what is wrong. Renewed opportunities of moral practice are given you, that you may go on from strength to strength until every part of that complicated moral machinery of which the human heart consists will work as it ought to work and is prepared to accomplish the mighty purposes for which your powers are designed. You are *on trial* — *on probation* now. You will enter upon *active service* in another world.

QUESTIONS. 1. How does the Bible consider this life? 2. What is a state of probation? 3. What is a steamboat? 4. Who invented it? 5. Was Robert Fulton an American? 6. What is meant by proving a steamboat? 7. What is the use of doing it? 8. Is there any resemblance between man and a steamboat? 9. If this life is our state of probation, what will a future state of existence be? 10. What difference is there between man's probation before the Fall and man's probation now?

SPELL AND DEFINE. 1. conveys   2. probation   3. discipline
4. illustrate 5. machinery 6. imperfection 7. workmanship 8. sufficient
9. engineer   10. cautiously   11. scrutinizes   12. apprehensively
13. ponderous 14. piston 15. obstacle 16. minutely 17. complicated
18. minutiae   19. lever   20. friction   21. bearing   22. reverses
23. alteration 24. equable 25. pressure 26. implicit 27. momentum
28. ethereal   29. reservoir   30. conflagration   31. unutterable
32. constructed   33. fatigue   34. susceptibilities   35. conception
36. conjecture 37. modify 38. rectify 39. renewed

LESSON LI

Paine's Age of Reason — Erskine

RULE. Stop at each comma long enough to take breath.

It seems, gentlemen, this is an age of reason, and the time and the person are at last arrived that are to dissipate the errors that have overspread the past generations of ignorance! The believers in Christianity are many, but it belongs to the few that are wise to correct their credulity! Belief is an act of reason, and superior reason may therefore dictate to the weak. In running the mind along the numerous list of sincere and devout Christians, I cannot help lamenting that Newton had not lived to this day, to have had his shallowness filled up with this new flood of light! But the subject is too awful for irony. I will speak plainly.

Newton was a Christian! Newton, whose mind burst forth from the fetters cast by nature upon our finite conceptions; Newton, whose science was truth and the foundation of whose knowledge of it was philosophy — not those visionary and arrogant assumptions which too often usurp its name but philosophy resting upon the basis of mathematics which, like figures, cannot lie. Newton, who carried the line and rule to the utmost barriers of creation and explored the principles by which, no doubt, all created matter is held together and exists.

But this extraordinary man, in the mighty reach of his mind, overlooked, perhaps, the errors which a minuter investigation of the created things on this earth might have taught him of the essence of his Creator. What shall then be said of the great Mr. Boyle, who looked into the organic structure of all matter, even to the inanimate substances which the foot treads on. Such a man may be supposed to have been equally qualified with Mr. Paine to "look through nature up to nature's God."

Yet the result of all his contemplation was the most confirmed and devout belief in all which the other holds in contempt as despicable and driveling superstition. But this error might, perhaps, arise from a want of due attention to the foundations of human judgment and the structure of that understanding which God has given us for the investigation of truth.

Let that question be answered by Mr. Locke, who was to the highest pitch of devotion and adoration, a Christian. Mr. Locke's office was to detect the errors of thinking by going up to the fountain of thought and to direct into the proper track of reasoning the devious mind of man by showing him its whole process, from the first perceptions of sense to the last conclusions of ratiocination, putting a rein besides upon false opinion by practical rules for the conduct of human judgment.

But these men were only deep thinkers and lived in their closet, unaccustomed to the traffic of the world and to the laws which partially regulate mankind. Gentlemen, in the place where you now sit to administer the justice of this great country, above a century ago the never-to-be-forgotten Sir Matthew Hale presided, whose faith in Christianity is an exalted commentary upon its truth. His life was a glorious example of its fruits, administering human justice with a wisdom drawn from the pure fountain of the Christian dispensation, which has been and will be, in all ages, a subject of the highest reverence and admiration. But it is said by Mr. Paine that the Christian fable is but the tale of the more notable superstitions of the world and may be easily comprehended by a proper understanding of the mythologies of the heathen.

Did Milton understand those mythologies? Was he less versed than Mr. Paine in the superstitions of the world? No, they were the subject of his immortal song, and though shut out from all recurrence to them, he poured them forth from the stores of a memory rich with all that man ever knew and laid them in their order as the illustration of that real and exalted faith, the unquestionable source of that fervid genius which cast a sort of shade upon all the other works of man.

> He passed the bounds of flaming space
> Where angels tremble while they gaze;
> He saw, till blasted with excess of light,
> He closed his eyes in endless night.

But it was the light of the body only that was extinguished; "the celestial light shone inward and enabled him to justify the ways of God to man."

Thus, gentlemen, you find all that is great or wise or splendid or illustrious among created beings, all the minds gifted beyond ordinary nature, if not inspired by their Universal Author for the advancement and dignity of the world, though divided by distant ages and by the clashing opinions which distinguish them from one another, yet joining, as it were, in one sublime chorus to celebrate the truths of Christianity and laying upon its holy altars the never-fading offerings of their immortal wisdom.

QUESTIONS. 1. Who and what was Paine?   2. What is said of Newton? 3. What of Boyle? 4. What of Locke? 5. These men, it might be said, were only great thinkers, unacquainted with practical life. Who is next brought forward to meet this? 6. What is Paine's argument in respect to the Bible and heathen mythology? 7. How is it met? 8. What is the argument for Christianity, deduced from the consideration of such individual cases?

SPELL AND DEFINE. 1. dissipate   2. overspread   3. credulity 4. shallowness   5. conceptions   6. philosophy   7. assumptions 8. mathematics   9. barriers   10. extraordinary   11. investigation 12. organic   13. contemplation   14. driveling   15. superstition 16. adoration   17. conclusions   18. ratiocination   19. judgment 20. unaccustomed 21. commentary 22. administering 23. dispensation 24. mythologies   25. recurrence   26. unquestionable   27. extinguished 28. illustrious

LESSON LII

Divine Providence — Job 5

RULE. In reading poetry that does not rhyme, there should be no pause at the end of a line except when it terminates with an important word, or the sense requires it.

Call now, if there be any that will answer thee;
And to which of the saints wilt thou turn?
For wrath killeth the foolish man,
And envy slayeth the silly one.
I have seen the foolish taking root:
But suddenly I cursed his habitation.
His children are far from safety,
And they are crushed in the gate,

Neither is there any to deliver them.
Whose harvest the hungry eateth up,
And taketh it even out of the thorns,
And the robber swalloweth up their substance.
Although affliction cometh not forth of the dust,
Neither doth trouble spring out of the ground;
Yet man is born unto trouble,
As the sparks fly upward.

I would seek unto God,
And unto God would I commit my cause:
Who doeth great things and unsearchable;
Marvelous things without number:
Who giveth rain upon the earth,
And sendeth waters upon the fields:
To set up on high those that be low;
That those which mourn may be exalted to safety.
He disappointeth the devices of the crafty,
So that their hands cannot perform their enterprise.
He taketh the wise in their own craftiness:
And the council of the froward is carried headlong.
They meet with darkness in the daytime,
And grope in the noonday as in the night.
But he saveth the poor from the sword,
From their mouth, and from the hand of the mighty.
So the poor hath hope,
And iniquity stoppeth her mouth.

Behold, happy is the man whom God correcteth:
Therefore despise not thou the chastening of the
    Almighty:
For he maketh sore, and bindeth up:
He woundeth, and his hands make whole.
He shall deliver thee in six troubles:
Yea, in seven there shall no evil touch thee.
In famine he shall redeem thee from death:
And in war from the power of the sword.

Thou shalt be hid from the scourge of the tongue:
Neither shalt thou be afraid of destruction when it
   cometh.
At destruction and famine thou shalt laugh:
Neither shalt thou be afraid of the beasts of the
   earth.
For thou shalt be in league with the stones of the
   field:
And the beasts of the field shall be at peace with thee.
And thou shalt know that thy tabernacle shall be in
   peace;
And thou shalt visit thy habitation, and shalt not sin.
Thou shalt know also that thy seed shall be great,
And thine offspring as the grass of the earth.
Thou shalt come to thy grave in a full age,
Like as a shock of corn cometh in in his season.
Lo this, we have searched it, so it is;
Hear it, and know thou it for thy good.

SPELL AND DEFINE. 1. habitation   2. crushed   3. swalloweth
4. affliction 5. unsearchable 6. marvelous 7. disappointeth 8. enterprise
9. froward 10. headlong 11. correcteth 12. destruction 13. tabernacle

LESSON LIII

The Righteous Never Forsaken — New York Spectator

RULE. Be careful to speak such little words as *by, in, on, a, and, at, of*
very distinctly and yet not to dwell on them so long as on other more
important words.

It was Saturday night, and the widow of the Pine Cottage
sat by her blazing fire with her five tattered children at her
side, endeavoring by listening to the artlessness of their
prattle to dissipate the heavy gloom that pressed upon her
mind. For a year, her own feeble hand had provided for her

helpless family, for she had no supporter. She thought of no friend in all the wide, unfriendly world around.

But that mysterious Providence, the wisdom of whose ways is above human comprehension, had visited her with wasting sickness, and her little means had become exhausted. It was now, too, midwinter and the snow lay heavy and deep through all the surrounding forests, while storms still seemed gathering in the heavens and the driving wind roared amid the bounding pines and rocked her puny mansion.

The last herring smoked upon the coals before her; it was the only article of food she possessed. No wonder her forlorn, desolate state brought up in her lone bosom all the anxieties of a mother when she looked upon her children. No wonder, forlorn as she was, if she suffered the heart swellings of despair to rise, even though she knew that He whose promise is to the widow and to the orphan cannot forget His word.

Providence had many years before taken from her her eldest son, who went from his forest home to try his fortune on the high seas. Since then she had heard no note of tidings of him. In her latter time He had, by the hand of death, deprived her of the companion and staff of her earthly pilgrimage, in the person of her husband. Yet to this hour she had been borne; she had not only been able to provide for her little flock but had never lost an opportunity of ministering to the wants of the miserable and destitute.

The indolent may well bear with poverty while the ability to gain sustenance remains. The individual who has but his own wants to supply may suffer with fortitude the winter of want; his affections are not wounded, his heart not wrung. The most desolate in populous cities may hope, for Charity has not quite closed her hand and heart and shut her eyes on misery.

But the industrious mother of helpless and depending children — far from the reach of human charity — has none of these to console her. Such a one was the widow of the Pine

Cottage. Yet as she bent over the fire and took up the last scanty remnant of food to spread before her children, her spirits seemed to brighten up, as by some sudden and mysterious impulse, and Cowper's beautiful lines came uncalled across her mind:

> Judge not the Lord by feeble sense,
> But trust Him for His grace;
> Behind a frowning Providence
> He hides a smiling face.

The smoked herring was scarcely laid upon the table when a gentle rap at the door and loud barking of a dog attracted the attention of the family. The children flew to open it, and a weary traveler in tattered garments and apparently indifferent health entered and begged a lodging and a mouthful of food. Said he, "It is now twenty-four hours since I tasted bread." The widow's heart bled anew as under a fresh complication of distresses, for her sympathies lingered not round her fireside. She hesitated not even now; rest and share of all she had she proffered to the stranger. "We shall not be forsaken," said she, "or suffer deeper for an act of charity."

The traveler drew near the table — but when he saw the scanty fare, he raised his eyes towards heaven with astonishment, "And is this *all* your store?" said he, "And a share of this do you offer to one you know not? Then never saw I *charity* before! But madam," said he, continuing, "do you not wrong your *children* by giving a part of your last mouthful to a stranger?"

"Ah," said the poor widow, and the teardrops gushed into her eyes as she said it, "I have a *boy,* a darling *son* somewhere on the face of the wide world, unless Heaven has taken him away, and I only act towards you as I would that others should act towards him. God, who sent manna from heaven, can provide for us as He did for Israel. How should I this night offend Him, if my son should be a wanderer, destitute as you, and He should have provided for him a home, even poor as this, were I to turn you unrelieved away."

The widow ended, and the stranger, springing from his seat, clasped her in his arms, "God indeed has provided your son a home and has given him wealth to reward the goodness of his benefactress — my mother! Oh, my mother!"

It was her long lost son returned to her bosom from the Indies. He had chosen that disguise that he might the more completely surprise his family. Never was surprise more perfect or followed by a sweeter cup of joy. That humble residence in the forest was exchanged for one comfortable, and indeed beautiful, in the valley. The widow lived long with her dutiful son in the enjoyment of worldly plenty and in the delightful employments of virtue. At this day the passerby is pointed to the willow that spreads its branches above her grave.

QUESTIONS. 1. Can you give a sketch of the widow's history? 2. Can evil ever come from judiciously obeying the dictates of benevolence?

SPELL AND DEFINE. 1. endeavoring   2. artlessness   3. supporter   4. mysterious   5. comprehension   6. exhausted   7. surrounding   8. anxieties 9. swellings 10. providence 11. pilgrimage 12. sustenance   13. individual   14. frowning   15. apparently   16. indifferent   17. sympathies   18. astonishment   19. unrelieved   20. benefactress   21. exchanged

LESSON LIV

Religion the Only Basis of Society — Channing

RULE. When two or more consonants come together, let the pupil be careful to sound every one distinctly.

EXERCISES UNDER THE RULE. It *exists* everywhere. Thou *smoothed'st* his rugged path. Thou *sat'st* upon thy *throne*. Do you see the *bird's nests?* Thou *call'st* in vain. Alkaline *earths*.

Religion is a social concern, for it operates powerfully on society, contributing in various ways to its stability and prosperity. Religion is not merely a private affair; the community is deeply interested in its diffusion, for it is the best support of the virtues and principles on which the social order rests. Pure and undefiled religion is to do good, and it follows very plainly that if God be the Author and Friend of society, then the recognition of Him must force all social duty, and enlightened piety must give its whole strength to public order.

Few men suspect, perhaps no man comprehends, the extent of the support given by religion to every virtue. No man, perhaps, is aware how much our moral and social sentiments are fed from this fountain; how powerless conscience would become without the belief of a God; how palsied would be human benevolence were there not the sense of a higher benevolence to quicken and sustain it; how suddenly the whole social fabric would quake and with what a fearful crash it would sink into hopeless ruin, were the ideas of a supreme Being, of accountableness, and of a future life to be utterly erased from every mind.

Let men thoroughly believe that they are the work and sport of chance, that no superior Intelligence concerns itself with human affairs, that all their improvements perish forever at death, that the weak have no guardian and the injured no avenger, that there is no recompense for sacrifices to uprightness and the public good, that an oath is unheard in heaven, that secret crimes have no witness but the perpetrator, that human existence has no purpose and human virtue no unfailing friend, that this brief life is everything to us and death is total, everlasting extinction. Once let them *thoroughly* abandon religion, and who can conceive or describe the extent of the desolation which would follow!

We hope, perhaps, that human laws and natural sympathy would hold society together. As reasonably might we believe that were the sun quenched in the heavens, *our* torches would illuminate and *our* fires quicken and fertilize the creation. What is there in human nature to awaken respect and tenderness, if man is the unprotected insect of a day? What is he more, if atheism be true?

Erase all thought and fear of God from a community, and selfishness and sensuality would absorb the whole man. Appetite, knowing no restraint, and suffering, having no solace or hope, would trample in scorn on the restraints of human laws. Virtue, duty, and principle would be mocked and spurned as unmeaning sounds. A sordid self-interest would supplant every feeling, and man would become, in fact, what the theory of atheism declares him to be — *a companion for brutes.*

QUESTIONS. 1. What is the operation of religion upon society? 2. What would be the effect of the removal of religion upon the whole fabric of virtue? 3. Why would not human laws and sympathies hold society together?

SPELL AND DEFINE. 1. contributing   2. community   3. diffusion 4. recognition 5. enlightened 6. comprehends 7. sentiments 8. powerless 9. conscience   10. accountableness   11. intelligence   12. recompense 13. perpetrator   14. illuminate   15. unprotected   16. selfishness 17. atheism

LESSON LV

Benevolence of the Supreme Being — Chalmers

RULE. Be careful to notice every comma and stop long enough to take breath.

It is saying much for the benevolence of God, to say that a single world or a single system is not enough for it, that it must have the spread of a mightier region on which it may pour forth a tide of exuberance throughout all its provinces; that, as far as our vision can carry us, it has strewed immensity with the floating receptacles of life and has stretched over each of them the garniture of such sky as mantles our own habitation; that, even from distances which are far beyond the reach of human eye, the songs of gratitude and praise may now be arising to the one God, who sits surrounded by the regards of His great and universal family.

Now, it is saying much for the benevolence of God to say that He sends forth these wide and distant emanations over the surface of a territory so ample that the world we inhabit, lying embedded as it does amid so much surrounding greatness, shrinks into a point that to the universal Eye might appear to be almost imperceptible.

Does it not add to the power and to the perfection of this universal Eye, that at the very moment it is taking a comprehensive survey of the vast, it can fasten a steady and undistracted attention on each minute and separate portion of it; that at the very moment it is looking at all worlds, it can look most pointedly and most intelligently to each of them; that at the very moment it sweeps the field of immensity, it can settle all the earnestness of its regards upon every distinct handbreadth of that field; that at the very moment at which it embraces the totality of existence, it can send a most thorough and penetrating inspection into each of its details and into every one of its endless diversities?

You cannot fail to perceive how much this adds to the power of the all-seeing Eye. Tell me, then, if it do not add as much perfection to the benevolence of God that while it is expatiating over the vast field of created things, there is not one portion of the field overlooked by it; that while it scatters blessings over the whole of an infinite range, it causes them to descend in a shower of plenty on every separate habitation; that while His arm is underneath and round about all worlds, He enters within the precincts of every one of them and gives a care and a tenderness to each individual of their teeming population.

Oh! does not the God, who is said to be love, shed over this attribute of His its finest illustration when, while He sits in the highest heaven and pours out His fullness on the whole subordinate domain of nature and of providence, He bows a pitying regard on the very humblest of His children and sends His reviving Spirit into every heart and cheers by His presence every home and provides for the wants of every family and watches every sickbed and listens to the complaints of every sufferer! While, by His wondrous mind the weight of universal government is borne, oh! is it not more wondrous and more excellent still, that He feels for every sorrow and has an ear open to every prayer!

QUESTIONS. 1. Compared with the whole universe, what is this single world? 2. What must, then, be the benevolence which could create such a universe? 3. What higher idea of the intellectual power, as well as goodness of the Creator, does it excite to reflect that not the smallest field of this immeasurable universe is left unnoticed or unprovided for? 4. Where is it said that "God is love"?

SPELL AND DEFINE. 1. mightier   2. exuberance   3. immensity
4. receptacles   5. garniture   6. surrounded   7. emanations   8. embedded
9. surrounding   10. imperceptible   11. comprehensive   12. undistracted
13. pointedly   14. intelligently   15. earnestness   16. totality
17. penetrating   18. inspection   19. diversities   20. expatiating
21. overlooked   22. teeming   23. population   24. subordinate
25. government 26. illustration

LESSON LVI

Love of Applause — Hawes

RULE. Do not let the voice grow weaker at the last words of a sentence.

To be insensible to public opinion or to the estimation in which we are held by others indicates anything rather than a good and generous spirit. It is indeed the mark of a low and worthless character, devoid of principle and therefore devoid of shame. A young man is not far from ruin when he can say, without blushing, *I don't care what others think of me.*

To have a proper regard to public opinion is one thing, but to make that opinion our rule of action is quite another. The one we may cherish consistently with the purest virtue and the most unbending rectitude, the other we cannot adopt without an utter abandonment of principle and disregard of duty.

The young man whose great aim is to please, who makes the opinion and favor of others his rule and motive of action, stands ready to adopt any sentiments or pursue any course of conduct, however false and criminal, provided only that it be popular. In every emergency his first question is, What will my companions, what will the world think and say of me if I adopt this or that course of conduct? Duty, the eternal laws of rectitude, are not thought of. Custom, fashion, popular favor — these are the things that fill his entire vision and decide every question of opinion and duty.

Such a man can never be trusted, for he has no integrity and no independence of mind to obey the dictates of rectitude. He is at the mercy of every casual impulse and change of popular opinion, and you can no more tell whether he will be right or wrong tomorrow than you can predict the course of the wind or what shape the clouds will then assume.

What is the usual consequence of this weak and foolish regard to the opinions of men? What the *end* of thus acting in compliance with custom in opposition to one's own convictions of duty? It is to lose the esteem and respect of the very men whom you thus attempt to please. Your defect of principle and hollow-heartedness are easily perceived, and though the persons to whom you thus sacrifice your conscience may affect to commend your complaisance, you may be assured that inwardly they despise you for it.

Young men hardly commit a greater mistake than to think of gaining the esteem of others by yielding to their wishes, contrary to their own sense of duty. Such conduct is always morally wrong and rarely fails to deprive one both of self-respect and the respect of others.

It is very common for young men just commencing business to imagine that, if they would advance their secular interests, they must not be very scrupulous in binding themselves down to the strict rules of rectitude. They must conform to custom, and if in buying and selling they sometimes say the things that are not true and do the things that are not honest, why, their neighbors do the same, and verily, there is no getting along without it. There is so much competition and rivalry that to be *strictly honest* and yet succeed in business is out of the question.

Now if it were indeed so, I would say to a young man — then, quit your business. Better dig, and beg too, than to tamper with conscience, sin against God, and lose your soul.

But, is it so? Is it necessary in order to succeed in business that you should adopt a standard of morals more lax and pliable than the one placed before you in the Bible? Perhaps for a time a rigid adherence to rectitude might bear hard upon you, but how would it be in the end? Possibly your neighbor, by being less scrupulous than you, may invent a more expeditious way of acquiring a fortune. If he is willing to violate the dictates of conscience, to lie and cheat, to trample on the rules of justice and honesty, he may, indeed, get the start of you and rise suddenly to wealth and distinction.

But would you envy him his riches or be willing to place yourself in his situation? Sudden wealth, especially when obtained by dishonest means, rarely fails of bringing with it sudden ruin. Those who acquire it are, of course, beggared in their morals and are often, very soon, beggared in property. Their riches are corrupted, and while they bring the curse of God on their immediate possessors, they usually entail misery and ruin upon their families.

If it be admitted then that strict integrity is not always the shortest way to success, is it not the surest, the happiest, and the best? A young man of thorough integrity may, it is true, find it difficult in the midst of dishonest competitors and rivals to start in his business or profession. But how long ere he will surmount every difficulty, draw around him patrons and friends, and rise in the confidence and support of all who know him?

What if, in pursuing this course, you should not, at the close of life, have so much money by a few hundred dollars? Will not a fair character, an approving conscience, and an approving God be an abundant compensation for this little deficiency of pelf?

O there is an hour coming when one whisper of an approving mind, one smile of an approving God will be accounted of more value than the wealth of a thousand worlds like this. In that hour, my young friends, nothing will sustain you but the consciousness of having been governed in life by worthy and good principles.

QUESTIONS. 1. What must be said of a total disregard of public opinion in a young man? 2. What is the effect of making public opinion the rule of life? 3. What erroneous opinion respecting strict honesty is common? 4. Is it a well-founded opinion?

SPELL AND DEFINE. 1. insensible   2. estimation   3. consistently
4. unbending   5. abandonment   6. criminal   7. companions   8. integrity
9. independence   10. compliance   11. hollow-hearted   12. commencing
13. neighbors   14. competition   15. conscience   16. adherence
17. expeditious 18. beggared 19. compensation 20. consciousness

LESSON LVII

Scripture Lesson — Job 38:1–27; 39:19–25

RULE. Sound the vowels correctly and very full.

EXERCISES UNDER THE RULE. Prolong the following vowel sounds that are italicized: *a*-ge, *a*-we, *a*-rm, *o*-ld, *ou*-r, *ee*-l, *oo*-ze, bu-*oy*, *i*-sle.

Then the Lord answered Job out of the whirlwind,
     and said,
  Who is this that darkeneth counsel
By words without knowledge?
Gird up now thy loins like a man;
For I will demand of thee, and answer thou me.

  Where wast thou when I laid the foundations of
     the earth?
Declare, if thou hast understanding.
Who hath laid the measures thereof, if thou knowest?
Or who hath stretched the line upon it?
Whereupon are the foundations thereof fastened?
Or who laid the corner stone thereof;
When the morning stars sang together,
And all the sons of God shouted for joy?

  Or who shut up the sea with doors,
When it brake forth, as if it had issued out of the
     womb?
When I made the cloud the garment thereof,
And thick darkness a swaddling band for it,
And brake up for it my decreed place,
And set bars and doors,
And said, Hitherto shalt thou come, but no further:
And here shall thy proud waves be stayed?

  Hast thou commanded the morning since thy
     days;
And caused the dayspring to know his place;
That it might take hold of the ends of the earth,
That the wicked might be shaken out of it?
It is turned as clay to the seal;
And they stand as a garment.
And from the wicked their light is withholden,
And the high arm shall be broken.

Hast thou entered into the springs of the sea?
Or hast thou walked in the search of the depth?
Have the gates of death been opened unto thee?
Or hast thou seen the doors of the shadow of death?
Hast thou perceived the breadth of the earth?
Declare if thou knowest it all.

Where is the way where light dwelleth?
And as for darkness, where is the place thereof,
That thou shouldest take it to the bound thereof,
And that thou shouldest know the paths to the house
        thereof?
Knowest thou it, because thou wast then born?
Or because the number of thy days is great?

Hast thou entered into the treasures of the snow?
Or hast thou seen the treasures of the hail,
Which I have reserved against the time of trouble,
Against the day of battle and war?

By what way is the light parted,
Which scattereth the east wind upon the earth?
Who hath divided a watercourse for the overflowing of
        waters,
Or a way for the lightning of thunder;
To cause it to rain on the earth, where no man is;
On the wilderness, wherein there is no man;
To satisfy the desolate and waste ground;
And to cause the bud of the tender herb to spring
        forth?

Hast thou given the horse strength?
Hast thou clothed his neck with thunder?
Canst thou make him afraid as a grasshopper?
The glory of his nostrils is terrible.
He paweth in the valley, and rejoiceth in his strength:

He goeth on to meet the armed men.

He mocketh at fear, and is not affrighted;
Neither turneth he back from the sword.
The quiver rattleth against him,
The glittering spear and the shield.
He swalloweth the ground with fierceness and rage:
Neither believeth he that it is the sound of the
      trumpet.
He saith among the trumpets, Ha, ha!
And he smelleth the battle afar off,
The thunder of the captains, and the shouting.

QUESTIONS. 1. Is this poetry? 2. Can you select a metaphor and a simile from the many to be found in this lesson?

SPELL AND DEFINE. 1. whirlwind   2. darkeneth   3. foundations
4. whereupon   5. dayspring   6. withholden   7. perceived   8. shouldest
9. watercourse   10. wilderness   11. grasshopper   12. affrighted
13. swalloweth 14. fierceness

LESSON LVIII

Ludicrous Account of English Taxes — Brougham

RULE. Do not read in a monotonous way, as if you were not interested in what you read.

Permit me to inform you, my friends, what are the inevitable consequences of being too fond of glory: taxes — upon every article which enters into the mouth or covers the back or is placed under the foot; taxes upon everything which it is pleasant to see, hear, feel, smell, or taste; taxes upon warmth, light, and locomotion; taxes on everything on earth and in the waters under the earth, on everything that comes from abroad or is grown at home; taxes on the raw material; taxes on every fresh value that is added to it by the industry of man; taxes on the sauce which pampers man's appetite and the drug which restores him to health, on the ermine which decorates the judge and the rope which hangs the criminal, on the poor man's salt and the rich man's spice, on the brass nails of the coffin and the ribbons of the bride, at bed or board, couchant or levant, we must pay.

The schoolboy whips his taxed top, the beardless youth manages his taxed horse with a taxed bridle on a taxed road, and the dying Englishman, pouring his medicine which has paid 7 percent into a spoon that has paid 15 percent, flings himself back upon his chintz bed which has paid 22 percent, makes his will on an eight pound stamp, and expires in the arms of an apothecary who has paid a license of a hundred pounds for the privilege of putting him to death.

His whole property is then immediately taxed from 2 to 10 percent. Besides the probate, large fees are demanded for burying him in the chancel, his virtues are handed down to posterity on taxed marble, and he is then gathered to his fathers — to be taxed no more.

In addition to all this, the habit of dealing with large sums will make the government avaricious and profuse. The system itself will infallibly generate the base vermin of spies and informers and a still more pestilent race of political tools and retainers of the meanest and most odious description. The prodigious patronage, which the collecting of this splendid revenue will throw into the hands of government, will invest it with so vast an influence and hold out such means and temptations to corruption that all the virtue and public spirit, even of republicans, will be unable to resist.

QUESTIONS. 1. Can you enumerate some of the benefits of a system of taxation? 2. What will be the effect of the system upon the probity and purity of government?

SPELL AND DEFINE. 1. inevitable   2. consequences   3. locomotion   4. pampers   5. appetite   6. ermine   7. decorates   8. couchant   9. levant

10. schoolboy   11. beardless   12. medicine   13. chintz   14. apothecary
15. immediately   16. probate   17. chancel   18. avaricious   19. infallibly
20. generate   21. prodigious   22. republicans

LESSON LIX

Christ and the Blind Man — John 9

RULE. Pronounce the consonant sounds very distinctly.

EXAMPLE. Prolong the consonant sounds that are italicized in the following words: or-*b*, ai-*d*, a-*ll*, ar-*m*, ow-*n*, so-*ng*, wa-*r*, sa-*ve*, ama-*ze*.

And as Jesus passed by, he saw a man which was blind from his birth. And his disciples asked him, saying, Master, who did sin, this man, or his parents, that he was born blind?

Jesus answered, Neither hath this man sinned, nor his parents: but that the works of God should be made manifest in him.

I must work the works of him that sent me, while it is day: the night cometh, when no man can work. As long as I am in the world, I am the light of the world.

When he had thus spoken, he spat on the ground, and made clay of the spittle, and he anointed the eyes of the blind man with the clay. And said unto him, Go, wash in the pool of Siloam, (which is by interpretation, Sent.)

He went his way therefore, and washed, and came seeing. The neighbors therefore, and they which before had seen him that he was blind, said, Is not this he that sat and begged?

Some said, This is he: others said, He is like him: but he said, I am he. Therefore said they unto him, How were thine eyes opened?

He answered and said, A man that is called Jesus made clay, and anointed mine eyes, and said unto me, Go to the pool of Siloam, and wash: and I went and washed, and I received sight. Then said they unto him, Where is he? He said, I know not.

They brought to the Pharisees him that aforetime was blind. And it was the sabbath day when Jesus made the clay, and opened his eyes.

Then again the Pharisees also asked him how he had received his sight. He said unto them, He put clay upon mine eyes, and I washed, and do see.

Therefore said some of the Pharisees, This man is not of God, because he keepeth not the sabbath day. Others said, How can a man that is a sinner do such miracles? And there was a division among them.

They say unto the blind man again, What sayest thou of him, that he hath opened thine eyes? He said, He is a prophet.

But the Jews did not believe concerning him, that he had been blind, and received his sight, until they called the parents of him that had received his sight.

And they asked them, saying, Is this your son, who ye say was born blind? how then doth he now see?

His parents answered them and said, We know that this is our son, and that he was born blind: But by what means he now seeth, we know not; or who hath opened his eyes, we know not: he is of age; ask him: he shall speak for himself.

These words spake his parents, because they feared the Jews: for the Jews had agreed already, that if any man did confess that he was Christ, he should be put out of the synagogue.

Therefore said his parents, He is of age; ask him. Then again called they the man that was blind, and said unto him, Give God the praise: we know that this man is a sinner.

He answered and said, Whether he be a sinner or no, I know not: one thing I know, that, whereas I was blind, now I see.

Then said they to him again, What did he to thee? how opened he thine eyes? He answered them, I have told you already, and ye did not hear: wherefore would ye hear it again? will ye also be his disciples?

Then they reviled him, and said, Thou art his disciple; but we are Moses' disciples. We know that God spake unto Moses: as for this fellow, we know not from whence he is.

The man answered and said unto them, Why herein is a marvelous thing, that ye know not from whence he is, and yet he hath opened mine eyes.

Now we know that God heareth not sinners: but if any man be a worshipper of God, and doeth his will, him he heareth. Since the world began was it not heard that any man opened the eyes of one that was born blind. If this man were not of God, he could do nothing.

They answered and said unto him, Thou wast altogether born in sins, and dost thou teach us? And they cast him out.

Jesus heard that they had cast him out; and when he had found him, he said unto him, Dost thou believe on the Son of God?

He answered and said, Who is he, Lord, that I might believe on him? And Jesus said unto him, Thou hast both seen him, and it is he that talketh with thee.

And he said, Lord, I believe. And he worshipped him.

And Jesus said, For judgment I am come into this world, that they which see not might see; and that they which see might be made blind.

And some of the Pharisees which were with him heard these words, and said unto him, Are we blind also?

Jesus said unto them, If ye were blind, ye should have no sin: but now ye say, We see; therefore your sin remaineth.

QUESTIONS. 1. From what part of the Bible was this lesson taken? 2. What miracle is recorded in it?   3. Who performed this miracle? 4. What means did He make use of?   5. Will clay, prepared in the same manner, restore sight to the blind now?   6. Would it ever, if prepared by any mere man?   7. Was Christ a mere man?   8. This miracle, and many others, were performed openly. Why were not the Jews convinced by them that He came from God?   9. How did the Jews treat the man whose sight was restored?   10. Why did they put him out of the synagogue?

SPELL AND DEFINE. 1. disciple   2. manifest   3. anointed
4. interpretation   5. neighbors   6. miracles   7. division   8. prophet
9. synagogue   10. reviled   11. marvelous   12. altogether   13. judgment
14. therefore

LESSON LX

The Ocean — Anonymous

RULE. In reading poetry that rhymes, there should be a slight pause
after the words that rhyme, even when the sense does not require it.

Likeness of heaven! agent of power!
Man is thy victim! shipwrecks thy dower!
Spices and jewels, from valley and sea,
Armies and banners are buried in thee!

What are the riches of Mexico's mines,
To the wealth that far down in thy deep water shines?
The proud navies that cover the conquering west —
Thou fling'st them to death with one heave of thy breast!

From the high hills that view thy wreck-making shore,
When the bride of the mariner shrieks at thy roar;
When, like lambs in the tempest or mews in the blast,
O'er ridge-broken billows the canvass is cast;

How humbling to one with a heart and a soul,
To look on thy greatness and list to its roll;
To think how that heart in cold ashes shall be,
While the voice of eternity rises from thee!

Yes! where are the cities of Thebes and of Tyre?
Swept from the nations like sparks from the fire;
The glory of Athens, the splendor of Rome,
Dissolved — and forever — like dew in the foam.

But thou art almighty, eternal, sublime,
Unweakened, unwasted — twin brother of time!
Fleets, tempests, nor nations, thy glory can bow;
As the stars first beheld thee, still chainless art thou!

But, hold! when thy surges no longer shall roll,
And that firmament's length is drawn back like a
     scroll;
Then — then shall the spirit that sighs by thee now,
Be more mighty, more lasting, more chainless than
     thou!

QUESTIONS. 1. How is the ocean an "agent of power"? 2. What comparison is made in verse 3, lines 3 and 4? 3. What sentiments are inspired by viewing the ocean (verse 4)? 4. How will the soul's duration and that of the ocean compare?

SPELL AND DEFINE. 1. likeness   2. shipwrecks   3. conquering
4. wreck-making   5. shrieks   6. ridge-broken   7. canvass   8. dissolved
9. almighty   10. eternal   11. sublime   12. unweakened   13. unwasted
14. chainless 15. firmaments

LESSON LXI

The Horrors of War — Robert Hall

RULE. Let each pupil observe and mention every syllable that is not sounded as each one reads.

Though the whole race of man is doomed to dissolution and we are hastening to our long home, yet at each successive moment Life and Death seem to divide between them the dominion of mankind, and Life appears to have the larger share. It is otherwise in war; Death reigns there without a rival and without control.

War is the work, the element, or rather the sport and triumph of Death, who here glories not only in the extent of his conquests but in the richness of his spoil. In the other methods of attack, in the other forms which Death assumes, the feeble and the aged, who at best can live but a short time, are usually the victims. Here they are the vigorous and the strong.

It is remarked by the most ancient of poets that, in peace, children bury their parents; in war, parents bury their children; nor is the difference small. Children lament their parents, sincerely, indeed, but with that moderate and tranquil sorrow which it is natural for those to feel who are conscious of retaining many tender ties, many animating prospects.

Parents mourn for their children with the bitterness of despair. The aged parent, the widowed mother loses, when she is deprived of her children, everything but the capacity of suffering. Her heart, withered and desolate, admits no other object, cherishes no other hope. It is Rachel weeping for her children and refusing to be comforted, because they are not.

To confine our attention to the number of the slain would give us a very inadequate idea of the ravages of the sword. The lot of those who perish instantaneously may be considered, apart from religious prospects, as comparatively happy, since they are exempt from those lingering diseases and slow torments to which others are so liable.

We cannot see an individual expire, though a stranger or an enemy, without being sensibly moved and prompted by compassion to lend him every assistance in our power. Every trace of resentment vanishes in a moment; every other emotion gives way to pity and terror. In the last extremities we remember nothing but the respect and tenderness due to our common nature.

What a scene, then, must a field of battle present, where thousands are left without assistance and without pity, with their wounds exposed to the piercing air while the blood, freezing as it flows, binds them to the earth amidst the trampling of horses and the insults of an enraged foe! If they are spared by the humanity of the enemy and carried from the field, it is but a prolongation of torment. Conveyed in uneasy vehicles, often to a remote distance, through roads almost impassable, they are lodged in ill-prepared receptacles for the wounded and sick. There the variety of distress baffles all the efforts of humanity and skill and renders it impossible to give to each the attention he demands.

Far from their native home, no tender assiduities of friendship, no well-known voice, no wife, mother, or sister is near to soothe their sorrows, relieve their thirst, or close their eyes in death! Unhappy man! Must you be swept into the grave unnoticed and unnumbered and no friendly tear be shed for your sufferings or mingled with your dust?

We must remember, however, that as a very small proportion of military life is spent in actual combat, so it is a very small part of its miseries which must be ascribed to this source. More are consumed by the rust of inactivity than by the edge of the sword, confined to a scanty or unwholesome diet, exposed in sickly climates, harassed with tiresome marches and perpetual alarms. Their life is a continual scene of hardships and dangers. They grow familiar with hunger, cold, and watchfulness. Crowded into hospitals and prisons, contagion spreads among their ranks till the ravages of disease exceed those of the enemy.

We have hitherto only adverted to the sufferings of those who are engaged in the profession of arms, without taking into our account the situation of the countries which are the scenes of hostilities. How dreadful to hold everything at the mercy of an enemy and to receive life itself as a boon dependent on the sword! How boundless the fears which such a situation must inspire, where the issues of life and death are determined by no known laws, principles, or customs, and no conjecture can be formed of our destiny except so far as it is dimly deciphered in characters of blood, in the dictates of revenge, and the caprices of power!

Conceive but for a moment the consternation which the approach of an invading army would impress on the peaceful villages in our own neighborhood. When you have placed yourselves for an instant in that situation, you will learn to sympathize with those unhappy countries which have sustained the ravages of arms. But how is it possible to give you an idea of these horrors?

Here you behold rich harvests, the bounty of heaven, and the reward of industry consumed in a moment or trampled under foot while famine and pestilence follow the steps of desolation. There the cottages of peasants given up to the flames; mothers expiring through fear, not for themselves but for their infants; the inhabitants flying with their helpless babes in all directions, miserable fugitives on their native soil! In another you witness opulent cities taken by storm. The streets, where no sounds were heard but those of peaceful industry, filled on a sudden with slaughter and blood, resounding with the cries of the pursuing and the pursued. The palaces of nobles are demolished, the houses of the rich pillaged, and every age, sex, and rank mingled in promiscuous massacre and ruin!

QUESTIONS. 1. In peace, does Life or Death reign? 2. How is it in war? 3. What is the difference between war and peace, according to the ancient poet? 4. Who are victims of war besides those killed outright? 5. Mention some of the most prominent evils of war.

SPELL AND DEFINE. 1. dissolution   2. successive   3. vigorous 4. inadequate   5. instantaneously   6. resentment   7. prolongation 8. unnumbered 9. unwholesome 10. contagion

LESSON LXII

The Bible — Grimke

RULE. Be careful to read the last words of every sentence in as full and loud a tone as the first part.

The Bible is the only book which God has ever sent and the only one He ever will send into this world. All other books are frail and transient as time since they are only the registers of time, but the Bible is durable as eternity, for its pages contain the records of eternity. All other books are weak and imperfect like their author, man; the Bible is a transcript of infinite power and perfection. Every other volume is limited in its usefulness and influence, but the Bible came forth conquering and to conquer, rejoicing as a giant to run his course and like the sun, "there is nothing hid from the heat thereof."

The Bible only, of all the myriad of books the world has seen, is equally important and interesting to all mankind. Its tidings, whether of peace or of woe, are the same to the poor, the ignorant, and the weak as to the rich, the wise, and the powerful.

Among the most remarkable of its attributes is justice, for it looks with impartial eyes on kings and on slaves, on the hero and the soldier, on philosophers and peasants, on the eloquent and the dumb. From all, it exacts the same obedience to its commandments. It promises to the good the fruits of his labors, to the evil the reward of his hands. Nor are the purity and holiness, the wisdom, the benevolence, and truth of the Scriptures less conspicuous than their justice.

In sublimity and beauty, in the descriptive and pathetic, in dignity and simplicity of narrative, in power and comprehensiveness, depth and variety of thought, in purity and elevation of sentiment, the most enthusiastic admirers of the heathen classics have conceded their inferiority to the Scriptures.

The Bible, indeed, is the only universal classic, the classic of all mankind, of every age and country, of time and eternity. It is more humble and simple than the primer of the child, more grand and magnificent than the epic and the oration, the ode and the drama, when Genius, with his chariot of fire and his horses of fire, ascends in whirlwind into the heaven of his own invention. It is the best classic the world has ever seen, the noblest that has ever honored and dignified the language of mortals!

If you boast that the Aristotles and the Platos and the Ciceros of the classic ages "dipped their pens in intellect," the sacred authors dipped theirs in inspiration. If those were the "secretaries of nature," these were the secretaries of the very Author of nature.

If Greece and Rome have gathered into their cabinet of curiosities the pearls of heathen poetry and eloquence, the diamonds of pagan history and philosophy, God himself has treasured up in the Scriptures the poetry and eloquence, the philosophy and history of sacred lawgivers, of prophets and apostles, of saints, evangelists, and martyrs. In vain may you seek for the pure and simple light of universal truth in the Augustan ages of antiquity. In the Bible only is the poet's wish fulfilled,

And, like the sun, be all one boundless eye.

QUESTIONS. 1. What does the word *Bible* mean? 2. How did the Bible come into the world? 3. Did God write the Bible? 4. If men wrote it, how can it be called God's book? 5. Was every part of the Bible written at the same time? 6. What is meant when it is said that the Bible contains the "records of eternity"? 7. How can you show it to be so? 8. Mention the six particulars in which the Bible differs from all other books?

SPELL AND DEFINE. 1. transient 2. record 3. eternity 4. transcript 5. conspicuous 6. comprehensiveness 7. enthusiastic 8. inferiority 9. magnificent 10. classic 11. curiosities 12. evangelists 13. martyrs

LESSON LXIII

Tit for Tat — Miss Edgeworth

RULE. Be careful not to allow the voice to grow weaker and weaker as you approach the end of each sentence.

Mrs. Bolingbroke. I wish I knew what is the matter with me this morning. Why do you keep the newspaper all to yourself, my dear?

Mr. Bolingbroke. Here it is for you, my dear. I have finished it.

Mrs. B. I humbly thank you for giving it to me when you have done with it. I hate stale news. Is there anything in the paper? for I cannot be at the trouble of hunting it.

Mr. B. Yes, my dear, there are the marriages of two of our friends.

Mrs. B. Who? Who?

Mr. B. Your friend, the widow Nettleby, to her cousin John Nettleby.

Mrs. B. Mrs. Nettleby! Dear! But why did you tell me?

Mr. B. Because you asked me, my dear.

Mrs. B. Oh, but it is a hundred times pleasanter to read the paragraph one's self. One loses all the pleasure of the surprise by being told. Well, whose was the other marriage?

Mr. B. Oh, my dear, I will not tell you. I will leave you the pleasure of the surprise.

Mrs. B. But you see I cannot find it. How provoking you are, my dear! Do pray tell me.

Mr. B. Our friend, Mr. Granby.

Mrs. B. Mr. Granby! Dear! Why did not you make me guess? I should have guessed him directly. But why do you call him *our* friend? I am sure he is no friend of mine, nor ever was. I took an aversion to him, as you remember, the very first day I saw him. I am sure he is no friend of mine.

Mr. B. I am sorry for it, my dear, but I hope you will go and see Mrs. Granby.

Mrs. B. Not I, indeed, my dear. Who was she?

Mr. B. Miss Cooke.

Mrs. B. Cooke! But there are so many Cookes. Can't you distinguish her any way? Has she no Christian name?

Mr. B. Emma, I think. Yes, Emma.

Mrs. B. Emma Cooke! No, it cannot be my friend Emma Cooke, for I am sure she was cut out for an old maid.

Mr. B. This lady seems to me to be cut out for a good wife.

Mrs. B. Maybe so — I am sure I'll never go to see her. Pray, my dear, how came you to see so much of her?

Mr. B. I have seen very little of her, my dear. I only saw her two or three times before she was married.

Mrs. B. Then, my dear, how could you decide that she was cut out for a good wife? I am sure you could not judge her by seeing her only two or three times, and before she was married.

Mr. B. Indeed, my love, that is a very just observation.

Mrs. B. I understand that compliment perfectly and thank you for it, my dear. I must own I can bear anything better than irony.

Mr. B. Irony! my dear. I was perfectly in earnest.

Mrs. B. Yes, yes, in earnest — so I perceive. I may naturally be dull of apprehension, but my feelings are quick enough; I comprehend too well. Yes — it is impossible to judge of a woman before marriage or to guess what sort of a wife she will make. I presume you speak from experience; you have been disappointed yourself and repent your choice.

Mr. B. My dear, what did I say that was like this? Upon my word, I meant no such thing. I really was not thinking of you in the least.

Mrs. B. No, you never think of me now. I can easily believe that you were not thinking of me in the least.

Mr. B. But I said that only to prove to you that I could not be thinking ill of you, my dear.

Mrs. B. But I would rather that you thought ill of me than that you did not think of me at all.

Mr. B. Well, my dear, I will even think ill of you, if that will please you.

Mrs. B. Do you laugh at me? When it comes to this, I am wretched indeed. Never man laughed at the woman he loved. As long as you had the slightest remains of love for me, you could not make me an object of derision. Ridicule and love are incompatible — absolutely incompatible. Well, I have done my best, my very best, to make you happy, but in vain. I see I am not *cut out* to be a good wife. Happy, happy Mrs. Granby!

Mr. B. Happy, I hope sincerely, that she will be with my friend, but my happiness must depend on you, my love. So for my sake, if not for your own, be composed, and do not torment yourself with such fancies.

Mrs. B. I do wonder whether this Mrs. Granby is really that Miss Emma Cooke. I'll go and see her directly. See her I must.

Mr. B. I am heartily glad of it, my dear, for I am sure a visit to his wife will give my friend Granby real pleasure.

Mrs. B. I promise you, my dear, I do not go to give him pleasure or you either, but to satisfy my own *curiosity.*

QUESTIONS. 1. Does Mrs. B. evince much good sense?   2. May not people realize their own fear by giving expression to their suspicions? 3. Is it wise for a husband or a wife to speak unfriendly to each other?

SPELL AND DEFINE. 1. newspaper   2. finished   3. marriages 4. paragraph   5. provoking   6. remember   7. distinguish   8. compliment 9. irony   10. apprehension   11. experience   12. disappointed 13. incompatible   14. curiosity

LESSON LXIV

Political Corruption — McDuffie

RULE. When similar sounds come at the end of one word and the beginning of the next word, they must not be blended into one.

EXERCISES. Malice seeks to destroy. The breeze sighs softly. The ice slowly melts.

We are apt to treat the idea of our own corruptibility as utterly visionary and to ask, with a grave affectation of dignity: What! do you think a member of Congress can be corrupted? Sir, I speak what I have long and deliberately considered when I say that, since man was created, there never has been a political body on the face of the earth that would not be corrupted under the same circumstances. Corruption steals upon us in a thousand insidious forms when we are least aware of its approaches.

Of all the forms in which it can present itself, the bribery of office is the most dangerous because it assumes the guise of patriotism to accomplish its fatal sorcery. We are often asked, Where is the evidence of corruption? Have you seen it? Sir, do you expect to see it? You might as well expect to see the embodied forms of Pestilence and Famine stalking before you as to see the latent operations of this insidious power. We may walk amidst it and breathe its contagion without being conscious of its presence.

All experience teaches us the irresistible power of temptation when vice assumes the form of virtue. The great enemy of mankind could not have consummated his infernal scheme for the seduction of our first parents but for the disguise in which he presented himself. Had he appeared as the devil in his proper form, had the spear of Ithuriel disclosed the naked deformity of the fiend of hell, the inhabitants of paradise would have shrunk with horror from his presence. But he came as the insinuating serpent and presented a beautiful apple, the most delicious fruit in all the garden. He told his glowing story to the unsuspecting victim of his guile: "It can be no crime to taste of this delightful fruit. It will disclose to you the knowledge of good and evil. It will raise you to an equality with the angels."

Such, sir, was the process, and in this simple but impressive narrative we have the most beautiful and philosophical illustration of the frailty of man and the power of temptation that could possibly be exhibited. Mr. Chairman, I have been forcibly struck with the similarity between our present situation and that of Eve after it was announced that Satan was on the borders of paradise. We, too, have been warned that the enemy are on our borders.

God forbid that the similitude should be carried any farther. Eve, conscious of her innocence, sought temptation and defied it. The catastrophe is too fatally known to us all. She went "with the blessings of heaven on her head and its purity in her heart," guarded by the ministry of angels. She returned, covered with shame, under the heavy denunciation of heaven's everlasting curse.

Sir, it is innocence that temptation conquers. If our first parent, pure as she came from the hand of God, were overcome by the seductive power, let us not imitate her fatal rashness, seeking temptation when it is in our power to avoid it. Let us not vainly confide in our own infallibility. We are liable to be corrupted. To an ambitious man, an honorable office will appear as beautiful and fascinating as the apple of paradise.

I admit, sir, that ambition is a passion at once the most powerful and the most useful. Without it, human affairs would become a mere stagnant pool. By means of his patronage, the president addresses himself in the most irresistible manner to this, the noblest and strongest of our passions. All that the imagination can desire — honor, power, wealth, ease — are held out as the temptation. Man was not made to resist such temptation. It is impossible to conceive, Satan himself could not devise a system which would more infallibly introduce corruption and death into our political Eden. Sir, the angels fell from heaven with less temptation.

QUESTIONS. 1. What is meant by the corruption of a political body? 2. What is the most dangerous form in which this can approach? 3. What is said of the passion of ambition? 4. By what is the progress of temptation in overcoming innocence illustrated?

SPELL AND DEFINE. 1. corruptibility 2. visionary 3. affectation 4. deliberately 5. circumstances 6. insidious 7. patriotism 8. accomplish 9. contagion 10. irresistible 11. consummated 12. deformity 13. insinuating 14. knowledge 15. impressive 16. philosophical 17. similitude 18. catastrophe 19. denunciation 20. infallibility 21. ambitious 22. fascinating 23. imagination 24. introduce

LESSON LXV

The Blind Preacher — Wirt

RULE. Be careful to observe the commas and stop long enough to take breath.

As I traveled through the county of Orange, my eye was caught by a cluster of horses tied near a ruinous, old, wooden house in the forest, not far from the roadside. Having frequently seen such objects before in traveling through these states, I had no difficulty in understanding that this was a place of religious worship.

Devotion alone should have stopped me to join in the duties of the congregation, but I must confess that curiosity to hear the preacher of such a wilderness was not the least of my motives. On entering, I was struck with his preternatural appearance. He was a tall and very spare old man. His head, which was covered with a white linen cap, his shriveled hands, and his voice were all shaking under the influence of a palsy. A few moments ascertained to me that he was perfectly blind.

The first emotions that touched my breast were those of mingled pity and veneration. How soon were all my feelings changed. The lips of Plato were never more worthy of a prognostic swarm of bees than were the lips of this holy man! It was a day of the administration of the sacrament, and his subject was, of course, the passion of our Savior. I had heard the subject handled a thousand times; I had thought it exhausted long ago. Little did I suppose that in the wild woods of America I was to meet with a man whose eloquence would give to this topic a new and more sublime pathos than I had ever before witnessed.

As he descended from the pulpit to distribute the mystic symbols, there was a peculiar, a more than human solemnity in his air and manners, which made my blood run cold and my whole frame shiver. He then drew a picture of the sufferings of our Savior, His trial before Pilate, His ascent up Calvary, His crucifixion. I knew the whole history, but never until then had I ever heard the circumstances so selected, so arranged, so colored! It was all new, and I seemed to have heard it for the first time in my life. His enunciation was so deliberate that his voice trembled on every syllable, and every heart in the assembly trembled in unison.

His peculiar phrases had that force of description that the original scene appeared to be at that moment acting before our eyes. We saw the very faces of the Jews, the staring, frightful distortions of malice and rage. We saw the buffet; my soul kindled with a flame of indignation, and my hands were involuntarily and convulsively clenched.

But when he came to touch on the patience and the forgiving meekness of our Savior, when he drew, to the life, His voice breathing to God a soft and gentle prayer of pardon on His enemies, "Father, forgive them, for they know not what they do," the voice of the preacher, which had all along faltered, grew fainter and fainter until, his utterance being entirely obstructed by the force of his feelings, he raised his handkerchief to his eyes and burst into a loud and irrepressible flood of grief. The effect is inconceivable. The whole house resounded with the mingled groans, sobs, and shrieks of the congregation.

It was some time before the tumult had subsided so far as to permit him to proceed. Indeed, judging by the usual but fallacious standard of my own weakness, I began to be very uneasy for the situation of the preacher. I could not conceive how he would be able to let his audience down from the height to which he had wound them without impairing the solemnity and dignity of his subject or perhaps shocking them by the abruptness of his fall. But — no, the descent was as beautiful and sublime as the elevation had been rapid and enthusiastic.

The first sentence with which he broke the awful silence was a quotation from Rousseau: "Socrates died like a philosopher, but Jesus Christ, like a God!"

I despair of giving you any idea of the effect produced by this short sentence, unless you could perfectly conceive the whole manner of the man as well as the peculiar crisis in the discourse. Never before did I completely understand what Demosthenes meant by laying such stress on delivery.

You are to bring before you the venerable figure of the preacher, his blindness constantly recalling to your recollection old Homer, Ossian, and Milton and associating with his performance the melancholy grandeur of their geniuses. You are to imagine that you hear his slow, solemn, well-accented enunciation and his voice of affecting trembling melody. You are to remember the pitch of passion and enthusiasm to which the congregation was raised and then the few moments of portentous, death-like silence which reigned throughout the house. The preacher, removing his white handkerchief from his aged face (even yet wet from the recent torrent of his tears) and slowly stretching forth the palsied hand which held it, begins the sentence, "Socrates died like a philosopher" — then pausing, raising his other, pressing them both, clasped together with warmth and energy to his breast, lifting his "sightless balls" to heaven and pouring his whole soul into his tremulous voice — "but Jesus Christ, like a God!"

If he had been indeed and in truth an angel of light, the effect could scarcely have been more divine. Whatever I had been able to conceive of the sublimity of Massilon or the force of Bourdaloue, had fallen far short of the power which I felt from the delivery of this simple sentence.

If this description give you the impression that this incomparable minister had anything of shallow, theatrical trick in his manner, it does him great injustice. I have never seen in any other orator such a union of simplicity and majesty. He has not a gesture, an attitude, or an accent to which he does not seem forced by the sentiment he is expressing. His mind is too serious, too earnest, too solicitous, and, at the same time, too dignified to stoop to artifice.

Although as far removed from ostentation as a man can be, yet it is clear from the train, the style, and substance of his thoughts that he is not only a polite scholar but a man of extensive and profound erudition. I was forcibly struck with a short yet beautiful character which he drew of your learned and amiable countryman, Sir Robert Boyle. He spoke of him as if "his noble mind had, even before death, divested itself of all influence from his frail tabernacle of flesh," and called him, in his peculiarly emphatic and impressive manner, "a pure intelligence, the link between men and angels."

This man has been before my imagination almost ever since. A thousand times, as I rode along, I dropped the reins of my bridle, stretched forth my hand, and tried to imitate his quotation from Rousseau. A thousand times I abandoned the attempt in despair and felt persuaded that his peculiar manner and power arose from an energy of soul which nature could give but which no human being could justly copy. As I recall, at this moment, several of his awfully striking attitudes, the chilling tide with which my blood begins to pour along my arteries reminds me of the emotions produced by the first sight of Gray's introductory picture of his bard.

QUESTIONS. 1. Can you describe the personal appearance of the blind preacher? 2. What effect was produced by his manner? 3. What by his language? 4. When he described the character and conduct of Christ, what was the effect on the congregation? 5. What effect was produced by the circumstance of his blindness? 6. What was the secret of the preacher's great power?

SPELL AND DEFINE. 1. congregation 2. preternatural 3. shriveled 4. ascertained 5. veneration 6. administration 7. symbols 8. enunciation 9. distortions 10. indignation 11. involuntarily 12. convulsively 13. obstructed 14. handkerchief 15. inconceivable 16. fallacious 17. enthusiastic 18. melancholy 19. tremulous

LESSON LXVI

Paradise Lost (Book 3, Lines 1–55) — Milton

RULE. Where two or more consonants come together, let the pupil be careful to sound every one distinctly.

EXERCISES UNDER THE RULE. Thou *indulged'st* thy appetite. O wind! that *waft'st* us o'er the main. Thou *tempted'st* him. Thou *loved'st* him fondly. Thou *credited'st* his story. The *lists* are open.

> Hail holy Light, ofspring of Heav'n first-born,
> Or of th' Eternal Coeternal beam
> May I express thee unblam'd? since God is light,
> And never but in unapproached light
> Dwelt from Eternitie, dwelt then in thee,
> Bright effluence of bright essence increate.
> Or hear'st thou rather pure Ethereal stream,
> Whose Fountain who shall tell? before the Sun,
> Before the Heav'ns thou wert, and at the voice
> Of God, as with a Mantle didst invest

The rising world of waters dark and deep,
Won from the void and formless infinite.
Thee I revisit now with bolder wing,
Escap't the *Stygian* Pool, though long detain'd
In that obscure sojourn, while in my flight
Through utter and through middle darkness borne
With other notes than to th' *Orphean* Lyre
I sung of *Chaos* and *Eternal Night,*
Taught by the heav'nly Muse to venture down
The dark descent, and up to reascend,
Though hard and rare: thee I revisit safe,
And feel thy sovran vital Lamp; but thou
Revisit'st not these eyes, that rowl in vain
To find thy piercing ray, and find no dawn;
So thick a drop serene hath quencht thir Orbs,
Or dim suffusion veild. Yet not the more
Cease I to wander where the Muses haunt
Cleer Spring, or shadie Grove, or Sunnie Hill,
Smit with the love of sacred Song; but chief
Thee Sion and the flowrie Brooks beneath
That wash thy hallowd feet, and warbling flow,
Nightly I visit: nor somtimes forget
Those other two equal'd with me in Fate,
So were I equal'd with them in renown,
Blind *Thamyris* and blind *Maeonides,*
And *Tiresias* and *Phineus* Prophets old.
Then feed on thoughts, that voluntarie move
Harmonious numbers; as the wakeful Bird
Sings darkling, and in shadiest Covert hid
Tunes her nocturnal Note. Thus with the Year
Seasons return, but not to me returns
Day, or the sweet approach of Ev'n or Morn,
Or sight of vernal bloom, or Summers Rose,
Or flocks, or heards, or human face divine;
But cloud in stead, and ever-during dark
Surrounds me, from the chearful wayes of men
Cut off, and for the Book of knowledge fair

Presented with a Universal blanc
Of Natures works to mee expung'd and ras'd,
And wisdom at one entrance quite shut out.
So much the rather thou Celestial light
Shine inward, and the mind through all her powers
Irradiate, there plant eyes, all mist from thence
Purge and disperse, that I may see and tell
Of things invisible to mortal sight.

QUESTIONS. 1. Why does Milton mention light so reverently?
2. What was the Stygian pool? 3. Orphean lyre? 4. Was Milton blind?
5. What bird does he call the "wakeful bird"?

SPELL AND DEFINE. 1. coeternal 2. increate 3. ethereal 4. infinite
5. chaos 6. reascend 7. suffusion 8. darkling 9. nocturnal 10. expunged
11. irradiate

LESSON LXVII

Procrastination — Young

RULE. Remember that the chief beauty and excellence of reading
consists in a clear and smooth articulation of the words and letters.

Be wise today, 'tis madness to defer;
Next day the fatal precedent will plead,
Thus on, till wisdom is pushed out of life.
Procrastination is the thief of time;
Year after year it steals, till all are fled,
And to the mercies of a moment leaves
The vast concerns of an eternal scene.
If not so frequent, would not this be strange?
That 'tis so frequent, this is stranger still.
Of man's miraculous mistakes, this bears
The palm, that all men are about to live
Forever on the brink of being born.

All pay themselves the compliment to think
They one day shall not drivel, and their pride
On this reversion takes up ready praise,
At least their own: their future selves applaud,
How excellent that life they ne'er will lead!
Time lodged in their own hands is folly's vails;
That lodged in Fate's, to wisdom they consign.
The thing they can't but purpose, they postpone;
'Tis not in folly, not to scorn a fool,
And scarce in human wisdom, to do more.
All promise is poor dilatory man,
And that through every stage: when young, indeed,
In full content we sometimes nobly rest
Unanxious for ourselves, and only wish,
As duteous sons, our fathers were more wise.
At thirty man suspects himself a fool;
Knows it at forty, and reforms his plan;
At fifty chides his infamous delay,
Pushes his prudent purpose to resolve;
In all the magnanimity of thought
Resolves, and re-resolves; then dies the same.

QUESTIONS. 1. What is meant by procrastination? 2. Name some of the evils of procrastination? 3. What is the meaning of lines 11 and 12? 4. What, of all things, are men most disposed to defer? 5. What did the ancients regard as the best kind of knowledge?

SPELL AND DEFINE. 1. defer   2. precedent   3. eternal   4. scene
5. miraculous   6. compliment   7. drivel   8. reversion   9. applaud
10. consign   11. postpone   12. dilatory   13. unanxious   14. duteous
15. infamous 16. magnanimity

LESSON LXVIII

America — Phillips

RULE. Let the pupil stand at as great a distance from the teacher as

possible and then try to read so loudly and distinctly that the teacher may
hear each syllable.

I appeal to History! Tell me, thou reverend chronicler of
the grave, can all the illusions of ambition realized, can all
the wealth of a universal commerce, can all the achievements of successful heroism or all the establishments of this
world's wisdom secure to empire the permanency of its
possessions? Alas! Troy thought so once, yet the land of
Priam lives only in song.

Thebes thought so once, yet her hundred gates have
crumbled, and her very tombs are as the dust they were
vainly intended to commemorate. So thought Palmyra — yet
where is she? So thought the countries of Demosthenes and
the Spartan, yet Leonidas is trampled by the timid slave and
Athens insulted by the servile, mindless, and enervate Ot-
toman.

In his hurried march, Time has but looked at their
imagined immortality, and all its vanities, from the palace to
the tomb, have, with their ruins, erased the very impression
of his footsteps! The days of their glory are as if they had
never been, and the island, that was then a speck, rude and
neglected in the barren ocean, now rivals the ubiquity of
their commerce, the glory of their arms, the fame of their
philosophy, the eloquence of their senate, and the inspiration of their bards.

Who shall say then, contemplating the past, that England, proud and potent as she appears, may not, one day, be
what Athens is and the young America yet soar to be what
Athens was? Who shall say that, when the European column
shall have moldered and the night of barbarism have obscured its very ruins, our mighty continent may not emerge
from the horizon to rule, for its time, sovereign of the
ascendant?

. . . .

Sir, it matters very little what immediate spot may have been the birthplace of such a man as Washington. No people can claim, no country can appropriate him. The boon of Providence to the human race, his fame is eternity and his residence creation. Though it was the defeat of our arms and the disgrace of our policy, I almost bless the convulsion in which he had his origin.

If the heavens thundered and the earth rocked, yet, when the storm had passed, how pure was the climate that it cleared! How bright, in the brow of the firmament, was the planet which it revealed to us! In the production of Washington, it does really appear as if Nature were endeavoring to improve upon herself and that all the virtues of the ancient world were but so many studies preparatory to the patriot of the new.

No doubt, there were individual instances that splendidly exemplified some singular quality: Caesar was merciful, Scipio was continent, Hannibal was patient. But it was reserved for Washington to blend them all in one and, like the lovely masterpiece of the Grecian artist, to exhibit, in one glow of associated beauty, the pride of every model and the perfection of every master.

As a general, he marshaled the peasant into a veteran and supplied by discipline the absence of experience; as a statesman, he enlarged the policy of the cabinet into the most comprehensive system of general advantage. Such was the wisdom of his views and the philosophy of his counsels, that, to the soldier and the statesman, he almost added the character of the sage!

A conqueror, he was untainted with the crime of blood; a revolutionist, he was free from any stain of treason — for aggression commenced the contest, and his country called him to the command. Liberty unsheathed his sword, necessity stained it, victory returned it. If he had paused here, history might have doubted what station to assign him, whether at the head of her citizens or her soldiers, her heroes or her patriots. But the last glorious act crowns his career and banishes all hesitation.

Who, like Washington, after having emancipated a hemisphere, resigned its crown and preferred the retirement of domestic life to the adoration of a land he might be said almost to have created?

Happy, proud America! The lightnings of heaven yield to your philosophy; the temptations of earth could not seduce your patriotism.

QUESTIONS. 1. What is the testimony of history on the permanence of national greatness? 2. What is said of the character of Washington? 3. How does he compare with Caesar, Scipio, Hannibal, Bonaparte?

SPELL AND DEFINE. 1. chronicler   2. achievements 3. establishments   4. permanence   5. crumbled   6. commemorate 7. enervate 8. immortality 9. impression 10. contemplating 11. emerge 12. ascendant   13. appropriate   14. convulsion   15. firmament 16. endeavoring   17. preparatory   18. marshaled   19. discipline 20. comprehensive   21. revolutionist   22. aggression   23. hemisphere 24. patriotism

LESSON LXIX

Thirsting after Righteousness — Psalm 42

RULE. Avoid reading in a monotonous way, as if you were not interested and do not understand what you read.

As the hart panteth after the water brooks,
So panteth my soul after thee, O God.
My soul thirsteth for God, for the living God:
When shall I come and appear before God?
My tears have been my meat day and night,
While they continually say unto me, Where is thy God?

When I remember these things, I pour out my soul in
      me:
For I had gone with the multitude, I went with them
      to the house of God,
With the voice of joy and praise,
With a multitude that kept holyday.

    Why art thou cast down, O my soul?
And why are thou disquieted within me?
Hope thou in God: for I shall yet praise him
For the help of his countenance.

    O my God! my soul is cast down within me:
Therefore will I remember thee from the land of Jor-
      dan, and of the Hermonites,
From the hill Mizar.
Deep calleth unto deep at the noise of thy water-
      spouts:
All thy waves and thy billows are gone over me.
Yet the Lord will command his loving-kindness in
      the daytime,
And in the night his song shall be with me,
And my prayer unto the God of my life.

    I will say unto God my rock, Why hast thou for-
      gotten me?
Why go I mourning because of the oppression of the
      enemy?
As with a sword in my bones, mine enemies reproach
      me;
While they say daily unto me, Where is thy God?

    Why art thou cast down, O my soul?
And why art thou disquieted within me?
Hope thou in God: for I shall yet praise him,
Who is the health of my countenance, and my God.

QUESTIONS. 1. From the first to seventh line, what feeling is described? 2. To whom are the second and fourth verses addressed? 3. What reasons to hope does this psalm give a believer in times of distress?

LESSON LXX

View from Mount Etna — London Encyc.

RULE. Be careful not to read in a faint and low tone.

The man who treads Mount Etna seems like a man above the world. He generally is advised to ascend before daybreak; the stars now brighten, shining like so many gems of flames, while others appear which were invisible below. The Milky Way seems like a pure flake of light lying across the firmament, and it is the opinion of some that the satellites of Jupiter might be discovered by the naked eye.

But when the sun arises, the prospect from the summit of Etna is beyond comparison the finest in nature. The eye rolls over it with astonishment and is lost. The diversity of objects, the extent of the horizon, the immense height, the country like a map at the feet, the ocean around, the heavens above all conspire to overwhelm the mind and affect it.

We must be allowed to extract Mr. Brydone's description of this scene. "There is not," he says, "on the surface of the globe, any one point that unites so many awful and sublime objects. The immense elevation from the surface of the earth, drawn as it were to a single point, without any neighboring mountain for the senses and imagination to rest upon and recover from their astonishment, in their way down to the world.

"This point or pinnacle, raised on the brink of a bottomless gulf, as old as the world, often discharges rivers of fire, and throws out burning rocks, with a noise that shakes the whole island. Add to this the unbounded extent of the prospect, comprehending the greatest diversity, and the most beautiful scenery in nature, with the rising sun advancing in the east, to illuminate the wondrous scene.

"The whole atmosphere by degrees kindles up, and shows dimly and faintly the boundless prospect around. Both sea and land appear dark and confused, as if only emerging from their original chaos, and light and darkness seem still undivided; till the morning, by degrees advancing, completes the separation. The stars are extinguished, and the shades disappear.

"The forests, which but just now seemed black and bottomless gulfs, from whence no ray was reflected to show their form or colors, appear a new creation rising to sight, catching life and beauty from every increasing beam. The scene still enlarges, and the horizon seems to widen and expand itself on all sides; till the sun, like the great Creator, appears in the east, and with his plastic ray completes the mighty scene.

"All appears enchantment: and it is with difficulty we can believe we are still on earth. The senses, unaccustomed to the sublimity of such a scene, are bewildered and confounded; and it is not till after some time, that they are capable of separating and judging of the objects that compose it.

"The body of the sun is seen rising from the ocean, immense tracts both of sea and land intervening; the islands of Lipari, Panari, Alicudi, Strombolo, and Volcano, with their smoking summits, appear under your feet; and you look down on the whole of Sicily as on a map; and can trace every river through all its windings, from its source to its mouth.

"The view is absolutely boundless on every side; nor is there any one object within the circle of vision to interrupt it, so that the sight is every where lost in the immensity; and I am persuaded, it is only from the imperfection of our organs, that the coasts of Africa, and even of Greece, are not discovered, as they are certainly above the horizon. The circumference of the visible horizon on the top of Etna, cannot be less than two thousand miles.

"At Malta, which is nearly two hundred miles distant they perceive all the eruptions from the second region: and that island is often discovered from about one half the elevation of the mountain: so that, at the whole elevation the horizon must extend to nearly double that distance, or four hundred miles, which makes eight hundred miles for the diameter of the circle, and two thousand four hundred for the circumference! But this is by much too vast for our senses. They are not intended to grasp so boundless a scene.

"The most beautiful part of the scene is certainly the mountain itself, the island of Sicily, and the numerous islands lying round it. All these, by a kind of magic in vision, that I am at a loss to account for, seem as if they were brought close round the skirts of Etna; the distances appearing reduced to nothing.

"Perhaps this singular effect is produced by the rays of light passing from a rarer medium into a denser, which, (from a well-known law in optics,) to an observer in the rare medium, appears to lift up objects that are at the bottom of the dense one, as a piece of money placed in a basin appears lifted up as soon as the basin is filled with water.

"The Regione Deserta, of the frigid zone of Etna, is the first object that calls your attention. It is marked out by a circle of snow and ice, which extends on all sides to the distance of about eight miles. In the center of this circle, the great crater of the mountain rears its burning head, and the regions of intense cold, and of intense heat, seem forever to be united in the same point.

"The Regione Deserta is immediately succeeded by the Sylvosa, or the woody region, which forms a circle or girdle of the most beautiful green, which surrounds the mountain on all sides, and is certainly one of the most delightful spots on earth."

QUESTIONS. 1. Where is Mount Etna? 2. How would you get there? How would someone in 1830 get there? 3. What is Mount Etna? 4. What is a volcano? 5. Are there any volcanoes in the United States? 6. When are travelers advised to ascend Mount Etna? 7. Describe the appearance of things at that time and afterwards, until sunrise. 8. How far can you see from the summit of Mount Etna? 9. Why cannot the shores of Africa and of Greece be seen from the top of Etna? 10. What is meant by saying, "as they are certainly above the horizon"? 11. How many miles does the circumference of vision embrace from the top of Etna? 12. Suppose you were at the top of the mountain, what different regions or kinds of country would you pass through before you would reach the bottom? 13. What islands are near Etna? 14. What cities? 15. If the country about Etna be so very delightful, would you not like to live there? 16. Why? (This question is intended to elicit a comparison of our own with foreign countries, both in point of natural scenery and civil institutions.)

SPELL AND DEFINE. 1. ascend   2. satellites   3. firmament
4. invisible   5. diversity   6. horizon   7. grandeur   8. astonishment
9. pinnacle   10. comprehending   11. wondrous   12. atmosphere
13. emerging 14. chaos 15. extinguished 16. plastic 17. unaccustomed
18. sublimity   19. bewildered   20. intervening   21. circumference
22. diameter

LESSON LXXI

Sublime Virtues Inconsistent with Infidelity — Robert Hall

RULE. Be careful to speak little words such as *a, in, at, on, to, by* very distinctly and yet not to dwell on them so long as on the more important words.

Infidelity is a soil as barren of great and sublime virtues as it is prolific in crimes. By "great and sublime virtues" are meant those which are called into action on great and trying occasions, which demand the sacrifice of the dearest interests and prospects of human life and sometimes life itself — the virtues which, by their rarity and splendor, draw admiration and have rendered illustrious the characters of patriots, martyrs, and confessors. It requires but little reflection to perceive that whatever veils a future world and contracts the limits of existence within the present life, must tend, in a proportionable degree, to diminish the grandeur and narrow the sphere of human agency.

You might as well expect exalted sentiments of justice from a professed gamester as look for noble principles in the man whose hopes and fears are all suspended on the present moment and who stakes the whole happiness of his being on the events of this vain and fleeting life.

If he ever be impelled to the performance of great achievements in a good cause, it must be solely by the hope of fame — a motive which, besides that it makes virtue the servant of opinion, usually grows weaker at the approach of death and which, however it may surmount the love of existence in the heat of battle or in the moment of public observation, can seldom be expected to operate with much force on the retired duties of a private station.

In affirming that infidelity is unfavorable to the higher class of virtues, we are supported as much by facts as by reason. We should be sorry to load our adversaries with unmerited reproach, but to what history, to what record will they appeal for the traits of moral greatness exhibited by their disciples? Where shall we look for the trophies of infidel magnanimity or atheistical virtue? Not that we mean to accuse them of inactivity; they have recently filled the world with the fame of their exploits — exploits of a different kind, indeed, but of imperishable memory and disastrous luster.

Though great and splendid actions are not the ordinary employments of life, but must from their nature be reserved for high and eminent occasions, yet that system is essentially defective which leaves no room for their production. They are important both from their immediate advantage and their remoter influence. They often save and always illustrate the age and nation in which they appear. They raise the standard of morals; they arrest the progress of degeneracy; they diffuse a luster over the path of life. Monuments of the greatness of the human soul, they present to the world the august image of virtue in her sublimest form, from which streams of light and glory issue to remote times and ages, while their commemoration, by the pen of historians and poets, awakens in distant bosoms the sparks of kindred excellence.

QUESTIONS. 1. What is meant by infidelity?   2. Are all infidels profane or immoral men?   3. Do they possess great and sublime virtues? 4. What is meant by "great and sublime virtues"?   5. To what is the infidel compared in paragraph 2?   6. Is the comparison just?   7. Do infidels possess no good qualities?   8. Do they perform no good actions?   9. What motive impels them ever to do good?   10. What is said of this motive? 11. What is the testimony of history on this point?

SPELL AND DEFINE. 1. infidelity   2. prolific   3. illustrious 4. proportionable 5. grandeur 6. sentiments 7. gamester 8. suspended 9. achievements   10. approach   11. unfavorable   12. adversaries 13. exhibited   14. disciples   15. magnanimity   16. atheistical 17. imperishable   18. disastrous   19. employment   20. essentially 21. production   22. immediate   23. remoter   24. degeneracy 25. monuments 26. august 27. commemoration

LESSON LXXII

The Alps — W. Gaylord Clark

RULE. In reading poetry, be careful to avoid the singsong tone which is made by marking too strongly with the voice all the accented syllables. In the example, the fault will appear if the words italicized are strongly accented.

EXAMPLE. Sweet *is* the *work* my *God* and *King*
To *praise* thy *name*, give *thanks* and *sing*.

Proud monuments of God! sublime ye stand
Among the wonders of His mighty hand:
With summits soaring in the upper sky,

Where the broad day looks down with burning eye;
Where gorgeous clouds in solemn pomp repose,
Flinging rich shadows on eternal snows:
Piles of triumphant dust, ye stand alone,
And hold, in kingly state, a peerless throne!

Like olden conquerors, on high ye rear
The regal ensign and the glittering spear:
Round icy spires the mists, in wreaths unrolled,
Float ever near, in purple or in gold;
And voiceful torrents, sternly rolling there,
Fill with wild music the unpillared air:
What garden, or what hall on earth beneath,
Thrills to such tones, as o'er the mountains breathe?

There, though long ages past, those summits shone
When morning radiance on their state was thrown;
There, when the summer day's career was done,
Played the last glory of the sinking sun;
There, sprinkling luster o'er the cataract's shade,
The chastened moon her glittering rainbow made;
And blent with pictured stars, her luster lay,
Where to still vales the free streams leaped away.

Where are the thronging hosts of other days,
Whose banners floated o'er the Alpine ways;
Who, through their high defiles, to battle, wound,
While deadly ordnance stirred the heights around?
Gone, like the dream that melts at early morn,
When the lark's anthem through the sky is borne.
Gone, like the wrecks that sink in ocean's spray,
And chill Oblivion murmurs, Where are they?

Yet "Alps on Alps" still rise, the lofty home
Of storms and eagles, where their pinions roam;
Still roam their peaks and magic colors lie,
Of morn and eve, imprinted on the sky.

And still, while kings and thrones shall fade and fall,
And empty crowns lie dim upon the pall;
Still shall their glaciers flash, their torrents roar,
Till kingdoms fail, and nations rise no more.

QUESTIONS. 1. In verse 1, what is the meaning of "piles of triumphant dust"? 2. What is an "anthem" (verse 4)? 3. And especially, what is a "lark's anthem"? 4. What hosts are referred to in verse 4, as crossing the Alps?

SPELL AND DEFINE. 1. monuments 2. gorgeous 3. flinging 4. triumphant 5. peerless 6. olden 7. ensign 8. voiceful 9. sprinkling 10. cataracts 11. ordnance 12. oblivion 13. murmurs 14. glaciers

LESSON LXXIII

Parallel between Pope and Dryden — Johnson

RULE. When two or more consonants come together, let the pupil be careful to sound every one distinctly.

EXERCISES UNDER THE RULE. He clenched his *fists*. He *lifts* his awful form. He makes his *payments*. Thou *smoothed'st* his rugged path. The *president's speech*.

Pope professed to have learned his poetry from Dryden, whom, whenever an opportunity was presented, he praised through his whole life with unvaried liberality. Perhaps, then, his character may receive some illustration, if he be compared with his master.

Integrity of understanding and the nicety of discernment were not allotted in less measure to Dryden than to Pope. The rectitude of Dryden's mind was sufficiently shown by the dismission of his poetic prejudices and the rejection of unnatural thoughts and rugged numbers. But Dryden never desired to apply all the judgment that he had. He wrote and professed to write merely for the people, and when he pleased others, he contented himself. He spent no time in struggles to rouse latent powers; he never attempted to make that better which was already good nor often to mend what he must have known to be faulty. He wrote, as he tells us, with very little consideration. When occasion or necessity called upon him, he poured out what the present moment happened to supply and, when once it had passed the press, ejected it from his mind, for, when he had no pecuniary interest, he had no further solicitude.

Pope was not content to satisfy; he desired to excel and, therefore, always endeavored to do his best. He did not court the candor but dared the judgment of his reader and, expecting no indulgence from others, showed none to himself. He examined lines and words with minute and punctilious observation and retouched every part with indefatigable diligence, till he had left nothing to be forgiven.

For this reason, he kept his pieces very long in his hands while he considered and reconsidered them. The only poems which can be supposed to have been written with such regard to the times as might hasten their publication were the two satires of *Thirty-eight,* of which Dodsley told me that they were brought to him by the author, that they might be fairly copied. "Every line," said he, "was then written twice over. I gave him a clean transcript which he sent sometime afterwards to me for the press, with every line written twice over a second time."

His declaration, that his care for his works ceased at their publication, was not strictly true. His parental attention never abandoned them. What he found amiss in the first edition, he silently corrected in those that followed. He appears to have revised the *Iliad* and freed it from some of its imperfections, and the *Essay on Criticism* received many improvements after its first appearance. It will seldom be found that he altered without adding clearness, elegance, or vigor. Pope had perhaps the judgment of Dryden, but Dryden certainly wanted the diligence of Pope.

In acquired knowledge, the superiority must be allowed to Dryden, whose education was more scholastic and who, before he became an author, had been given more time for study, with better means of information. His mind has a larger range, and he collects his images and illustrations from a more extensive circumference of science. Dryden knew more of man in his general nature and Pope, in his local manners. The notions of Dryden were formed by comprehensive speculation and those of Pope by minute attention. There is more dignity in the knowledge of Dryden and more certainty in that of Pope.

Poetry was not the sole praise of either, for both excelled likewise in prose. But Pope did not borrow his prose from his predecessor. The style of Dryden is capricious and varied, that of Pope cautious and uniform. Dryden obeys the motions of his own mind; Pope constrains his mind to his own rules of composition. Dryden is sometimes vehement and rapid; Pope is always smooth, uniform, and gentle. Dryden's page is a natural field, rising into inequalities and diversified by the varied exuberance of abundant vegetation; Pope's is a velvet lawn, shaven by the scythe and leveled by the roller.

Of genius — that power which constitutes a poet, that quality without which judgment is cold and knowledge inert, that energy which collects, combines, amplifies, and animates — the superiority must, with some hesitation, be allowed to Dryden. It must not be inferred that of this poetic vigor Pope had only a little because Dryden had more. Every other writer since Milton must give place to Pope, and even of Dryden it must be said that if he has brighter paragraphs, he has not better poems.

Dryden's performances were always hasty, either excited by some external occasion or extorted by domestic necessity. He composed without consideration and published without correction. What his mind could supply at call or gather in one excursion was all that he sought and all that he gave.

The dilatory caution of Pope enabled him to condense his sentiments, to multiply his images, and to accumulate all that study might produce or chance might supply. If the flights of Dryden, therefore, are higher, Pope continues longer on the wing. If the blaze of Dryden's fire is brighter, the heat of Pope's is more regular and constant. Dryden often surpasses expectation, and Pope never falls below it. Dryden is read with frequent astonishment and Pope with perpetual delight.

This parallel will, I hope, when it is well considered, be found just. If the reader should suspect me, as I suspect myself, of some partial fondness for the memory of Dryden, let him not too hastily condemn me, for meditation and inquiry may, perhaps, show him the reasonableness of my determination.

QUESTIONS. 1. During whose reigns did Pope and Dryden live? 2. Did Dryden labor his poems, as did Pope? 3. Which excelled in native genius? 4. Which in education? 5. Can you mention any of the poems of either author?

SPELL AND DEFINE. 1. illustration 2. punctilious 3. indefatigable 4. transcript 5. exuberance 6. amplifies 7. dilatory

LESSON LXXIV

Happy Consequences of American Independence — Maxcy

RULE. When similar sounds come at the end of one word and at the beginning of the next word, they must not be blended into one.

EXERCISES. He sinks sorrowing to the tomb. Man loves society. Time flies swiftly. The birds sing.

In a full persuasion of the excellency of our government, let us shun those vices which tend to its subversion and cultivate those virtues which will render it permanent and transmit it in full vigor to all succeeding ages. Let not the haggard forms of intemperance and luxury ever lift up their destroying visages in this happy country. Let economy, frugality, moderation, and justice at home and abroad mark the conduct of all our citizens. Let it be our constant care to diffuse knowledge and goodness through all ranks of society.

The people of this country will never be uneasy under its present form of government, provided they have sufficient information to judge of its excellency. No nation under heaven enjoys so much happiness as the Americans.

Convince them of this, and will they not shudder at the thought of subverting their political constitution, of suffering it to degenerate into aristocracy or monarchy? Let a sense of our happy situation awaken in us the warmest sensations of gratitude to the Supreme Being. Let us consider Him as the author of all our blessings, acknowledging Him as our beneficent parent, protector, and friend. The predominant tendency of His providences towards us as a nation evinces His benevolent designs. Every part of His conduct speaks in a language plain and intelligible. Let us open our ears, let us attend, let us be wise.

While we celebrate the anniversary of our independence, let us not pass over in silence the defenders of our country. Where are those brave Americans whose lives were torn down in the tempest of battle? Are they not bending from the bright abodes? A voice from the altar cries, "These are they who loved their country, these are they who died for liberty." We now reap the fruit of their agony and toil. Let their memories be eternally embalmed in our bosoms. Let the infants of all posterity prattle their fame and drop tears of courage for their fate.

The consequences of American independence will soon reach to the extremities of the world. The shining car of freedom will soon roll over the necks of kings and bear off the oppressed to scenes of liberty and peace. The clamors of war will cease under the whole heaven. The tree of liberty will shoot its top up to the sun. Its boughs will hang over the ends of the whole world, and wearied nations will lie down and rest under its shade.

Here in America stands the asylum for the distressed and persecuted of all nations. The vast temple of freedom rises majestically fair. Founded on a rock, it will remain unshaken by the force of tyrants, undiminished by the flight of time. Long streams of light emanate through its portals and chase the darkness from distant nations. Its turrets will swell into the heavens, rising above every tempest, and the pillar of divine glory, descending from God, will rest forever on its summit.

QUESTIONS. 1. How does the form of government of the United States compare with those of all other nations? 2. What is our happiness compared with that of other nations? 3. What should we do to perpetuate our political institutions? 4. Is the last sentence true?

SPELL AND DEFINE. 1. persuasion   2. excellency   3. government 4. subversion   5. permanent   6. succeeding   7. intemperance   8. economy 9. information   10. political   11. constitution   12. degenerate 13. aristocracy   14. monarchy   15. acknowledging   16. beneficent 17. predominant   18. providences   19. intelligible   20. independence 21. consequences   22. extremities   23. asylum   24. majestically 25. undiminished   26. summit

LESSON LXXV

Paradise Lost (Book 2, Lines 629–726) — Milton

RULE. Let each pupil in the class observe and mention every syllable that is not correctly sounded as each one reads.

Mean while the Adversary of God and Man,
Satan with thoughts inflam'd of highest design,
Puts on swift wings, and towards the Gates of Hell
Explores his solitary flight; som times

He scours the right hand coast, som times the left,
Now shaves with level wing the Deep, then soars
Up to the fiery Concave towering high.
As when farr off at Sea a Fleet descri'd
Hangs in the Clouds, by *AEquinoctial* Winds
Close sailing from *Bengala,* or the Iles
Of *Ternate* and *Tidore,* whence Merchants bring
Thir spicie Drugs: they on the Trading Flood
Through the wide *Ethiopian* to the Cape
Ply stemming nightly toward the Pole. So seem'd
Farr off the flying Fiend: at last appeer
Hells bounds high reaching to the horrid Roof,
And thrice threefold the Gates; three folds were
    Brass,
Three Iron, three of Adamantine Rock,
Impenetrable, impal'd with circling fire,
Yet unconsum'd. Before the Gates there sat
On either side a formidable shape;
The one seem'd Woman to the waste, and fair,
But ended foul in many a scaly fould
Voluminous and vast, a Serpent arm'd
With mortal sting: about her middle round
A cry of Hell Hounds never ceasing bark'd
With wide *Cerberean* mouths full loud, and rung
A hideous Peal: yet, when they list, would creep,
If aught disturb'd thir noyse, into her woomb,
And kennel there, yet there still bark'd and howl'd,
Within unseen. Farr less abhorr'd than these
Vex'd *Scylla* bathing in the Sea that parts
Calabria from the hoarce *Trinacrian* shore:
Nor uglier follow the Night-Hag, when call'd
In secret, riding through the Air she comes
Lur'd with the smell of infant blood, to dance
With *Lapland* Witches, while the labouring Moon
Eclipses at thir charms. The other shape,
If shape it might be call'd that shape had none
Distinguishable in member, joynt, or limb,

Or substance might be call'd that shadow seem'd,
For each seem'd either; black it stood as Night,
Fierce as ten Furies, terrible as Hell,
And shook a dreadful Dart; what seem'd his head
The likeness of a Kingly Crown had on.
Satan was now at hand, and from his seat
The Monster moving onward came as fast
With horrid strides, Hell trembled as he strode.
Th'undaunted Fiend what this might be admir'd,
Admir'd, not fear'd; God and his Son except,
Created thing naught valu'd he nor shun'd;
And with disdainful look thus first began.

Whence and what art thou, execrable shape,
That dar'st, though grim and terrible, advance
Thy miscreated Front athwart my way
To yonder Gates? through them I mean to pass,
That be assur'd, without leave askt of thee:
Retire, or taste thy folly, and learn by proof,
Hell-born, not to contend with Spirits of Heav'n.

To whom the Goblin full of wrauth, reply'd,
Art thou that Traitor Angel, art thou hee,
Who first broke peace in Heav'n and Faith, till then
Unbrok'n, and in proud rebellious Arms
Drew after him the third part of Heav'ns Sons
Conjur'd against the highest, for which both Thou
And they outcast from God, are here condemn'd
To waste Eternal dayes in woe and pain?
And reck'n'st thou thy self with Spirits of Heav'n,
Hell-doom'd, and breath'st defiance here and scorn,
Where I reign King, and to enrage thee more,
Thy King and Lord? Back to thy punishment,
False fugitive, and to thy speed add wings,
Least with a whip of Scorpions I pursue
Thy lingring, or with one stroke of this Dart
Strange horror seise thee, and pangs unfelt before.

So spake the grieslie terrour, and in shape,
So speaking and so threatning, grew tenfold

More dreadful and deform: on th' other side
Incenst with indignation *Satan* stood
Unterrifi'd, and like a Comet burn'd,
That fires the length of *Ophiucus* huge
In th' Artick Sky, and from his horrid hair
Shakes Pestilence and Warr. Each at the Head
Level'd his deadly aim; thir fatall hands
No second stroke intend, and such a frown
Each cast at th' other, as when two black Clouds
With Heav'ns Artillery fraught, come rattling on
Over the *Caspian,* then stand front to front
Hov'ring a space, till Winds the signal blow
To joyn their dark Encounter in mid air:
So frownd the mighty Combatants, that Hell
Grew darker at their frown, so matcht they stood;
For never but once more was either like
To meet so great a foe: and now great deeds
Had been achiev'd, whereof all Hell had rung,
Had not the Snakie Sorceress that sat
Fast by Hell Gate, and kept the fatal Key,
Ris'n, and with hideous outcry rush'd between.

QUESTIONS. 1. What beautiful comparison is there in the first fifteen lines? 2. Where are Bengala, Ternate, and Tidore? 3. What is meant by "Cerberean mouths"? 4. What is the fable to which allusion is made in lines 35–39 and so on. 5. Who was the "Snakie Sorceress"? 6. Why is Death represented as the son of Satan and Sin?

SPELL AND DEFINE. 1. solitary   2. concave   3. stemming
4. adamantine 5. impenetrable 6. miscreated 7. fraught 8. sorceress

LESSON LXXVI

Evils of Dismemberment — Webster

RULE. While each pupil reads, let the rest observe and then mention which syllables were pronounced wrong and which were omitted or indistinctly sounded.

Gentlemen, the political prosperity which this country has attained and which it now enjoys, it has acquired mainly through the instrumentality of the present government. While this agent continues, the capacity of attaining to still higher degrees of prosperity exists also.

We have, while this lasts, a political life capable of beneficial exertion, with power to resist or overcome misfortunes, to sustain us against the ordinary accidents of human affairs, and to promote, by active efforts, every public interest.

But dismemberment strikes at the very being which preserves these faculties. It would lay its rude and ruthless hand on this great agent itself. It would sweep away not only what we possess but also all power of regaining lost, or acquiring new, possessions. It would leave the country not only bereft of its prosperity and happiness but also without limbs and organs or faculties by which to exert itself, hereafter, in the pursuit of that prosperity and happiness.

Other misfortunes may be borne or their effects overcome. If disastrous war should sweep our commerce from the ocean, another generation may renew it; if it exhaust our treasury, future industry may replenish it; if it desolate and lay waste our fields, still, under a new cultivation, they will grow green again and ripen to future harvests.

It were but a trifle, even if the walls of yonder capitol were to crumble, if its lofty pillars should fall and its gorgeous decorations be all covered by the dust of the valley. All these might be rebuilt. But who shall reconstruct the fabric of demolished government? Who shall rear again the well-proportioned columns of constitutional liberty? Who shall frame together the skillful architecture which unites national sovereignty with states' rights, individual security, and public prosperity?

No, gentlemen, if these columns fall, they will be raised not again. Like the Coliseum and the Parthenon, they will be destined to a mournful, a melancholy immortality. Bitterer tears, however, will flow over them than were ever shed over the monuments of Roman or Grecian art, for they will be the remnants of a more glorious edifice than Greece or Rome ever saw — the edifice of constitutional American liberty.

But, gentlemen, let us hope for better things. Let us trust in that gracious Being who has hitherto held our country as in the hollow of His hand. Let us trust to the virtue and the intelligence of the people and to the efficacy of religious obligation. Let us trust to the influence of Washington's example. Let us hope that that fear of heaven, which expels all other fear, and that regard to duty, which transcends all other regard, may influence public men and private citizens and lead our country still onward in her happy career. Full of these gratifying anticipations and hopes, let us look forward to the end of that century which is now commenced.

May the disciples of Washington then see, as we now see, the flag of the Union floating on the top of the capitol. Then, as now, may the sun in his course visit no land more free, more happy, more lovely than this our own country!

QUESTIONS. 1. How was the political prosperity of our country obtained? 2. So long as this government lasts, what will be our situation? 3. What will be the effect of dismemberment? 4. Why would the destruction of our present form of government be an irretrievable loss of liberty? 5. In what is our chief hope for the permanency of our government to be placed?

SPELL   AND   DEFINE.   1. instrumentality   2. government 3. beneficial 4. misfortunes 5. dismemberment 6. ruthless 7. disastrous 8. replenish   9. gorgeous   10. decorations   11. demolished   12. well-proportioned   13. constitutional   14. architecture   15. sovereignty 16. Coliseum   17. Parthenon   18. melancholy   19. immortality 20. constitutional 21. transcends 22. anticipations

LESSON LXXVII

No Excellence without Labor — Wirt

RULE. Be careful to pronounce the little words like a, the, and, in distinctly and not to join them to the next word.

The education, moral and intellectual, of every individual must be, chiefly, his own work. Rely upon it that the ancients were right — both in morals and intellect — we give their final shape to our characters and thus become, emphatically, the architects of our own fortune. How else could it happen that young men who have had precisely the same opportunities should be continually presenting us with such different results and rushing to such opposite destinies?

Difference of talent will not solve it, because that difference is very often in favor of the disappointed candidate. You shall see issuing from the walls of the same college — nay, sometimes from the bosom of the same family — two young men, of whom the one shall be admitted to be a genius of high order, the other, scarcely above the point of mediocrity. Yet you shall see the genius sinking and perishing in poverty, obscurity, and wretchedness, while on the other hand, you shall observe the mediocre plodding his slow but sure way up the hill of life, gaining steadfast footing at every step and mounting, at length, to eminence and distinction, an ornament to his family, a blessing to his country.

Now, whose work is this? Manifestly their own. They are the architects of their respective fortunes. The best seminary of learning that can open its portals to you can do no more than to afford you the opportunity of instruction. It must depend, at last, on yourselves whether you will be instructed or not, or to what point you will push your instruction.

Of this be assured — I speak, from observation, a certain truth: There is no excellence without great labor. It is the fiat of fate from which no power of genius can absolve you.

Genius, unexerted, is like the poor moth that flutters around a candle until it scorches itself to death. If genius be desirable at all, it is only of that great and magnanimous kind which, like the condor of South America, pitches from the summit of Chimborazo, above the clouds, and sustains itself, at pleasure, in that empyreal region, with an energy rather invigorated than weakened by the effort.

It is this capacity for high and long-continued exertion, this vigorous power of profound and searching investigation, this careering and wide-spreading comprehension of mind, and those long reaches of thought that

> Pluck bright honor from the pale-faced moon,
> Or dive into the bottom of the deep,
> Where fathom line could never touch the ground,
> And drag up drowned honor by the locks.

This is the prowess, and these the hardy achievements which are to enroll your names among the great men of the earth.

QUESTIONS. 1. What did the ancients say in respect to education? 2. How does it appear from facts that it is labor rather than genius which gives eminence?

SPELL AND DEFINE. 1. intellectual   2. individual   3. ancients 4. emphatically 5. architects 6. continually 7. disappointed 8. obscurity 9. wretchedness   10. mediocre   11. manifestly   12. respective 13. opportunity   14. instruction   15. excellence   16. magnanimous 17. empyreal   18. invigorated   19. investigation   20. comprehension 21. profound 22. achievements

LESSON LXXVIII

Thoughts in a Place of Public Worship — Hannah More

RULE. In reading poetry that does not rhyme, there should be no pause at the end of a line, except when it terminates with an important word or the sense requires it.

And here we come and sit, time after time,
And call it social worship; Is it thus?
Oh Thou! whose searching all-pervading eye
Scans every secret movement of the heart,
And sees us as we are, Why mourns my soul
On these occasions? Why so dead and cold
My best affections? I have found Thee, oft
In my more secret seasons, in the field,
And in my chamber — even in the stir
Of outward occupations has my mind
Been drawn to Thee, and found Thy presence life.
But here I seek in vain, and rarely find
Thy ancient promise to the few that wait
In singleness upon Thee, reach to us.
Most sweet it is to feel the unity
Of soul-cementing love, gathering in one,
Flowing from heart to heart, and like a cloud
Of mingled incense rising to the throne
Of love itself! Then much of heaven is felt
By minds drawn thitherward and closely linked
In the celestial union; 'tis in this
Sweet element alone that we can live
To any purpose, or expect our minds
Clothed with that covering which alone prepares
For social worship. Therefore mourns my soul
In secret, and like one amidst the vast
And widely peopled earth, would seek to hide
Myself and sorrows from the motley crowd

Of human observation. But oh, Thou
Whose bowels of compassion never fail
Towards the creatures fashioned by Thy hand,
Reanimate the dead! and give to those
Who never felt Thy presence in their souls
Nor saw Thy beauty, both to see and feel
That Thou art lovely, and Thy presence life:
Restore the wanderer and support the weak
With Thy sustaining arm, for strength is Thine.
And oh! preserve this tempest-beaten bark
From sinking in the wave, whose swelling surge
Threatens to overwhelm; forsake her not,
But be her Pilot, though no sun nor star
Appear amid the gloom; for if a ray
From Thy all-cheering presence light her course,
She rides the storm secure, and in due time
Will reach her destined port, and be at peace.

QUESTIONS. 1. What is blank verse? 2. How many feet are there to
a line in blank verse? 3. What is a foot? 4. What feeling is most necessary
to social worship? 5. What is the petition offered in the last ten lines?
6. What is a figure of speech? 7. Is there one in this lesson? 8. Where?

SPELL AND DEFINE. 1. singleness   2. cementing   3. celestial
4. element   5. prepares   6. peopled   7. observation   8. compassion
9. bowels   10. wanderer   11. restore   12. sustaining   13. surge   14. pilot
15. destined

LESSON LXXIX

A Plea for Common Schools — Samuel Lewis

RULE. Give a full and distinct sound to all the consonant sounds.

In rising to address an assembly at the seat of government of the state of Ohio on the subject of education, I
cannot but recur to the times when I first heard of the

beautiful rivers and plains of the West. My earliest recollections are associated with the glowing pictures that were drawn of the immense advantages that must result to all that would help to people this new state. When not more than eight years of age and in the neighborhood of that spot rendered almost sacred by the landing of the pilgrims nearly two hundred years before, I stood and listened, with all the curiosity of a child, to the questions of parents, grandparents, and neighbors put to those who pretended to know anything relating to this then almost heathen land.

You all recollect how highly this country was spoken of, and the most glowing panegyric was always finished by giving positive assurance that provision, the most ample, was made to educate the children of the rising state. I well recollect that this was considered one of its greatest advantages, and parents who proposed to emigrate were more particular in their inquiries on this than on any other subject.

I will add that nothing did more to secure an early sale and settlement of the lands of government than the appropriations for schools. I more than once heard the resolute but affectionate mother, when surrounded by friends dissuading her from emigration, assign it as a sufficient inducement to go to the far west: "*My* children will there be entitled to education as well as the children of the *rich*." With that ambition to see their children elevated, which only such mothers feel, did many a young mother tear herself from parents, brothers, sisters, and the home of her youth and, with only her husband and weeping children, throw herself into this valley to realize those hopes that had been inspired by government and the agents of different land companies.

To what extent these hopes, so far as education is concerned, have been realized, you all know. Here let me contradict, in the most positive manner, the assertion so often made by the older states, that the general government has been liberal to this and the other western states in educational endowments. Ohio has never received the first farthing in money nor the first acre of land from this source as a donation for educational purposes. True, there was a vast tract of uncultivated land owned by government, which she desired to sell, and to do this she had to devise some plan that would allure men to the purchase. She accordingly assigned a certain portion for education. But she did not give it — it was *a part of the consideration paid* — the very same plan adopted by men who laid out new towns. They gave away a part to secure a sale of the residue, and no part of the immense public domain has ever brought into the treasury so great a return as that devoted to schools.

The impression that ample provision was made became so general and remained so long that for years our legislature omitted all action on the subject, and to this cause alone do I attribute what would, otherwise, seem to be an unpardonable neglect. Many subjects, important in themselves, have claimed the attention of those who have from time to time been called to legislate for us. Where so much was to be done and in so short a time, it is not strange that some things have been overlooked; it is indeed wonderful that so much has been accomplished.

Our state, instead of requiring centuries to gain a standing among her elder sisters, has passed, almost by magic, from infancy to maturity. To maturity, did I say! Look at the gigantic plans of improvement just begun and those in contemplation. Look at your immense facilities for agriculture, manufactures, and commerce. Above all, look at the enterprise and public spirit manifested throughout your state. With all these in view, instead of saying that Ohio is at her maturity, must we not exclaim that she has just entered upon youth with all her energies — but that in her very youth she is greater than states and nations were wont to be in maturity?

We have not attained this exalted place without incurring corresponding responsibilities to the world and to posterity. Among these responsibilities, none rests with greater weight than our obligation to educate the rising generation.

In this sentiment all will doubtless agree, and leaving to others to excuse themselves and hold back the general cause on the plea of hostility in the people, I venture to affirm that there is no subject which, if properly presented, would find greater favor with our citizens than the subject of general education.

After a residence of more than twenty years in this state and observing public sentiment with some care, I affirm that I have never seen twenty men who would for themselves oppose a system of general instruction adapted to the wants of the community. I have heard some professed friends of common schools express fears that others would not sustain an improvement of the system, and I have heard those to whose care the schools were entrusted excuse themselves from taking measures to meet the demands of the community by casting on that community the reproach of hostility. But I am much mistaken if, on a direct appeal to the people by cities and townships, there would be found one town in ten that would not sustain the most efficient measures.

Patronize education, establish common schools, and sustain them well and you will, most assuredly, provide a place where all classes will, in childhood, become familiar before the influence of pride, wealth, and family can bias the mind. An acquaintance thus formed will last as long as life itself. Take fifty lads in a neighborhood, including rich and poor — send them in childhood to the same school, let them join in the same sports, read and spell in the same classes until their different circumstances fix their business for life: some go to the field, some to the mechanic's shop, some to their merchandise; one becomes eminent at the bar, another in the pulpit; some become wealthy; the majority live on with a mere competency — a few are reduced to beggary!

But let the most eloquent orator that ever harangued a popular assembly attempt to prejudice the minds of one part against the other, and so far from succeeding, the poorest of the whole would consider himself insulted and from his own knowledge stand up in defense of his more fortunate schoolmate. I appeal to all who hear me, Have the ties of friendship formed at school not outlived every other? Can the oldest man in this assembly meet the schoolmate of bygone days without feelings that almost hallow the greeting? These are the feelings that I would, by common schools, establish in the bosoms of every son and daughter of Ohio. Distinction will soon enough find its way into society from considerations of wealth and influence. It should be the duty of our legislature to provide an antidote against all its evil consequences. Now you have the power. Now your state is American in all its feelings. Wait not until those who are hostile to such a measure are able to make head against you. We ought to remember that occupy new ground in the world. We look to the past, but rather as a beacon than a guide.

No state before us has ever presented a spectacle so magnificent. Less than forty years ago the state of Ohio was only in prospect; since that time she has come into being. Behold her now, the fourth state in the bright catalog of all the states, with more than a million people, intelligent and enterprising, with her four hundred miles of canals, her turnpikes, railroads constructing and projected. See her steamboats, her mills, her factories, her fields, and her flocks! She sustains, at the same time, the highest credit both at home and abroad. Does even ancient fable tell of anything like this?

Add to all this that our government is of the most popular kind. Public will gives law and enforces obedience. Public sentiment, then, is the unlimited sovereign of this state. Other nations have hereditary sovereigns, and one of the most important duties of their governments is to take care of the education of the heir to the throne. *These children about your streets, some of whom cannot even speak your language, are to be your future sovereigns.* Is it not important, then, that they should be well educated? Is it not important that they should understand the genius of your constitution and your laws? Should they not be able to read the daily issues from your different presses, civil and religious? Can you calculate highly on their judgment, either in governing themselves or selecting others for posts of honor, if they themselves are not intelligent?

All nations are looking on our experiment. Individuals bid us Godspeed. But every court in Europe would rejoice to see us do as they have long prophesied we must do, dissolve in anarchy — after having been, for a brief space, made the sport of contending factions, and when our houses had been burned, our fields made desolate, and our families destroyed, hail as our deliverer the fortunate tyrant who had the address to seize the reins of government, hold them steadily enough to secure our lives and property, and trample upon our liberties.

From such a state all are ready to say, good Lord deliver us! And many, perhaps, are disposed to say, the speaker dreams. But let me refer you to the history of other nations and other times. Did not France desire to be free? Did not she *deserve* to be free — if a sacrifice of blood and treasure could merit freedom? Nor was she without learning among the privileged orders. No court was ever so crowded with men of learning as that of the unfortunate Louis. But the great mass of the community were uneducated. Hence, they were imposed upon by the few, and the people, after achieving all that patriotism, bravery, wealth, and numbers could do — and breasting the opposition of combined Europe with success — ultimately threw themselves into the arms of a Corsican soldier. Yes, they passed under the yoke of the most galling tyranny, to save themselves from the ravages of an outraged and ignorant mob!

QUESTIONS. 1. What high panegyric has been pronounced upon the state of Ohio? 2. What was one great cause of the early and rapid settlement of this state? 3. Is it true that the general government has made donations to the western states for educational purposes? 4. What did it do? 5. What has been the progress of this state in respect to education? 6. What obligations rest upon her in consequence of this?

SPELL AND DEFINE. 1. government 2. neighborhood 3. panegyric
4. appropriations 5. dissuading 6. ambition 7. realized 8. endowments
9. educational   10. uncultivated   11. consideration   12. legislature
13. unpardonable   14. overlooked   15. agriculture   16. manufactures
17. enterprise 18. responsibilities

LESSON LXXX

Midnight Musings — Young

RULE. Avoid reading in a monotonous way, as if you were not
interested and do not understand what you read.

The bell strikes One. We take no note of time
But from its loss; to give it then a tongue
Is wise in man. As if an angel spoke
I feel the solemn sound. If heard aright,
It is the knell of my departed hours.
Where are they? With the years beyond the flood.
It is the signal that demands dispatch:
How much is to be done! My hopes and fears
Start up alarm'd, and o'er life's narrow verge
Look down — on what? A fathomless abyss.
A dread eternity! how surely mine!
And can eternity belong to me,
Poor pensioner on the bounties of an hour?

How poor, how rich, how abject, how august,
How complicate, how wonderful is man!
How passing wonder He who made him such!
Who center'd in our make such strange extremes,
From different natures marvelously mix'd,
Connection exquisite of distant worlds!
Distinguish'd link in being's endless chain!
Midway from nothing to the Deity!
A beam ethereal, sullied, and absorbed!
Though sullied and dishonor'd, still divine!

Dim miniature of greatness absolute!
An heir of glory! a frail child of dust!
Helpless immortal! insect infinite!
A worm! a god! — I tremble at myself,
And in myself am lost. At home a stranger,
Thought wanders up and down, surpris'd, aghast,
And wondering at her own. How reason reels!
O what a miracle to man is man!
Triumphantly distress'd! what joy! what dread!
Alternately transported and alarm'd;
What can preserve my life! or what destroy!
An angel's arm can't snatch me from the grave;
Legions of angels can't confine me there.

'Tis past conjecture; all things rise in proof.
While o'er my limbs Sleep's soft dominion spread,
What though my soul fantastic measures trod
O'er fairy fields, or mourn'd along the gloom
Of pathless woods, or down the craggy steep
Hurl'd headlong, swam with pain the mantled pool,
Or scal'd the cliff, or danc'd on hollow winds
With antic shapes, wild natives of the brain!
Her ceaseless flight, though devious, speaks her nature
Of subtler essence than the trodden clod;
Active, aerial, towering, unconfin'd,
Unfetter'd with her gross companion's fall.
Ev'n silent night proclaims my soul immortal;
Ev'n silent night proclaims eternal day!
For human weal Heaven husbands all events;
Dull sleep instructs, nor sport vain dreams in vain.

QUESTIONS. 1. What leads us to "take note of time"? 2. Repeat some of the epithets applied to man. 3. What conclusion is deduced from the activity of mind during sleep?

SPELL AND DEFINE. 1. verge   2. fathomless   3. pensioner
4. complicate   5. exquisite   6. triumphantly   7. legions   8. fantastic
9. craggy   10. antic   11. devious

LESSON LXXXI

Omnipresence of God — Psalm 139:1–12

RULE. In reading such lessons as the following, be careful to read slowly and with great deliberation and seriousness. When sentences are short and yet contain a great deal of meaning, you must allow the hearer a little time to gather the sense and to dwell upon it.

O Lord, thou hast searched me, and known me. Thou knowest my downsitting and mine uprising, thou understandest my thought afar off.

Thou compassest my path and my lying down, and art acquainted with all my ways. For there is not a word in my tongue, but, lo, O Lord, thou knowest it altogether. Thou hast beset me behind and before, and laid thine hand upon me.

Such knowledge is too wonderful for me; it is high, I cannot attain unto it.

Whither shall I go from thy Spirit? or whither shall I flee from thy presence? If I ascend up into heaven, thou art there: if I make my bed in hell, behold, thou art there. If I take the wings of the morning, and dwell in the uttermost parts of the sea; Even there shall thy hand lead me, and thy right hand shall hold me.

If I say, Surely the darkness shall cover me; even the night shall be light about me. Yea, the darkness hideth not from thee; but the night shineth as the day: the darkness and the light are both alike to thee.

QUESTIONS. 1. Can we do anything without God's seeing and knowing it?   2. Does He know what we speak and what we think, as well as what we do?   3. What is meant by, "if I make my bed in hell, behold, thou art there"?   4. How should the sentiments of this psalm influence our conduct?

SPELL AND DEFINE. 1. searched 2. understandest 3. compassest 4. acquainted 5. attain 6. ascend 7. uttermost

LESSON LXXXII

Henry Martyn and Lord Byron — Miss Beecher

RULE. Be careful to give a full sound to the vowels. Regard to this rule will correct the common flat, clipping, and uninteresting way in which many read.

EXERCISES. Prolong the italicized vowels: H*ai*l! holy l*i*ght!
We pr*ai*se thee, *O* Lord God.

These names of the Deity are seldom pronounced with that full and solemn sound that is proper. *Lud* and *Law-ard* and *Gud* and *Gawd* are too frequently used instead of the proper sounds. If the pupil can learn to speak the three words *O Lord God* properly, it will be worth no little attention. Every pupil ought to be exercised on these words till he pronounces them properly and in a full and solemn tone.

By reasoning from the known laws of mind, we gain the position that obedience to the divine law is the surest mode of securing every kind of happiness attainable in this state of existence.

The recorded experience of mankind does no less prove that obedience to the law of God is the true path to happiness. To exhibit this, some specific cases will be selected. Perhaps a fairer illustration cannot be presented than the contrasted records of two youthful personages who have made the most distinguished figures in the Christian and the literary world: Henry Martyn, the missionary, and Lord Byron, the poet.

Martyn was richly endowed with ardent feelings, keen susceptibilities, and superior intellect. He was the object of many affections and in the principal university of Great Britain won the highest honors, both in classic literature and mathematical science. He was flattered, caressed, and admired; the road to fame and honor lay open before him, and the brightest hopes of youth seemed ready to be realized.

But the hour came when he looked upon a lost and guilty world in the light of eternity, when he realized the full meaning of the sacrifice of our incarnate God, when he assumed his obligations to become a fellow worker in recovering a guilty world from the dominion of sin and all its future woes.

"The love of God constrained him," and without a murmur, for wretched beings on a distant shore whom he never saw, of whom he knew nothing but that they were miserable and guilty, he relinquished the wreath of fame, forsook the path of worldly honor, severed the ties of kindred, and gave up friends, country, and home. With every nerve throbbing in anguish at the sacrifice, he went forth alone to degraded heathen society, to solitude and privation, to weariness and painfulness, and to all the trials of missionary life.

He spent his days in teaching the guilty and degraded the way of pardon and peace. He lived to write the law of his God in the language of the Persian nation and to place a copy in the hands of its king. He lived to contend with the chief mullahs of Muhammad in the mosques of Shiraz and to kindle a flame in Persia more undying than its fabled fires.

He lived to endure rebuke and scorn, to toil and suffer in a fervid clime, to drag his weary steps over burning sands with the daily dying hope that at last he might be laid to rest among his kindred and on his native shore. Yet even this last earthly hope was not attained, for after spending all his youth in ceaseless labors for the good of others, at the early age of thirty-two he was laid in an unknown and foreign grave.

He died *alone* — a stranger in a strange land — with no friendly form around to sympathize and soothe him. Yet this was the last record of his dying hand: "I sat in the orchard and thought with sweet comfort and peace of my God! in solitude, my company! my friend! my comforter!"

In reviewing the record of his short yet blessed life — even if we forget the exulting joy with which such a benevolent spirit must welcome to heaven the thousands he toiled to save — if we look only at his years of self-denying trial, where were accumulated all the sufferings he was ever to feel, we can find more evidence of *true happiness* than is to be found in the records of the youthful poet who was gifted with every susceptibility of happiness, who spent his days in search of selfish enjoyment, who had every source of earthly bliss laid open, and drank to the very dregs.

We shall find that a mind that obeys the law of God is happier when bereft of the chief joys of this world than a worldly man can be when possessed of them all. The remains of Lord Byron present one of the most mournful exhibitions of a noble mind in all the wide chaos of ruin and disorder. He, also, was naturally endowed with overflowing affections, keen sensibilities, quick conceptions, and a sense of moral rectitude. He had all the constituents of a mind of first-rate order, but he passed through existence amid the wildest disorder of a ruined spirit.

His mind seemed utterly unbalanced, teeming with rich thoughts and overbearing impulses, the sport of the strangest fancies and the strongest passions, bound down by no habit, restrained by no principle — a singular combination of great conceptions and fantastic caprices, of manly dignity and childish folly, of nobler feeling and babyish weakness.

The lord of Newstead Abbey, the heir of a boasted line of ancestry, a peer of the realm, the pride of the social circle, the leading star of poesy, the hero of Greece, the wonder of the gaping world can now be followed to his secret haunts. There the mere child of the nursery might be amused at some of his silly weaknesses and ridiculous conceits — distressed about the cut of a collar, fuming at the color of his dress, intensely anxious about the whiteness of his hands, deeply engrossed with monkeys and dogs, and flying about from one whim to another with a reckless earnestness as ludicrous as it is disgusting.

At times this boasted hero and genius seemed naught but an overgrown child that had broken his leading strings and overmastered his nurses. At other times he is beheld in all the rounds of dissipation and the haunts of vice, occasionally filling up his leisure in recording and disseminating the disgusting minutiae of his weakness and shame with an effrontery and stupidity equaled only by that of the friend who retails them to the insulted world.

Again, we behold him philosophizing like a sage and moralizing like a Christian, while often from his bosom burst forth the repinings of a wounded spirit. He sometimes seemed to gaze upon his own mind with wonder, to watch its disordered powers with curious inquiry, to touch its complaining strings and start at the response, while often with maddening sweep he shook every chord and sent forth its deep wailings to entrance a wondering world.

Both Henry Martyn and Lord Byron shared the sorrows of life, and their records teach the different workings of the Christian and the worldly mind. Byron lost his mother, and when urged not to give way to sorrow, he burst into an agony of grief, saying, "I had but *one* friend in the world, and now she is gone!" On the death of some of his early friends, he thus writes: "My friends fall around me, and I shall be left a lonely tree before I am withered. *I have no resource but my own reflections,* and they present no prospect here or hereafter, except the selfish satisfaction of surviving my betters. I am indeed most wretched!"

Thus Henry Martyn mourns the loss of one most dear: "Can it be that she has been lying so many months in the cold grave? Would that I could always remember it or always forget it, but to think a moment on other things and then feel the remembrance of it come, as if for the first time, rends my heart asunder. O my gracious God, what should I do without Thee! But now Thou art manifesting Thyself as 'the God of all consolation.' Never was I so near Thee. There is nothing in the world for which I could wish to live, except because it may please God to appoint me some work to do. O Thou incomprehensibly glorious Savior, what Thou hast done to alleviate the sorrows of life!"

It is recorded of Byron that in society he generally appeared humorous and prankish, yet when rallied on his melancholy turn of writing, his constant answer was that though thus merry and full of laughter, he was at heart one of the most miserable wretches in existence.

Thus he writes: "Why, at the very height of desire and human pleasure, worldly, amorous, ambitious, or even avaricious, does there mingle a certain sense of doubt and sorrow — a fear of what is to come — a doubt of what is? If it were not for hope, what would the future be — a hell! As for the past, what predominates in memory — hopes baffled! From whatever place we commence, we know *where it must all end.* And yet what good is there in knowing it? It does not make men wiser or better. If I were to live over again, I do not know what I would change in my life, unless it were — *not to have lived at all.* All history and experience, and the rest, teach us that good and evil are pretty equally balanced in this existence and that what is *most to* be desired is an *easy passage out of it.* What can it give us but years, and these have *little of good but their ending.*"

Thus Martyn writes: "I am happier here in this remote land, where I seldom hear what happens in the world, than I was in England, where there are so many calls to look at things that are seen. The precious *Word* is now my only study, by means of translations. Time flows on with great rapidity. It seems as if life would all be gone before anything is done. I sometimes rejoice that I am but twenty-seven and that unless God should ordain it otherwise, I may double this number in constant and successful labor. But I shall not cease from my happiness and scarcely from my labor by passing into the other world."

Thus they make their records at anniversaries, when the mind is called to review life and its labors. Byron writes: "At twelve o'clock I shall have completed thirty-three years! I go to my bed with a heaviness of heart at having lived so long and to so little purpose. It is now three minutes past twelve, and I am thirty-three!

'Alas, my friend, the years pass swiftly by.'

But I do not regret them so much for what I have done as for what I *might* have done."

Thus Martyn: "I like to find myself employed usefully, in a way I did not expect or foresee. The coming year is to be a perilous one, but my life is of little consequence, whether I finish the Persian New Testament or not. I look back with pity on myself when I attached so much importance to my life and labors. The more I see of my own works the more I am ashamed of them, for coarseness and clumsiness mar all the works of man. I am sick when I look at the wisdom of man but am relieved by reflecting that we have a city whose builder and maker is God. The least of *His* works is refreshing. A dried leaf or a straw makes me feel *in good company,* and complacency and admiration take the place of disgust. What a momentary duration is the life of man! 'It glides along, rolling onward forever,' may be affirmed of the river, but men pass away as soon as they begin to exist. Well, let the moments pass!"

They waft us sooner o'er
This life's tempestuous sea,
Soon we shall reach the blissful shore
Of blest eternity!

Such was the experience of those who in youth completed their course. The poet has well described his own career:

A wandering mass of shapeless flame,
A pathless comet and a curse,
The menace of the universe;
Still rolling on with innate force,
Without a sphere, without a course,
A bright deformity on high,
The monster of the upper sky!

In Holy Writ we read of those who are "raging waves of the sea, foaming out their own shame; wandering stars, to whom is reserved the blackness of darkness for ever." The lips of man may not apply these terrific words to any whose doom is yet to be disclosed, but there is a passage which none can fear to apply. "And they that be wise shall shine as the brightness of the firmament; and they that turn many to righteousness, as the stars for ever and ever."

QUESTIONS. 1. What truth have we gained by reasoning from the known laws of mind? 2. What else furnishes us with evidence of the same truth, and what two characters are given as examples? 3. What is said of Henry Martyn? 4. Why did he give up home, country, and the honors and pleasures of life? 5. Do you suppose he was happier in this world than he would have been if he had lived simply to seek pleasure for himself? 6. Will he be happier in heaven for the sacrifices he made on earth? 7. Who had the most of this world to enjoy — Martyn or Byron? 8. What is said of Byron? 9. Which had the most comfort in seasons of affliction? 10. How did Byron feel when he was enjoying himself the most? 11. How did Martyn feel when he was cut off from most of the pleasures that Bryon was seeking? 12. What was the difference in their feelings at their birthdays? 13. What two passages of Scripture indicate the future prospects of two such minds as Byron and Martyn?

SPELL AND DEFINE. 1. overmastered 2. disseminating 3. entrance 4. resource 5. gracious 6. melancholy 7. predominates 8. anniversaries 9. perilous

LESSON LXXXIII

Byron — Pollock

RULE. Where two or more consonants come together, let the pupil be careful to sound every one distinctly.

EXERCISES UNDER THE RULE. Thou *indulged'st* thy appetite. O wind! that *waft'st* us o'er the main. Thou *tempted'st* him. Thou *loved'st* him fondly. Thou *credited'st* his story. The *lists* are open.

He touched his harp and nations heard, entranced.
As some vast river of unfailing source,
Rapid, exhaustless, deep, his numbers flowed,
And oped new fountains in the human heart.
Where fancy halted, weary in her flight
In other men, his, fresh as morning rose,
And soared untrodden heights, and seemed at home
Where angels bashful looked. Others, though great,
Beneath their argument seemed struggling whiles;
He from above descending, stooped to touch
The loftiest thought; and proudly stooped, as though
It scarce deserved his verse. With Nature's self
He seemed an old acquaintance, free to jest
At will with all her glorious majesty.
He laid his hand upon "the ocean's mane,"
And played familiar with his hoary locks.
Stood on the Alps, stood on the Apennines;
And with the thunder talked, as friend to friend;
And wove his garland of the lightning's wing,
In sportive twist — the lightning's fiery wing,
Which, as the footsteps of the dreadful God,
Marching upon the storm in vengeance seemed —
Then turned, and with the grasshopper, who sung
His evening song beneath his feet, conversed.
Suns, moons, and stars, and clouds his sisters were;
Rocks, mountains, meteors, seas, and winds, and storms
His brothers — younger brothers, whom he scarce
As equals deemed.
As some fierce comet of tremendous size,
To which the stars did reverence as it passed,
So he through learning and through fancy took
His flight sublime and on the loftiest top
Of fame's dread mountain sat; not soiled and worn,
As if he from the earth had labored up,
But as some bird of heavenly plumage fair
He looked, which down from higher regions came,

And perched it there, to see what lay beneath.
Great man! the nations gazed and wondered much,
And praised — and many called his evil good.
Wits wrote in favor of his wickedness,
And kings to do him honor took delight.
Thus full of titles, flattery, honor, fame;
Beyond desire, beyond ambition full —
He died — he died of what? Of wretchedness.
Drank every cup of joy, heard every trump
Of fame; drank early, deeply drank; drank draughts
That common millions might have quenched — then
    died
Of thirst, because there was no more to drink.
His goddess, Nature, wooed, embraced, enjoyed,
Fell from his arms abhorred; his passions died,
Died, all but dreary, solitary pride;
And all his sympathies in being died.
As some ill-guided bark, well built and tall,
Which angry tides cast on our desert shore,
And then retiring, leave it there to rot
And molder in the winds and rains of heaven;
So he, cut from the sympathies of life
And cast ashore from pleasure's boisterous surge,
A wandering, weary, worn, and wretched thing,
Scorched and desolate and blasted soul,
A gloomy wilderness of dying thought —
Repined and groaned and withered from the earth.

QUESTIONS. 1. Who was Byron? 2. Where did he die? 3. Why is he compared to a comet? 4. What was his character? 5. Are talents a blessing or curse to such a man as Byron?

SPELL AND DEFINE. 1. entranced 2. exhaustless 3. Apennines 4. struggling 5. nature 6. familiar 7. garland 8. meteors 9. tremendous 10. fancy 11. sublime 12. soiled 13. wits 14. flattery 15. goddess 16. sympathies 17. tides 18. boisterous 19. wilderness

LESSON LXXXIV

Chesterfield and Paul — Miss Beecher

RULE. Speak every syllable distinctly, and do not slip over the little words nor pronounce them wrong.

To these youthful witnesses [Martyn and Byron] whose remains show the difference between the happiness of those who obey or disobey the law of God, may be added the testimony of two who had fulfilled their years. The first was the polished, the witty, the elegant, and admired Earl of Chesterfield, who tried every source of earthly enjoyment and at the end makes this acknowledgment.

"I have seen," says he, "the silly rounds of business and of pleasure and have done with them all. I have enjoyed all the pleasures of the world and consequently know their futility and do not regret their loss. I appraise them at their real value, which is, in truth, very low. Whereas, those that have not experienced always overrate them. They only see their gay outside and are dazzled at the glare.

"But I have been behind the scenes. I have seen all the coarse pulleys and dirty ropes which exhibit and move the gaudy machines; I have seen and smelt the tallow candles which illuminate the whole decoration, to the astonishment and admiration of the ignorant audience.

"When I reflect on what I have seen, what I have heard, and what I have done, I can hardly persuade myself that all that frivolous hurry of bustle and pleasure of the world had any reality. I look upon all that is passing as one of those romantic dreams which opium commonly occasions, and I do by no means desire to repeat the nauseous dose for the sake of the fugitive dream.

"Shall I tell you that I bear this melancholy situation with that meritorious constancy and resignation which most people boast of? No, for I really cannot help it. I bear it because I *must* bear it, whether I will or no! I think of nothing but killing Time the best way I can, now that he is become my enemy. It is my resolution to *sleep in the carriage* during the remainder of the journey of life."

The other personage was Paul, the Aged. For Christ and the salvation of those for whom Christ died, Paul "suffered the loss of all things." This is the record of his course: "in labors more abundant, in stripes above measure, in prisons more frequent, in deaths oft.... In journeyings often, in perils of waters, in perils of robbers, in perils by mine own country-men, in perils by the heathen, in perils in the city, in perils in the wilderness, in perils in the sea, in perils among false brethren; In weariness and painfulness, in watchings often, in hunger and thirst, in fastings often, in cold and naked-ness. Beside those things that are without, that which cometh upon me daily, the care of all the churches....

"We are troubled on every side, yet not distressed; we are perplexed, but not in despair; persecuted, but not forsaken; cast down, but not destroyed.... But though our outward man perish, yet the inward man is renewed day by day. For our light affliction, which is but for a moment, worketh for us a far more exceeding and eternal weight of glory."

And as the time drew near when he was to be "offered up," and he looked back on the past course of his life, these are his words of triumphant exultation: "I have fought a good fight, I have finished my course, I have kept the faith: Henceforth there is laid up for me a crown of righteousness, which the Lord, the righteous judge, shall give me at that day."

To this testimony may be added other parts of Scripture: "Whoso trusteth in the Lord, happy is he. Behold, the fear of the Lord, that is wisdom; and to depart from evil is under-standing. For wisdom is better than rubies; and all the things that may be desired are not to be compared to it. Her ways are ways of pleasantness, and all her paths are peace. Keep sound wisdom and discretion: So shall they be life unto thy soul, and grace to thy neck. Then shalt thou walk in thy way safely, and thy foot shall not stumble. When thou liest down, thou shalt not be afraid: yea, thou shalt lie down, and thy sleep shall be sweet."

And thus the Redeemer invites to His service: "Come unto me, all ye that labor and are heavy laden, and I will give you rest. Take my yoke upon you, and learn of me; for I am meek and lowly in heart: and ye shall find rest unto your souls."

QUESTIONS. 1. What two persons who lived to be old have left their testimony in regard to the way to be happy? 2. What is said of Lord Chesterfield? 3. How did he look on past life? 4. What did he resolve to do? 5. What is said of Paul? 6. Which was the happier man of the two? 7. What does the Bible say respecting the way of happiness?

SPELL AND DEFINE. 1. acknowledgment   2. consequently 3. illuminate 4. nauseous 5. resignation 6. salvation 7. persecuted 8. triumphant 9. compared 10. Redeemer

LESSON LXXXV

Henry the First after the Death of His Son — Hemans

RULE. Let each pupil in the class observe and mention every syllable that is not sounded as each one reads.

> The bark that held the prince went down,
>   The sweeping waves rolled on —
> And what was England's glorious crown
>   To him that wept a son?
> He lived — for life may long be borne,
>   Ere sorrow breaks its chain;
> Still comes not death to those who mourn;
>   He never smiled again!
>
> There stood proud forms before his throne,
>   The stately and the brave;

But which could fill the place of one,
    That one beneath the wave?
Before him passed the young and fair,
    In pleasure's reckless train;
But seas dashed o'er his son's bright hair —
    He never smiled again!

He sat where festal bowls went round;
    He heard the minstrel sing;
He saw the tourney's victor crowned
    Amid the mighty ring —
A murmur of the restless deep
    Mingled with every strain,
A voice of winds that would not sleep —
    He never smiled again!

Hearts in that time closed o'er the trace
    Of vows once fondly poured,
And strangers took the kinsman's place
    At many a joyous board;
Graves, which true love had bathed with tears,
    Were left to heaven's bright rain;
Fresh hopes were born for other years —
    He never smiled again!

QUESTIONS. 1. Relate the historical event upon which this poem is founded. 2. Is there anything in earthly splendor that can soothe the suffering heart? 3. What is the allusion in the third verse?

SPELL AND DEFINE. 1. bark   2. reckless   3. festal   4. tourney
5. vows 6. kinsman 7. joyous

LESSON LXXXVI

The Miser — Pollok

RULE. Observe the commas and stop at each long enough to take
breath.

Gold many hunted, sweat and bled for gold,
Waked all the night, and labored all the day;
And what was this allurement, dost thou ask?
A dust dug from the bowels of the earth,
Which, being cast into the fire, came out
A shining thing that fools admired, and called
A god — and in devout and humble plight
Before it kneeled, the greater to the less.
And on its altar, sacrificed ease, peace,
Truth, faith, integrity, good conscience, friends,
Love, charity, benevolence, and all
The sweet and tender sympathies of life;
And to complete the horrid murderous rite,
And signalize their folly, offered up
Their souls, and an eternity of bliss,
To gain them; What? an hour of dreaming joy,
A feverish hour that hasted to be done,
And ended in the bitterness of woe.
Most, for the luxuries it bought, the pomp,
The praise, the glitter, fashion, and renown,
This yellow phantom followed and adored.
But there was one in folly, farther gone,
With eye awry, incurable, and wild,
The laughingstock of devils and of men,
And by his guardian angel quite given up —
The miser, who with dust inanimate
Held intimate communion.
                              Ill-guided wretch!
Thou mightst have seen him at the midnight hour,

When good men slept, and in light-winged dreams
Ascended up to God, in wasteful hall,
With vigilance and fasting worn to skin
And bone, and wrapped in most debasing rags;
Thou mightst have seen him bending o'er his heaps,
And holding strange communion with his gold;
And as his thievish fancy seemed to hear
The night-man's foot approach, starting alarmed,
And in his old, decrepit, withered hand,
That palsy shook, grasping the yellow earth
To make it sure.
                                Of all God made upright,
And in their nostrils breathed a living soul,
Most fallen, most prone, most earthy, most debased;
Of all that sold Eternity for Time,
None bargained on so easy terms with Death.
Illustrious fool! Nay, most inhuman wretch!
He sat among his bags and, with a look
Which hell might be ashamed of, drove the poor
Away unalmsed, and midst abundance died,
Sorest of evils! died of utter want.

QUESTIONS. 1. What is the subject of this extract? 2. What are some of the evil consequences of the love of money? 3. What good can wealth bestow on its votaries? 4. What are some of the marks of a miserly character? 5. What are the effects of avarice upon body and mind? 6. What is the miser's fate?

SPELL AND DEFINE. 1. allurement   2. bowels   3. admired
4. integrity 5. conscience 6. benevolence 7. sympathies 8. murderous
9. signalize   10. phantom   11. awry   12. incurable   13. laughingstock
14. inanimate 15. vigilance 16. decrepit 17. illustrious

LESSON LXXXVII

True Wisdom — Job 28:12–28

RULE. Read slowly and distinctly and pronounce every syllable.

But where shall wisdom be found?
And where is the place of understanding?
Man knoweth not the price thereof;
Neither is it found in the land of the living.
The deep saith, It is not in me:
And the sea saith, It is not with me.
It cannot be gotten for gold,
Neither shall silver be weighed for the price thereof.
It cannot be valued with the gold of Ophir,
With the precious onyx, or the sapphire.
The gold and the crystal cannot equal it:
And the exchange of it shall not be for jewels of fine
    gold.
No mention shall be made of coral, or of pearls:
For the price of wisdom is above rubies.
The topaz of Ethiopia shall not equal it,
Neither shall it be valued with pure gold.

Whence then cometh wisdom?
And where is the place of understanding?
Seeing it is hid from the eyes of all living,
And kept close from the fowls of the air.
Destruction and death say,
We have heard the fame thereof with our ears.
God understandeth the way thereof,
And he knoweth the place thereof.
For he looketh to the ends of the earth,
And seeth under the whole heaven;
To make the weight for the winds;
And he weigheth the waters by measure.

When he made a decree for the rain,
And a way for the lightning of the thunder;
Then did he see it, and declare it;
He prepared it, yea, and searched it out.
And unto man he said,
Behold, the fear of the Lord, that is wisdom;
And to depart from evil is understanding.

QUESTIONS. 1. What are onyx and sapphire? 2. What is true wisdom?

SPELL AND DEFINE. 1. wisdom   2. understanding   3. onyx
4. sapphire   5. crystal   6. topaz   7. destruction   8. weigheth   9. decree
10. lightning   11. prepared

LESSON LXXXVIII

The Wife — W. Irving

RULE. Be careful to speak such little words as *the, of, a, in, from, at, by* very distinctly and yet not to dwell on them so long as on the other more important words.

I have often had occasion to remark concerning the fortitude with which women sustain the most overwhelming reverses of fortune. Those disasters which break down the spirit of a man and prostrate him in the dust seem to call forth all the energies of the softer sex and give such intrepidity and elevation to their character that at times it approaches to sublimity.

Nothing can be more touching than to behold a soft and tender female, who had been all weakness and dependence and alive to every trivial roughness while treading the prosperous paths of life, suddenly rising in mental force to be the comforter and supporter of her husband under misfortune and abiding, with unshrinking firmness, the most bitter blasts of adversity. As the vine which has long twined its graceful foliage about the oak and been lifted by it into sunshine will, when the hardy plant is rifted by the thunderbolt, cling around it with its caressing tendrils and bind up its shattered boughs, so is it beautifully ordered by Providence that woman, who is the dependent and ornament of man in his happier hours, should be his stay and solace when smitten with sudden calamity, winding herself into the rugged recesses of his nature, tenderly supporting the drooping head, and binding up the broken heart.

I was once congratulating a friend who had around him a blooming family, knit together in the strongest affection. "I can wish you no better lot," said he, with enthusiasm, "than to have a wife and children. If you are prosperous, there they are to share your prosperity; if otherwise, there they are to comfort you."

Indeed, I have observed that a married man falling into misfortune is more apt to retrieve his situation in the world than a single one, partly because he is more stimulated to exertion by the necessities of the helpless and beloved beings who depend upon him for subsistence, but chiefly because his spirits are soothed and relieved by domestic endearments and his self-respect kept alive by finding that, though all abroad is darkness and humiliation, yet there is still a little world of love at home of which he is the monarch. Whereas, a single man is apt to run to waste and self-neglect, to fancy himself lonely and abandoned, and his heart to fall to ruin like some deserted mansion for want of an inhabitant.

QUESTIONS. 1. What is said of the fortitude of the female sex? 2. What effect is produced on the mind by the view of this trait? 3. To what natural object is it beautifully compared? 4. Why should man have a family? 5. What is apt to be the case with the single man, as to character and comfort? 6. Do married persons generally live longer than unmarried?

SPELL AND DEFINE. 1. fortitude   2. overwhelming   3. disasters
4. intrepidity   5. sublimity   6. dependence   7. roughness   8. unshrinking
9. adversity   10. foliage   11. thunderbolt   12. rifted   13. shattered
14. beautifully   15. solace   16. recesses   17. rugged   18. tendrils
19. congratulating   20. enthusiasm   21. prosperous   22. stimulated
23. retrieve 24. necessities 25. subsistence 26. domestic 27. abandoned

LESSON LXXXIX

Duty of the American Orator — Grimke

RULE. Be careful to give all the consonants their full sound in each
word.

One theme of duty still remains, and I have placed it
alone because of its peculiar dignity, sacredness, and importance. Need I tell you that I speak of the union of the states?
Let the American orator discharge all other duties but this,
if indeed it be not impossible, with the energy and eloquence
of John Rutledge and the disinterested fidelity of Robert
Morris, yet shall he be counted a traitor if he attempt to
dissolve the Union.

His name, illustrious as it may have been, shall then be
gibbeted on every hilltop throughout the land, a monument
of his crime and punishment and of the shame and grief of
his country. If indeed he believe, and doubtless there may be
such, that wisdom demands the dissolution of the Union,
that the South should be severed from the North, the West
be independent of the East, let him cherish the sentiment,
for his own sake, in the solitude of his breast or breathe it
only in the confidence of friendship.

Let him rest assured that as his country tolerates the
monarchist and the aristocrat of the Old World, she tolerates him. Should he plot the dismemberment of the Union,
the same trial, judgment, and execution await him as would
await them should they attempt to establish the aristocracy

of Venice or the monarchy of Austria on the ruins of our confederacy. To him, as to them, she leaves freedom of speech and the very licentiousness of the press and permits him to write even in the spirit of scorn and hatred and unfairness.

She trembles not at such effort, reckless and hostile as they may be. She smiles at their impotence while she mourns over their infatuation. But let them lift the hand of parricide in the insolence of pride or the madness of power, to strike their country and her countenance, and all the severity and terrors of a parent's wrath shall smite them with amazement and horror. Let them strike, and the voices of millions of freemen from the city and hamlet, from the college and the farmhouse, from the cabins amid the western wilds and our ships scattered around the world, shall utter the stern irrevocable judgment: self-banishment for life, or ignominious death.

Be it then among the noblest offices of American eloquence to cultivate, in the people of every state, a deep and fervent attachment to the Union. The Union is to us the marriage bond of states, indissoluble in life, to be dissolved, we trust, only on that day when nations shall die in a moment, never to rise again. Let the American orator discountenance, then, all the arts of intrigue and corruption which not only pollute the people and dishonor republican institutions but also prepare the way for the ruin of both — how secretly, how surely, let history declare. Let him banish from his thoughts and his lips the hypocrisy of the demagogue, equally deceitful and degraded.

> With smooth dissimulation, skill'd to grace
> A devil's purpose, with an angel's face.

Let that demagogue and those arts, his instruments of power, be regarded as pretended friends but secret and dangerous enemies of the people. Let it never be forgotten that to him and to them we owe all the licentiousness and violence, all the unprincipled and unfeeling persecution of party spirit. Let the American orator labor, then, with all the solemnity of a religious duty, with all the intensity of filial love, to convince his countrymen that the danger to liberty in this country is to be traced to those sources. Let the European tremble for his institutions in the presence of military power and for the warrior's ambition.

Let the American dread, as the archenemy of republican institutions, the shock of exasperated parties and the implacable revenge of demagogues. The discipline of standing armies is the terror of freedom in Europe, but the tactics of parties, the standing armies of America, are still more formidable to liberty with us.

Let the American orator frown, then, on that ambition which, pursuing its own aggrandizement and gratification, perils the harmony and integrity of the Union and counts the grief, anxiety, and expostulations of millions as the small dust of the balance. Let him remember that ambition, like the Amruta cup of Indian fable, gives to the virtuous an immortality of glory and happiness, but to the corrupt an immortality of ruin, shame, and misery.

Let not the American orator, in the great questions on which he is to speak or write, appeal to the mean and groveling qualities of human nature. Let him love the people and respect himself too much to dishonor them and degrade himself by an appeal to selfishness and prejudice, to jealousy, fear, and contempt. The greater the interests and the more sacred the rights which may be at stake, the more resolutely should he appeal to the generous feelings, the noble sentiments, the calm considerate wisdom which become a free, educated, peaceful Christian people. Even if he battle against criminal ambition and base intrigue, let his weapons be a logic — manly, intrepid, honorable — and an eloquence magnanimous, disinterested, and spotless.

What a contrast between his duties and those of Athenian eloquence! where the prince of orators was but the prince of demagogues. How could it be otherwise! with a religion that commanded no virtue and prohibited no vice; with deities the model of every crime and folly which deform and pollute even man; with a social system in which refinement, benevolence, and forbearance found no place. How could it be otherwise! with a political system in which war was the chief element of power and honor in the individual and of strength, security, and glory in the state, while the ambition or resentment of rulers found a cheerful response in the love of conquest, plunder, or revenge on the part of the people.

How could it be otherwise! with such domestic relations between the republics as made it the duty of the ancient orator to aggrandize his own at the expense of all the rest, to set state against state, to foment jealousies and bickerings among them, to deceive and weaken the strong, to oppress and seize on the feeble. How could it be otherwise! when such were the domestic and foreign relations, viewed as a whole, that the duty of the ancient orator was to cultivate the union of the states not as a matter of deep and lasting importance at home, not as the very life of peace and harmony there but only as an expedient against foreign invasion, while partial and hostile combinations, headed by Athens or Thebes or Sparta, were the current events of their domestic policy.

Compared to such duties and such scenes, who can turn to the obligations and field of American eloquence without a thrill of spirit-stirring admiration and gratitude? His office in our union, how full of benignity and peace, of justice, majesty, and truth. Where, except in the Christian pulpit, shall we find its parallel? Why do we find it there? but that the Christian ministry is, like him, the advocate of purity, forbearance, and love. How delightful, how honorable the task to calm the angry passions, to dissipate error, to reconcile prejudice, to banish jealousy, and silence the voice of selfishness!

American eloquence must likewise cultivate a fixed, unalterable devotion to the Union — a frank, generous, ardent attachment of section to section, of state to state, and in the citizen, liberal sentiments towards his rulers and cordial love for his countrymen. Nor is this all. Let the American orator comprehend and live up to the grand conception that the Union is the property of the world no less than of ourselves, that it is a part of the divine scheme for the moral government of the earth as the solar system is a part of the mechanism of the heavens, that it is destined, whilst traveling from the Atlantic to the Pacific like the ascending sun, to shed its glorious influence backward on the states of Europe and forward on the empires of Asia.

Let him comprehend its sublime relations to time and eternity, to God and man, to the most precious hopes, the most solemn obligations, and the highest happiness of humankind. What an eloquence must that be whose source of power and wisdom is God himself, the objects of whose influence are all the nations of the earth, whose sphere of duty is coextensive with all that is sublime in religion, beautiful in morals, commanding in intellect, and touching in humanity. How comprehensive and, therefore, how wise and benevolent must then be the genius of American eloquence compared to the narrow-minded, narrow-hearted, and therefore selfish eloquence of Greece and Rome.

How striking is the contrast between the universal social spirit of the former and the individual, exclusive character of the latter. The boundary of this is the horizon of a plain, the circle of that the horizon of a mountain summit. Be it then the duty of American eloquence to speak, to write, to act in the cause of Christianity, patriotism, and literature; in the cause of justice, humanity, virtue, and truth; in the cause of the people, of the Union, of the whole human race, and of the unborn of every clime and age. Then shall American eloquence, the personification of truth, beauty, and love,

> Walk the earth, that she may hear her name
> Still hymn'd and honor'd by the grateful voice
> Of humankind, and in her fame rejoice.

QUESTIONS. 1. How shall the orator be regarded who attempts to dissolve the Union? 2. Suppose he believe a separation desirable, what shall he do with his opinion? 3. Why is freedom of speech and the press allowed both to bad and good? 4. What feeling towards the Union must be cherished in every American bosom? 5. How should the American regard party spirit and the arts of demagogues? 6. To what sentiments of the human mind should he always appeal, and to what others never? 7. Contrast the American with the Athenian orator, paragraphs 10–13. 8. While the orator cherishes union of state to state, of section to section, how shall he regard the country in respect to the world? 9. To time (eternity)? 10. Sum up the contrast contained in the close of this lesson between what ancient eloquence was and what American eloquence ought to be.

SPELL AND DEFINE. 1. disinterested   2. gibbeted   3. independent   4. dissolution   5. monarchist   6. aristocrat   7. confederacy   8. irrevocable   9. indissoluble   10. dissimulation   11. demagogues   12. combinations   13. comprehend

LESSON XC

The Patriotism of Western Literature — Dr. Drake

RULE. Be careful to give the vowels their proper sound.

Our literature cannot fail to be patriotic, and its patriotism will be American — composed of a love of country, mingled with an admiration for our political institutions.

The slave, whose very mind has passed under the yoke, and the senseless ox, whom he goads onward in the furrow, are attached to the spot of their animal companionship and may even fight for the cabin and the field where they came into existence. This affection, considered as an ingredient of patriotism, although the most universal, is the lowest, and to rise into a virtue it must be discriminating and comprehensive, involving a varied association of ideas and embracing the beautiful of the natural and moral world as they appear around us.

To feel in his heart and infuse into his writings the inspiration of such a patriotism, the scholar must feast his taste on the delicacies of our scenery and dwell with enthusiasm on the genius of our constitution and laws. Thus sanctified in its character, this sentiment becomes a principle of moral and intellectual dignity — an element of fire, purifying and subliming the mass in which it glows.

As a guiding star to the will, its light is inferior only to that of Christianity. Heroic in its philanthropy, untiring in its enterprises, and sublime in the martyrdoms it willingly suffers, it justly occupies a high place among the virtues which ennoble the human character. A literature animated with this patriotism is a national blessing, and such will be the literature of the West.

The literature of the whole Union must be richly endowed with this spirit, but a double portion will be the lot of the interior, because the foreign influences, which dilute and vitiate this virtue in the extremities, cannot reach the heart of the continent, where all that lives and moves is American.

Hence, a native of the West may be confided in as his country's hope. Compare him with the native of a great maritime city on the verge of the nation — his birthplace the fourth story of a house hemmed in by surrounding edifices, his playground a pavement, the scene of his juvenile rambles an arcade of shops, his young eyes feasted on the flags of a hundred alien governments, the streets in which he wanders crowded with foreigners, and the ocean, common to all nations, forever expanding to his view.

Estimate *his* love of country, as far as it depends on local and early attachments, and then contrast him with the young backwoodsman, born and reared amid objects, scenes, and events which you can all bring to mind — the jutting rocks in the great road, half-alive with organic remains or sparkling with crystals; the quiet old walnut tree dropping its nuts upon the yellow leaves as the morning sun melts the October frost; the grapevine swing; the chase after the cowardly black snake until it creeps under the rotten log; the sitting down to rest upon the crumbling trunk and an idle examination of the mushrooms and mosses which grow from its ruins; the wading in the shallow stream and upturning of the flat stones to find bait with which to fish in the deeper waters; the plunder of a bird's nest to make necklaces of the speckled eggs for her who has plundered him of his young heart; the beech tree, with its smooth body, on which he cuts the initials of her name interlocked with his own; the great hollow stump by the path that leads up the valley to the log schoolhouse, its dry bark peeled off and the stately polk weed growing from its center and bending with crimson berries which invite him to sit down and write upon its polished wood. How much pleasanter it is to extract ground squirrels from beneath its roots than to extract the square root under that laborsaving machine, the ferule of a teacher!

The affections of one who is blest with such reminiscences, like the branches of our beautiful trumpet flower, strike their roots into every surrounding object and derive support from all which stand within their reach. The love of country is with him a constitutional and governing principle. If he be a mechanic, the wood and iron which he molds into form are dear to his heart because they remind him of his own hills and forests; if a husbandman, he holds companionship with growing corn as the offspring of his native soil; if a legislator, his dreams are filled with sights of national prosperity to flow from his beneficent enactments. If he be a scholar devoted to the interests of literature — in his lone and excited hours of midnight study, while the winds are hushed and all animated nature sleeps, when the silence is so profound that the stroke of his own pen grates loudly and harshly upon his ear and fancy — from the great deep of his luminous intellect, he draws up new forms of smiling beauty and solemn grandeur. The genius of his country hovers nigh and sheds over its pages an essence of patriotism sweeter than the honeydew which the summer night distills upon the leaves of our forest trees.

QUESTIONS. 1. What is American patriotism? 2. Where is this kind of patriotism most likely to be found, in the cities of the seashore or in the West? 3. What are the causes which make it greater in the West?

SPELL AND DEFINE. 1. patriotism 2. discriminating 3. intellectual 4. arcade 5. backwoods 6. initials 7. reminiscences 8. constitutional

LESSON XCI

Childe Harold's Pilgrimage (Canto 4, Verses 78–84, 106– 110, 112) — Byron

RULE. In poetry that does not rhyme, no pause need be made at the end of such lines as terminate with unimportant words, except when the sense requires it.

Oh, Rome! my Country! City of the Soul!
The orphans of the heart must turn to thee,
Lone Mother of dead Empires! and control
In their shut breasts their petty misery.
What are our woes and sufferance? Come and see
The cypress — hear the owl — and plod your way
O'er steps of broken thrones and temples — Ye!
Whose agonies are evils of a day —
A world is at our feet as fragile as our clay.

The Niobe of nations! there she stands,
Childless and crownless, in her voiceless woe;
An empty urn within her withered hands,
Whose holy dust was scattered long ago;
The Scipios' tomb contains no ashes now;
The very sepulchres are tenantless
Of their heroic dwellers: dost thou flow,
Old Tiber! through a marble wilderness?
Rise, with thy yellow waves, and mantle her distress.

The Goth, the Christian — Time — War — Flood,
   and Fire,
Have dealt upon the seven-hilled City's pride;
She saw her glories star by star expire,
And up the steep barbarian Monarchs ride,
Where the car climbed the Capitol; far and wide
Temple and tower went down, nor left a site: —
Chaos of ruins! who shall trace the void,
O'er the dim fragments cast a lunar light,
And say, "here was, or is," where all is doubly night?

The double night of ages, and of her,
Night's daughter, Ignorance, hath wrapt and wrap
All round us; we but feel our way to err:
The Ocean hath his chart, the Stars their map,
And Knowledge spreads them on her ample lap;
But Rome is as the desert — where we steer
Stumbling o'er recollections; now we clap
Our hands, and cry "Eureka!" "it is clear" —
When but some false Mirage of ruin rises near.

Alas! the lofty city! and, alas,
The trebly hundred triumphs! and the day
When Brutus made the dagger's edge surpass
The Conqueror's sword in bearing fame away!
Alas, for Tully's voice, and Virgil's lay,
And Livy's pictured page! — but these shall be
Her resurrection; all beside — decay.
Alas, for Earth, for never shall we see
That brightness in her eye she bore when Rome was
   free!

Oh, thou, whose chariot rolled on Fortune's wheel,
Triumphant Sylla! Thou, who didst subdue
Thy country's foes ere thou wouldst pause to feel
The wrath of thy own wrongs, or reap the due
Of hoarded vengeance till thine Eagles flew

O'er prostrate Asia; — thou, who with thy frown
Annihilated senates; — Roman, too,
With all thy vices — for thou didst lay down
With an atoning smile a more than earthly crown,

Thy dictatorial wreath — couldst thou divine
To what would one day dwindle that which made
Thee more than mortal? and that so supine,
By aught than Romans, Rome should thus be laid? —
She who was named Eternal, and arrayed
Her warriors but to conquer — she who veiled
Earth with her haughty shadow, and displayed,
Until the o'er-canopied horizon failed,
Her rushing wings — Oh! she who was Almighty
      hailed!

. . . .

Then let the Winds howl on! their harmony
Shall henceforth be my music, and the Night
The sound shall temper with the owlets' cry,
As now I hear them, in the fading light
Dim o'er the bird of darkness' native site,
Answering each other on the Palatine,
With their large eyes, all glistening grey and bright,
And sailing pinions. — Upon such a shrine
What are our petty griefs? — let me not number
      mine.

Cypress and ivy, weed and wallflower grown
Matted and massed together — hillocks heaped
On what were chambers — arch crushed, column
      strown
In fragments — choked up vaults, and frescos steeped
In subterranean damps, where the owl peeped,
Deeming it midnight: — Temples — Baths — or
      Halls?
Pronounce who can: for all that Learning reaped

From her research hath been, that these are walls —
Behold the Imperial Mount! 'tis thus the Mighty
    falls.

There is the moral of all human tales;
'Tis but the same rehearsal of the past,
First Freedom, and then Glory — when that fails,
Wealth — Vice — Corruption, — Barbarism at last:
And History, with all her volumes vast,
Hath but *one* page, — 'tis better written here,
Where gorgeous Tyranny had thus amassed
All treasures, all delights, that Eye or Ear,
Heart, Soul could seek — Tongue ask — Away with
    words! draw near,

Admire — exult — despise — laugh — weep, — for
    here
There is such matter for all feeling: — Man!
Thou pendulum betwixt a smile and tear,
Ages and Realms are crowded in this span,
This mountain, whose obliterated plan
The pyramid of Empires pinnacled,
Of Glory's gewgaws shining in the van
Till the Sun's rays with added flame were filled!
Where are its golden roofs? where those who dared to
    build?

Tully was not so eloquent as thou,
Thou nameless column with the buried base!
What are the laurels of the Caesar's brow?
Crown me with ivy from his dwelling-place.
Whose arch or pillar meets me in the face,
Titus or Trajan's? No! — 'tis that of Time:
Triumph, arch, pillar, all he doth displace
Scoffing; and apostolic statues climb
To crush the Imperial urn, whose ashes slept sub-
    lime,

. . . . ? . . .

Where is the rock of Triumph, the high place
Where Rome embraced her heroes? where the steep
Tarpeian? — fittest goal of Treason's race,
The Promontory whence the Traitor's Leap
Cured all ambition? Did the conquerors heap
Their spoils here? Yes; and in yon field below,
A thousand years of silenced factions sleep —
The Forum, where the immortal accents glow,
And still the eloquent air breathes — burns with
    Cicero!

QUESTIONS. 1. Why does Byron call Rome "my Country"? 2. Who was Niobe, and what was her story? 3. How is Rome the Niobe of nations? 4. Upon what site was Rome built? 5. What "double night" rests upon Rome? 6. What ancient Grecian exclaimed "Eureka," and why? 7. What great men of Rome are mentioned in verse 5? 8. What is narrated of Sylla in verses 6 and 7? 9. Is Rome a mere mass of ruins, or are these descriptions of parts of the city? 10. In verse 10, what moral is drawn from the rehearsal of the past? 11. What beautiful metaphor is found in verse 11? 12. What is said of the imperial urn, and what fact is referred to? 13. What is said of the Forum? 14. What was the Forum? 15. What was the Tarpeian?

SPELL AND DEFINE. 1. cypress 2. fragile 3. crownless 4. voiceless 5. sepulchres 6. barbarian 7. fragments 8. lunar 9. stumbling 10. recollections 11. hundred 12. triumphs 13. triumphant 14. annihilated 15. dictatorial 16. o'er-canopied 17. harmony 18. palatine 19. subterranean 20. rehearsal 21. pyramid 22. Tarpeian

LESSON XCII

Rebellion in Massachusetts State Prison — Buckingham

RULE. Be careful not to slip over or mispronounce the small words.

A more impressive exhibition of moral courage, opposed to the wildest ferocity under the most appalling circumstances, was never seen than that which was witnessed by the officers of our state prison in the rebellion which occurred about five years ago.

Three convicts had been sentenced under the rules of the prison to be whipped in the yard, and by some effort of one of the other prisoners, a door had been opened at midday, communicating with the great dining hall and through the warden's lodge with the street.

The dining hall is long, dark, and damp from its situation near the surface of the ground. In this all the prisoners assembled with clubs and such tools as they could seize in passing through the workshops. Knives, hammers, and chisels, with every variety of such weapons, were in the hands of the ferocious spirits who are drawn away from their encroachments on society, forming a congregation of strength, vileness, and talent that can hardly be equaled on earth, even among the famed brigands of Italy.

Men of all ages and characters, guilty of every variety of infamous crime, dressed in the motley and peculiar garb of the institution and displaying the wild and demoniac appearance that always pertains to imprisoned wretches, were gathered together for the single purpose of preventing the punishment which was to be inflicted on the morrow upon their comrades.

The warden, the surgeon, and some other officers of the prison were there at the time and were alarmed at the consequences likely to ensue from the conflict necessary to restore order. They huddled together and could scarcely be said to consult, as the stoutest among them lost all presence of mind in overwhelming fear. The news rapidly spread through the town, and a subordinate officer, of most mild and kind disposition, hurried to the scene and came calm and collected into the midst of the officers. The most equable tempered and the mildest man in the government was in this hour of peril the firmest.

He instantly dispatched a request to Major Wainwright, commander of the marines stationed at the navy yard, for assistance and declared his purpose to enter into the hall and try the force of firm demeanor and persuasion upon the enraged multitude.

All his brethren exclaimed against an attempt so full of hazard, but in vain. They offered him arms, a sword and pistols, but he refused them. He said that he had no fear, and in case of danger, arms would do him no service. Alone, with only a little rattan, which was his usual walking stick, he advanced into the hall to hold parley with the selected, congregated, and enraged villains of the whole commonwealth.

He demanded their purpose in thus coming together with arms, in violation of the prison laws. They replied that they were determined to obtain the remission of the punishment of their three comrades. He said it was impossible; the rules of the prison must be obeyed, and they must submit.

At the hint of submission they drew a little nearer together and prepared their weapons for service. They were dimly seen in the further end of the hall by those who observed from the gratings that opened up to the day, and a more appalling sight cannot be conceived, nor one of more moral grandeur, than that of the single man standing within their grasp and exposed to be torn limb from limb instantly if a word or look should add to the already intense excitement.

That excitement, too, was of a most dangerous kind. It broke not forth in noise and imprecations but was seen only in the dark looks and the strained nerves that showed a deep determination. The officer expostulated. He reminded them of the hopelessness of escape, that the town was alarmed and that the government of the prison would submit to nothing but unconditional surrender. He said that all those who would go quietly away should be forgiven for this offense, but that if every prisoner were killed in the contest, power enough would be obtained to enforce the regulations of the prison.

They replied that they expected that some would be killed, that death would be better than such imprisonment, and with that look and tone which bespeaks an indomitable purpose, they declared that not a man should leave the hall alive till the flogging was remitted. At this period of the discussion, their evil passions seemed to be more inflamed, and one or two offered to destroy the officer, who still stood firmer and with a more temperate pulse than did his friends who saw from above but who could not avert the danger that threatened him.

Just at this moment, about fifteen minutes from the commencement of the tumult, the officer saw the feet of the marines, whose presence alone he relied on for succor, filing by the small upper lights. Without any apparent anxiety, he had repeatedly turned his attention to their approach. Now he knew that it was his only time to escape, before a conflict for life became, as was expected, one of the most dark and dreadful in the world.

He stepped slowly backwards, still urging them to depart before the officers were driven to use the last resort of firearms. When he was within three or four feet of the door, it was opened, and closed instantly again as he sprang through and was thus unexpectedly restored to his friends.

Major Wainwright was requested to order his men to fire down upon the convicts through the little windows, first with powder and then with ball, till they were willing to retreat. But he took a wiser as well as a bolder course, relying upon the effect which firm determination would have upon men so critically situated. He ordered the door to again be opened and marched in at the head of twenty or thirty men who filed through the passage and formed at the end of the hall, opposite to the crowd of criminals huddled together at the other.

He stated that he was empowered to quell the rebellion, that he wished to avoid shedding blood, but that he should not quit that hall alive until every convict had returned to his duty. They seemed balancing the strength of the two parties and replied that some of them were ready to die and only waited for an attack to see which was the most powerful, swearing that they would fight to the last unless the punishment were remitted, for they would not submit to any such punishment in the prison. Major Wainwright ordered his marines to load their pieces, and that they might not be suspected of trifling, each man was made to hold up to view the bullet which he afterwards put in his gun.

This only caused a growl of determination, and no one blenched or seemed disposed to shrink from the foremost exposure. They knew that their number would enable them to bear down and destroy the handful of marines after the first discharge and before their pieces could be reloaded. Again they were ordered to retire, but they answered with more ferocity than ever. The marines were ordered to take their aim so as to be sure and kill as many as possible. Their guns were presented, but not a prisoner stirred except to grasp more firmly his weapon.

Still desirous to avoid such a tremendous slaughter as must have followed the discharge of a single gun, Major Wainwright advanced a step or two and spoke even more firmly than before, urging them to depart. Again, and while looking directly into the muzzles of the guns which they had seen loaded with ball, they declared their intention "to fight it out." This intrepid officer then took out his watch and told his men to hold their pieces aimed at the convicts but not to fire until they had orders. Then, turning to the prisoners, he said, "You must leave this hall — I give you three minutes to decide. If at the end of that time a man remains, he shall be shot dead."

No situation of greater interest than this can be conceived. At one end of the hall a fearful multitude of the most desperate and powerful men in existence waiting for the assault — at the other, a little band of disciplined men waiting with arms presented and ready, upon the least motion or sign, to begin the carnage, their tall and imposing commander holding up his watch to count the lapse of three minutes given as the reprieve to the lives of hundreds. No poet or painter can conceive of a spectacle of more dark and terrible sublimity. No human heart can conceive a situation of more appalling suspense.

For two minutes not a person nor a muscle was moved, not a sound was heard in the unwonted stillness of the prison except the labored breathings of the infuriated wretches as they began to pant between fear and revenge. At the expiration of two minutes, during which they had faced the ministers of death with unblenching eyes, two or three of those in the rear and nearest the further entrance went slowly out. A few more followed the example, dropping out quietly and deliberately. Before half of the last minute had gone, every man was struck by the panic and crowded for an exit. The hall was cleared as if by magic. Thus the steady firmness of moral force and the strong effect of determination, acting deliberately, awed the most savage men and suppressed a scene of carnage which would have instantly followed the least precipitancy or exertion of physical force.

QUESTIONS. 1. What is the use of the state prison? 2. Where is the penitentiary of this state?   3. What accounts for the conduct of the subordinate officer who, though ordinarily the mildest, was on this occasion the firmest?   4. Suppose Major Wainwright had fired through the windows as he was advised, what would have been, in all probability, the result?   5. Narrate the substance of the final two paragraphs. 6. What gained this bloodless victory?

SPELL AND DEFINE. 1. impressive   2. ferocity   3. appalling 4. rebellion   5. encroachment   6. brigands   7. motley   8. demoniac 9. warden   10. subordinate   11. demeanor   12. expostulated 13. indomitable   14. empowered   15. blenched   16. sublimity 17. precipitancy

LESSON XCIII

The Life and Death of King John (Act 4, Scene 1) —
Shakespeare

RULE. When two or more consonants come together, let the pupil be careful to sound every one distinctly.

EXERCISES UNDER THE RULE. He clenched his *fists*. He *lifts* his awful form. He makes his *payments*. Thou *smoothed'st* his rugged path. The *president's speech*.

Hubert. Heat me these irons hot, and look thou stand
Within the arras. When I strike my foot
Upon the bosom of the ground, rush forth
And bind the boy which you shall find with me
Fast to the chair. Be heedful. Hence, and watch.
   First Executioner. I hope your warrant will bear out the deed.
   Hub. Uncleanly scruples! fear not you. Look to't.
                                  [Exeunt Executioners.]
Young lad, come forth; I have to say with you.
                                     [Enter Arthur.]
   Arth. Good morrow, Hubert.
   Hub. Good morrow, little prince.
   Arth. As little prince, having so great a title
To be more prince, as may be. You are sad.
   Hub. Indeed I have been merrier.
   Arth.   Mercy on me!
Methinks nobody should be sad but I.
Yet I remember, when I was in France,
Young gentlemen would be as sad as night,
Only for wantonness. By my christendom,
So I were out of prison and kept sheep,
I should be merry as the day is long;
And so I would be here, but that I doubt
My uncle practices more harm to me.

He is afraid of me and I of him.
Is it my fault that I was Geffrey's son?
No indeed is't not; and I would to heaven
I were your son, so you would love me, Hubert.

Hub. [*Aside.*] If I talk to him, with his innocent prate
He will awake my mercy, which lies dead;
Therefore I will be sudden, and dispatch.

Arth. Are you sick, Hubert? You look pale to-day.
In sooth, I would you were a little sick,
That I might sit all night and watch with you.
I warrant I love you more than you do me.

Hub. [*Aside.*] His words do take possession of my bosom.
Read here, young Arthur. [*Showing a paper.*]
                    [*Aside.*] How now, foolish rheum?
Turning dispiteous torture out of door?
I must be brief, lest resolution drop
Out at mine eyes in tender womanish tears. —
Can you not read it? Is it not fair writ?

Arth. Too fairly, Hubert, for so foul effect.
Must you with hot irons burn out both mine eyes?

Hub. Young boy, I must.

Arth.   And will you?

Hub.   And I will.

Arth. Have you the heart? When your head did but ache,
I knit my handkerchief about your brows
(The best I had, a princess wrought it me)
And I did never ask it you again;
And with my hand at midnight held your head;
And like the watchful minutes to the hour,
Still and anon cheer'd up the heavy time,
Saying, "What lack you?" and "Where lies your grief?"
Or "What good love may I perform for you?"
Many a poor man's son would have lien still,
And ne'er have spoke a loving word to you;
But you at your sick service had a prince.
Nay, you may think my love was crafty love,
And call it cunning. Do, and if you will;

If heaven be pleas'd that you should use me ill,
Why then you must. Will you put out mine eyes,
These eyes that never did nor never shall
So much as frown on you?

Hub. I have sworn to do it;
And with hot irons must I burn them out.

Arth. Ah, none but in this iron age would do it!
The iron of itself, though heat red-hot,
Approaching near these eyes, would drink my tears,
And quench its fiery indignation,
Even in the matter of mine innocence;
Nay, after that, consume away in rust,
But for containing fire to harm mine eye.
Are you more stubborn-hard than hammer'd iron?
And if an angel should have come to me
And told me Hubert should put out mine eyes,
I would not have believ'd him — no tongue but Hubert's.

Hub. Come forth.   [*Stamps.*]
                    [*Enter Executioners with cord, irons, etc.*]
Do as I bid you do.

Arth. O, save me, Hubert, save me! My eyes are out
Even with the fierce looks of the bloody men.

Hub. Give me the iron, I say, and bind him here.

Arth. Alas, what need you be so boist'rous-rough?
I will not struggle, I will stand stone-still.
For heaven sake, Hubert, let me not be bound!
Nay, hear me, Hubert, drive these men away,
And I will sit as quiet as a lamb;
I will not stir, nor wince, nor speak a word,
Nor look upon the iron angrily.
Thrust but these men away, and I'll forgive you,
What ever torment you do put me to.

Hub. Go stand within; let me alone with him.

First Exec. I am best pleas'd to be from such a deed.
                    [*Exeunt Executioners.*]

Arth. Alas, I then have chid away my friend!
He hath a stern look, but a gentle heart.

Let him come back, that his compassion may
Give life to yours.

  Hub.   Come, boy, prepare yourself.

  Arth. Is there no remedy?

  Hub.   None, but to lose your eyes.

  Arth. O heaven! that there were but a mote in yours,
A grain, a dust, a gnat, a wandering hair,
Any annoyance in that precious sense!
Then feeling what small things are boisterous there,
Your vile intent must needs seem horrible.

  Hub. Is this your promise? Go to, hold your tongue.

  Arth. Hubert, the utterance of a brace of tongues
Must needs want pleading for a pair of eyes.
Let me not hold my tongue, let me not, Hubert;
Or, Hubert, if you will, cut out my tongue,
So I may keep mine eyes. O, spare mine eyes,
Though to no use but still to look on you!
Lo, by my troth, the instrument is cold,
And would not harm me.

  Hub.   I can heat it, boy.

  Arth. No, in good sooth; the fire is dead with grief,
Being create for comfort, to be us'd
In undeserv'd extremes. See else yourself,
There is no malice in this burning coal;
The breath of heaven hath blown his spirit out,
And strew'd repentant ashes on his head.

  Hub. But with my breath I can revive it, boy.

  Arth. And if you do, you will but make it blush
And glow with shame of your proceedings, Hubert.
Nay, it perchance will sparkle in your eyes;
And, like a dog that is compell'd to fight,
Snatch at his master that does tarre him on.
All things that you should use to do me wrong
Deny their office; only you do lack
That mercy which fierce fire and iron extends,
Creatures of note for mercy-lacking uses.

  Hub. Well, see to live; I will not touch thine eye

For all the treasure that thine uncle owes.
Yet I am sworn, and I did purpose, boy,
With this same very iron to burn them out.

Arth. O now you look like Hubert! All this while
You were disguis'd.

Hub.   Peace; no more. Adieu.
Your uncle must not know but you are dead.
I'll fill these dogged spies with false reports;
And, pretty child, sleep doubtless and secure
That Hubert, for the wealth of all the world,
Will not offend thee.

Arth.   O heaven! I thank you, Hubert.

Hub. Silence, no more. Go closely in with me;
Much danger do I undergo for thee.

QUESTIONS. 1. Who was Prince Arthur?   2. Where did he live?
3. Who was Hubert?   4. Who had instigated Hubert to perpetrate such
cruelty?   5. What does Hubert mean in saying, "How now, foolish rheum?"
6. Enumerate the motives by which the prince induces Hubert to spare
him.

SPELL AND DEFINE. 1. arras   2. exeunt   3. wantonness
4. dispiteous 5. indignation 6. boisterous 7. wince

LESSON XCIV

The Child's Inquiry — Doane

RULE. In reading poetry, be careful to avoid the singsong tone which
is made by marking too strongly with the voice all the accented syllables.
In the example, the fault will appear if the words italicized are strongly
accented.

EXAMPLE. Sweet *is* the *work* my *God* and *King*
                To *praise* thy *name*, give *thanks* and *sing*.

What is that, Mother?

                The lark, my child.

The morn has just looked out, and smiled,

When he starts from his humble grassy nest,

And is up and away with the dew on his breast,

And a hymn in his heart, to yon pure bright sphere

To warble it out in his Maker's ear.

Ever, my child, be thy morn's first lays,

Tuned, like the lark's, to thy Maker's praise.

What is that, Mother?

                The dove, my son.

And that low sweet voice, like a widow's moan,

Is flowing out from her gentle breast,

Constant and pure by that lonely nest,

As the wave is poured from some crystal urn,

For her distant dear one's quick return.

Ever, my son, be thou like the dove,

In friendship as faithful, as constant in love.

What is that, Mother?

                The eagle, my boy,

Proudly careering his course of joy,

Firm, in his own mountain vigor relying,

Breasting the dark storm, the red bolt defying.

His wing on the wind, and his eye on the sun,

He swerves not a hair, but bears onward, right on.

Boy, may the eagle's flight ever be thine,

Onward and upward, and true to the line.

What is that, Mother?

                The swan, my love.

He is floating down from his native grove,

No loved one now, no nestling nigh;

He is floating down by himself, to die.

Death darkens his eye, and unplumes his wings,

Yet his sweetest song is the last he sings.

Live so, my love, that when death shall come,
Swanlike and sweet may it waft thee home.

QUESTIONS. 1. May we not often derive useful instruction from
observation of nature? 2. What lesson is drawn from the lark? 3. What
from the dove? 4. The eagle? 5. The swan? 6. What beautiful figure in
verse 2?

SPELL AND DEFINE. 1. sphere 2. warble 3. friendship 4. careering
5. swerves 6. nestling 7. unplumes

LESSON XCV

*Christian Hymn of Triumph (from "The Martyr of Anti-
och")* — Milman

RULE. In reading poetry that rhymes, there should be a slight pause
after the words that rhyme, even when the sense does not require it.

Sing to the Lord! let harp and lute and voice,
Up to the expanding gates of heaven rejoice,
    While the bright martyrs to their rest are borne!
Sing to the Lord! their blood-stained course is run,
And every head its diadem hath won,
    Rich as the purple of the summer morn —
Sing the triumphant champions of their God,
While burn their mounting feet along their skyward
        road.

Sing to the Lord! for her, in beauty's prime,
Snatched from this wintry earth's ungenial clime,
    In the eternal spring of paradise to bloom;
For her the world displayed its brightest treasure,
And the airs panted with the songs of pleasure.
    Before earth's throne she chose the lowly tomb,

The vale of tears with willing footsteps trod,
Bearing her cross with thee, incarnate Son of God.

Sing to the Lord! it is not shed in vain,
The blood of martyrs! from its freshening rain
    High springs the church like some fount-shadowing
        palm:
The nations crowd beneath its branching shade,
Of its green leaves are kingly diadems made,
    And, wrapt within its deep, embosoming calm,
Earth shrinks to slumber like the breezeless deep,
And war's tempestuous vultures fold their wings and
    sleep.

Sing to the Lord! no more the angels fly —
Far in the bosom of the stainless sky —
    The sound of fierce, licentious sacrifice.
From shrin'd alcove and stately pedestal,
The marble gods in cumbrous ruin fall;
    Headless, in dust, the awe of nations lies;
Jove's thunder crumbles in his moldering hand,
And mute as sepulchres the hymnless temples stand.

QUESTIONS. 1. Explain the last line of the first verse. 2. Explain the last line of the second. 3. With what propriety can vultures be called "tempestuous"? 4. Who is "Jove"?

SPELL AND DEFINE. 1. triumphant   2. champion   3. skyward
.4. ungenial   5. incarnate   6. diadem   7. tempestuous   8. vultures
9. licentious 10. alcove 11. pedestal 12. cumbrous 13. sepulchres

LESSON XCVI

Charles de Moor's Remorse — Schiller

RULE. When similar sounds come at the end of one word and the beginning of the next word, they must not be blended into one.

EXERCISES. Malice seeks to destroy. The breeze sighs softly. The ice slowly melts.

I must rest here. My joints are shaken asunder. My tongue cleaves to my mouth, it is dry as a potsherd. I would beg of some of you to fetch me a little water in the hollow of your hand, from yonder brook, but all of you are weary to death.

How glorious, how majestic yonder setting sun! 'Tis thus the hero falls, 'tis thus he dies — in godlike majesty! When I was a boy, a mere child, it was my favorite thought to live and die like that sun.

'Twas an idle thought, a boy's conceit. There was a time — leave me, my friends, alone — there was a time when I could not sleep if I had forgotten my prayers. Oh, that I were a child once more!

What a lovely evening, what a pleasing landscape. That scene is noble, this world is beautiful, the earth is grand! I am hideous in this world of beauty — a monster on this magnificent earth — the prodigal son. My innocence! Oh, my innocence! All nature expands at the sweet breath of spring, but, O God, this paradise — this heaven is a hell to me! All is happiness around me, all in the sweet spirit of peace; the world is one family, but its Father there above is not my father.

I am an outcast — the prodigal son, the companion of murderers, of viperous fiends, bound down enchained to guilt and horror! Oh, that I could return once more to peace and innocence, that I hung an infant on the breast, that I were born a beggar — the meanest kind — a peasant of the field.

I would toil, till the sweat of blood dropped from my brow, to purchase the luxury of one sound sleep, the rapture of a single tear. There was a time when I could weep with ease. Oh, days of bliss! Oh, mansion of my fathers! Scenes of my infant years, enjoyed by fond enthusiasm, will you no more return? Will you no more exhale your sweets to cool this burning bosom?

O never, never shall they return. No more shall they refresh this bosom with the breath of peace. They are gone, gone forever!

QUESTIONS. 1. Who was Schiller? 2. Can you conceive of a being so wretched as here represented?

SPELL AND DEFINE. 1. potsherd   2. majestic   3. favorite
4. landscape   5. hideous   6. magnificent   7. innocence   8. outcast
9. viperous   10. enchained   11. luxury   12. rapture   13. mansion
14. enthusiasm 15. refresh

LESSON XCVII

Value of Mathematics — E. D. Mansfield

RULE. Be careful to give the right sound to the vowels.

Man may construct his works by irregular and uncertain rules, but God has made an unerring law for his whole creation, and made it, too, in respect to the physical system, upon principles which, as far as we now know, can never be understood without the aid of mathematics.

Let us suppose a youth who despises, as many do, these *cold* and *passionless abstractions of mathematics.* Yet, he is intellectual; he loves knowledge. He would explore nature and know the reason of things, but he would do it without aid from this *rigid, syllogistic, measuring, calculating science.* He seeks, indeed, no "royal road to geometry," but he seeks one not less difficult to find, in which geometry is not needed.

He begins with mechanics. He takes the lever and readily understands that a weight will move it, but the principle upon which *different* weights, at *different* distances, move it, he is forbidden to know, for *they* depend upon *ratios* and *proportions.* He passes to the inclined plane but quits it in disgust when he finds its action depends upon the relations of angles and triangles. The screw is still worse, and when he comes to the wheel and axle, he gives them up forever; they are *all mathematical!*

He would investigate the laws of falling bodies and moving fluids and would know why their motion is *accelerated* at different periods and upon what their momentum depends. But roots and squares, lines, angles and curves float before him in the mazy dance of a disturbed intellect. The very first proposition is a mystery, and he soon discovers that mechanics is little better than mathematics itself.

However, he still has his *senses;* he will, at least, not be indebted to diagrams and equations for their enjoyment. He gazes with admiration upon the phenomena of light, the many-colored rainbow upon the bosom of the clouds, the clouds themselves reflected with all their changing shades from the surface of the quiet waters. Whence comes this beautiful imagery? He investigates and finds that every hue in the rainbow is made by a different *angle of refraction* and that each ray reflected from the mirror has its angle of incidence equal to its angle of reflection. As he pursues the subject further, in the construction of lenses and telescopes, the whole family of triangles, ratios, proportions, and conclusions arise to alarm his excited vision.

He turns to the heavens and is charmed with its shining host moving in solemn procession "through the halls of the sky," each star, as it rises and sets, marking time on the records of nature. He would know the structure of this beautiful system and search out, if possible, the laws which regulate those distant lights. But Astronomy forever banishes him from her presence; she will have none near her to whom mathematics is not a *familiar friend.* What can *he* know of her parallaxes, anomalies, and precessions, who has never studied the conic sections or the higher orders of analysis? She sends him to some wooden orrery from which he may gather as much knowledge of the heavenly bodies as a child does of armies from the gilded troopers of the toy shop.

If he can have no companionship with optics nor astronomy nor mechanics, there *are* sciences, he thinks, which have better taste and less austerity of manners. He flies to chemistry, and her garments float loosely around him. For a while he goes gloriously on, illuminated by the *red lights* and *blue lights* of crucibles and retorts. But soon he comes to compound bodies, to the composition of the elements around him, and finds them all in fixed relations. He finds that gases and fluids will combine with each other and with solids only in a certain *ratio* and that all possible compounds are formed by nature in *immutable proportion.* Then starts up the whole doctrine of chemical equivalents, and mathematics again stares him in the face.

Affrighted, he flies to mineralogy. Stones he may pick up, jewels he may draw from the bosom of the earth and be no longer alarmed at the stern visage of this terrible science. Even here, however, he is not safe. The first stone that he finds — quartz — contains a *crystal,* and that crystal assumes the dreaded form of geometry. Crystallization allures him on. As he goes, cubes and hexagons, pyramids and dodecagons arise before him in beautiful array. He would understand more about them but must wait at the portal of the temple until introduced within by that honored of time and science, our friendly *Euclid.*

So now, where shall this student of nature, without the aid of mathematics, go for his knowledge or his enjoyments? Is it to natural history? The very *birds* cleave the air in the form of the cycloid, and mathematics proves it the *best.* Their feathers are formed upon calculated mechanical principles; the muscles of their frame are moved by them. The cell of the little bee is constructed in the very geometrical figure and with the precise angles which mathematicians, after ages of investigation, have demonstrated to be that which contain the *greatest economy of space and strength.*

Yes, he who would shun mathematics must fly the bounds of "flaming space," and in the realms of chaos, that "dark, illimitable ocean" where Milton's Satan wandered from the wrath of heaven, he may *possibly* find some spot visited by no figure of geometry and no harmony of proportion. But nature, this beautiful creation of God, has no resting place for him. All its construction is *mathematical,* all its uses *reasonable,* all its ends *harmonious.* It has no elements mixed without regulated law, no broken chord to make a false note in the music of the spheres.

QUESTIONS. 1. How is it illustrated that without mathematics it is impossible for the student to understand the principles of the physical system? 2. Suppose he turns to mechanics? 3. Suppose he trusts to the senses? 4. Turns to chemistry? 5. To mineralogy? 6. To natural history?

SPELL AND DEFINE. 1. mathematics 2. syllogistic 3. abstractions 4. geometry 5. accelerated 6. proportions 7. momentum 8. mechanics 9. diagrams 10. equations 11. phenomena 12. imagery 13. refraction 14. telescopes 15. parallaxes 16. anomalies 17. precessions 18. companionship 19. composition 20. immutably 21. cycloid 22. illimitable

LESSON XCVIII

Value of Mathematics — continued

RULE. Do not slide over the little words nor omit any syllable of any word.

Let us take *another student,* with whom mathematics is neither despised nor neglected. He sees in it the means of past success to others, he reads in its history the progress of universal improvement, and he believes that what has contributed so much to the civilization of the world, what is even now contributing so much to all that humanizes society and what the experience of all mankind has sanctioned, *may,* perchance, be useful to his own intellectual development.

He opens a volume of geometry and steadily pursues its abstractions from the definition of a line through the elegant properties of the right triangle, the relations of similar figures, and the laws of curved surfaces. He finds a chain of *unbroken* and *impregnable* reasoning and is at once possessed of all the knowledge of postulates, syllogisms, and conclusions which the most accomplished school of rhetoric could have taught him.

He looks upon society, and wherever he turns, arts, sciences, and their results — from carpentry to civil engineering, from architecture to hydraulics, from the ingenious lock upon a canal to the useful mill upon its sides — disclose their operations, no longer mysterious to his enlightened understanding. Many an interesting repository of knowledge this key has opened to his vision, and as he thus walks through the *vestibule* of science, he longs to penetrate those deep aisles and ascend that magnificent stairway which lead up to the structure of the universe.

With the properties of the ellipsis, the laws of motion demonstrated by mathematics, and two facts drawn from observation (that bodies fall towards the earth and that the motion of the planets is regular), he demonstrates beyond the power of refutation the laws of the celestial system. He traces star after star, however eccentric its course, through the unseen immensity of space and calculates with unfailing certainty the hour of its return, after ages have passed away.

He does more. He weighs matter in the balances of creation and finds that to complete the harmony of the system, a planet is wanting in some distant corner of its wide domain. No mortal eye has ever seen it, no tradition tells of its existence. Yet, with the confidence and zeal of prophecy, he announces that it *must exist,* for *demonstration has proved it.* The prediction is recorded in the volume of science.

Long after, astronomy, by the aid of mathematics, discovers the long lost tenant of the skies, fractured though it be, while its members perform their revolution. No living soul can be permitted to doubt the worth of mathematics or the powers of his own immortal mind.

What were the glorious contemplations of that pupil of mathematical philosophy as he passed behind the clouds of earth to investigate the machinery of celestial spheres! Alone, yet not solitary, amid the glowing lights of heaven, he sends his spirit forth through the works of God. He has risen by the force of cultivated intellect to heights which mortal fancy had never reached.

He has taken line and figure and measure, and from proposition to proposition and from conclusion to conclusion, riveting link after link, he has bound the universe to the throne of its Creator by that "golden, everlasting chain, whose strong embrace holds heaven and earth and main."

Is there no *moral* instruction in this? Does he learn no lesson of wisdom? Do no strong emotions of love and gratitude arise towards that Supreme Being who thus delights him with the charms of intellectual enjoyment and blesses him with the multiplied means of happiness? *Harder* than the adamant of his own reasoning, *colder* than the abstractions in which he is *falsely* supposed to move must be he who thus conducted by the handmaid of the arts and sciences through whatever humanizes man, through whatever is sublime in his progress to a higher state, through all the vast machinery which the Almighty has made tributary to his comfort and happiness, feels no livelier sentiment of duty towards Him, no kinder or more peaceful spirit towards his fellow man.

QUESTIONS. 1. In what light does the student regard mathematics? 2. Can you sketch his career?   3. What is the moral instruction to be derived from this?

SPELL AND DEFINE. 1. civilization 2. humanizes 3. impregnable 4. postulates   5. accomplished   6. engineering   7. architecture

8. hydraulics   9. vestibule   10. ellipsis   11. demonstrated   12. prophecy
13. universe   14. adamant

LESSON XCIX

Washing Day — Mrs. Hemans

RULE. In reading poetry that does not rhyme, there should be no
pause at the end of a line except when it terminates with an important
word or the sense requires it.

The Muses are turned gossips; they have lost
The buskined step and clear high-sounding phrase,
Language of gods. Come then, domestic Muse,
In slipshod measure loosely prattling on
Of farm or orchard, pleasant curds and cream,
Or drowning flies, or shoe lost in the mire
By little whimpering boy with rueful face;
Come, Muse, and sing the dreaded Washing Day.
Ye who beneath the yoke of wedlock bend,
With bowed soul, full well ye know the day
Which week, smooth sliding after week, brings on
Too soon — for to that day no peace belongs
Nor comfort — ere the first gray streak of dawn,
The red-armed washers come and chase repose.
Nor pleasant smile, nor quaint device of mirth,
E'er visited that day; the very cat,
From the wet kitchen scared, and reeking hearth,
Visits the parlor — an unwonted guest.
The silent breakfast meal is soon dispatched,
Uninterrupted, save by anxious looks
Cast at the lowering sky, if sky should lower.
From that last evil, O preserve us, heavens!
For should the skies pour down, adieu to all
Remains of quiet; then expect to hear

Of sad disasters — dirt and gravel stains
Hard to efface, and loaded lines at once
Snapped short, and linen horse by dog thrown down,
And all the petty miseries of life.
Saints have been calm while stretched upon the rack,
And Guatimozin smiled on burning coals;
But never yet did housewife notable
Greet with a smile a rainy washing day.
But grant the welkin fair, require not thou
Who call'st thyself perchance the master there,
Or study swept, or nicely dusted coat,
Or usual 'tendance — ask not, indiscreet,
Thy stockings mended, though the yawning rents
Gape wide as Erebus; nor hope to find
Some snug recess impervious. Shouldst thou try
The 'customed garden walks, thine eye shall rue
The budding fragrance of thy tender shrubs,
Myrtle or rose, all crushed beneath the weight
Of coarse checked apron, with impatient hand
Twitched off when showers impend; or crossing lines
Shall mar thy musings, as the wet cold sheet
Flaps in thy face abrupt. Woe to the friend
Whose evil stars have urged him forth to claim
On such a day the hospitable rites!
Looks, blank at best, and stinted courtesy,
Shall he receive. Vainly he feeds his hopes
With dinner of roast chickens, savory pie,
Or tart or pudding; pudding he nor tart
That day shall eat, nor, though the husband try,
Mending what can't be helped, to kindle mirth
From cheer deficient, shall his consort's brow
Clear up propitious. The unlucky guest
In silence dines, and early slinks away.
I well remember when a child, the awe
This day struck into me; for then the maids,
I scarce knew why, looked cross, and drove me from
    them.

Nor soft caress could I obtain, nor hope
Usual indulgences; jelly or creams,
Relic of costly suppers, and set by
For me their petted one, or buttered toast,
When butter was forbid, or thrilling tale
Of ghost or witch or murder — so I went
And sheltered me beside the parlor fire.
There my dear grandmother, eldest of forms,
Tended the little ones, and watched from harm,
Anxiously fond, though oft her spectacles
With elfin cunning hid, and oft the pins
Drawn from her raveled stockings, might have soured
One less indulgent.
At intervals my mother's voice was heard,
Urging dispatch: briskly the work went on,
All hands employed to wash, to rinse, to wring,
To fold, and starch, and clap, and iron, and plait.
Then would I sit me down and ponder much
Why washings were. Sometimes through hollow bowl
Of pipe amused we blew, and sent aloft
The floating bubbles; little dreaming then
To see, Mongolfier, thy silken ball
Ride buoyant through the clouds — so near approach
The sports of children and the toils of men.

QUESTIONS. 1. What is meant by "buskined step"?   2. Who was
Guatimozin? What was his history?   3. What was Erebus?   4. Who was
Mongolfier?

SPELL AND DEFINE. 1. muses 2. gossips 3. whimpering 4. quaint
5. device   6. reeking   7. dispatched   8. uninterrupted   9. efface
10. housewife 11. welkin 12. impervious 13. musings 14. propitious
15. indulgences 16. elfin 17. buoyant

LESSON C

Capturing the Wild Horse — W. Irving

RULE. When similar sounds come at the end of one word and at the beginning of the next word, they must not be blended into one.

EXERCISES. He sinks sorrowing to the tomb. Man loves society. Time flies swiftly. The birds sing.

We left the buffalo camp about eight o'clock and had a toilsome and harassing march of two hours over ridges of hills covered with a ragged forest of scrub oaks and broken by deep gullies.

About ten o'clock in the morning, we came to where this line of rugged hills swept down into a valley, through which flowed the north fork of the Red River. A beautiful meadow, about half a mile wide and enameled with yellow autumnal flowers, stretched for two or three miles along the foot of the hills. The meadow was bordered on the opposite side by the river, whose banks were fringed with cottonwood trees, the bright foliage of which refreshed and delighted the eye after being wearied by the contemplation of monotonous wastes of brown forest.

The meadow was finely diversified by groves and clumps of trees so happily disposed that they seemed as if set out by the hand of art. As we cast our eyes over this fresh and delightful valley, we beheld a troop of wild horses quietly grazing on a green lawn, about a mile distant to our right. To our left, at nearly the same distance, were several buffaloes, some feeding, others reposing and ruminating among the high, rich herbage under the shade of a clump of cottonwood trees. The whole had the appearance of a broad, beautiful tract of pastureland on the highly ornamented estate of some gentleman farmer, with his cattle grazing about the lawns and meadows.

A council of war was now held, and it was determined to profit by the present favorable opportunity and try our hand at the grand hunting maneuver which is called "ringing the wild horse." This requires a large party of horsemen, well mounted.

They extend themselves in each direction, at certain distances apart, and gradually form a ring of two or three miles in circumference, so as to surround the game. This must be done with extreme care, for the wild horse is the most readily alarmed inhabitant of the prairie and can scent a hunter at a great distance if to windward.

The ring being formed, two or three ride toward the horses, which start off in an opposite direction. Whenever they approach the bounds of the ring, however, a huntsman presents himself and turns them from their course. In this way, they are checked and driven back at every point and kept galloping round and round this magic circle until, being completely tired down, it is easy for the hunters to ride up beside them and throw the lariat over their heads. The prime horses of the most speed, courage, and bottom, however, are apt to break through and escape, so that, in general, it is the second rate horses that are taken.

Preparations were now made for a hunt of this kind. The pack horses were now taken into the woods and firmly tied to trees, lest in a rush of wild horses they should break away.

Twenty-five men were then sent, under the command of a lieutenant, to steal along the edge of the valley, within the strip of wood that skirted the hills. They were to station themselves about fifty yards apart, within the edge of the woods, and not advance or show themselves until the horses dashed in that direction. Twenty-five men were sent across the valley to steal in like manner along the riverbank that bordered the opposite side and to station themselves among the trees.

A third party of about the same number was to form a line stretching across the lower part of the valley, so as to connect the two wings. Beatte and our other half-breed, Antoine, together with the ever officious Tonish, were to make a circuit through the woods so as to get to the upper part of the valley, in the rear of the horses, and drive them forward into the kind of sack that we had formed, while the two wings should join behind them and make a complete circle.

The flanking parties were quietly extending themselves out of sight on each side of the valley, and the residue were stretching themselves like the links of a chain across it, when the wild horses gave signs that they scented an enemy — snuffing the air, snorting, and looking about. At length, they pranced off slowly toward the river and disappeared behind a green bank.

Here, had the regulations of the chase been observed, they would have been quietly checked and turned back by the advance of a hunter from among the trees. Unfortunately, however, we had our wildfire, jack-o'-lantern little Frenchman to deal with.

Instead of keeping quietly up the right side of the valley to get above the horses, the moment he saw them move toward the river, he broke out of the covert of woods and dashed furiously across the plain in pursuit of them. This put an end to all system. The half-breeds and a half a score of rangers joined in the chase.

Away they all went over the green bank. In a moment or two the wild horses reappeared and came thundering down the valley, with Frenchman, half-breeds, and rangers galloping and yelling behind them. It was in vain and the line drawn across the valley attempted to check and turn back the fugitives; they were too hotly pressed by their pursuers. In their panic, they dashed through the line and clattered down the plain.

The whole troop joined in the headlong chase, some of the rangers without hats or caps, their hair flying about their ears, and others with handkerchiefs tied round their heads. The buffaloes, which had been calmly ruminating among the herbage, heaved up their huge forms, gazed for a moment at the tempest that came scouring down the meadow, then turned and took to heavy rolling flight. They were soon overtaken. The promiscuous throng was pressed together by the contracting sides of the valley. Away they went, pell-mell, hurry-scurry, wild buffalo, wild horse, wild huntsman, with clang and clatter and whoop and halloo that made the forest ring.

At length, the buffaloes turned into a green brake on the riverbank while the horses dashed up a narrow defile of the hills with their pursuers close at their heels. Beatte passed several of them, having fixed his eye upon a fine Pawnee horse that had his ears slit and saddle marks upon his back.

He pressed him gallantly but lost him in the woods. Among the wild horses was a fine black mare, which in scrambling up the defile, tripped and fell. A young ranger sprang from his horse and seized her by the mane and muzzle. Another ranger dismounted and came to his assistance. The mare struggled fiercely, kicking and biting and striking with her forefeet, but a noose was slipped over her head, and her struggles were in vain.

It was some time, however, before she gave over rearing and plunging and lashing out with her feet on every side. The two rangers then led her along the valley by two strong lariats, which enabled them to keep at a sufficient distance on each side, to be out of the reach of her hoofs. Whenever she struck out in one direction, she was jerked in the other. In this way her spirit was gradually subdued.

As to Tonish, who had marred the whole scheme by his precipitancy, he had been more successful than he deserved, having managed to catch a beautiful cream colored colt, about seven months old, that had not strength to keep up with its companions. The mercurial little Frenchman was beside himself with exultation. It was amusing to see him with his prize. The colt would rear and kick and struggle to get free, when Tonish would take him about the neck, wrestle with him, jump on his back, and cut as many antics as a monkey with a kitten.

Nothing surprised me more, however, than to witness how soon these poor animals, thus taken from the unbounded freedom of the prairie, yielded to the dominion of man. In the course of two or three days, the mare and colt went with the lead horses and became quite docile.

QUESTIONS. 1. Near what river did this expedition commence? 2. Where is that river? 3. Describe the country, scenery, etc. 4. What animated objects presented themselves to view upon the right and the left? 5. To what is the whole scene compared? 6. What hunting maneuver was commenced? Describe it. 7. What is the lariat? 8. Describe the proceedings of the party in this maneuver. 9. What interrupted its successful completion? 10. Give the striking contrast between the flight of the wild horses and that of the buffaloes. 11. Describe the capture of the black mare. 12 What was the conduct of the captured animals in respect to being tamed? 13. Was not this cruel sport?

SPELL AND DEFINE. 1. buffalo   2. harassing   3. enameled 4. autumnal   5. contemplation   6. monotonous   7. ruminating 8. maneuver   9. circumference   10. windward   11. huntsman 12. preparations   13. flanking   14. regulations   15. wildfire   16. jack-o'-lantern   17. reappeared   18. handkerchief   19. scrambling   20. mercurial 21. exultation   22. unbounded   23. prairie

LESSON CI

The Gods of the Heathen — Psalm 115

RULE. Be careful and give a full sound to the vowels. Regard to this rule will correct the common flat, clipping, and uninteresting way in which many read.

EXERCISES.   Prolong the italicized vowels: H*ai*l! holy l*i*ght. We pr*ai*se thee, *O* Lord God.

These names of the Deity are seldom pronounced with that full and solemn sound that is proper. *Lud* and *Law-ard* and *Gud* and *Gawd* are too frequently used instead of the proper sounds. If the pupil can learn to speak the three words *O Lord God* properly, it will be worth no little attention. Every pupil ought to be exercised on these words till he pronounces them properly and in a full and solemn tone.

Not unto us, O Lord, not unto us,
But unto thy name give glory,
For thy mercy, and for thy truth's sake.
Wherefore should the heathen say,
Where is now their God?
But our God is in the heavens:
He hath done whatsoever he hath pleased.

Their idols are silver and gold,
The work of men's hands.
They have mouths, but they speak not:
Eyes have they, but they see not:
They have ears, but they hear not:
Noses have they, but they smell not:
They have hands, but they handle not:
Feet have they, but they walk not:
Neither speak they through their throat.
They that make them are like unto them;
So is every one that trusteth in them.

O Israel, trust thou in the Lord:
He is their help and their shield.
O house of Aaron, trust in the Lord:
He is their help and their shield.
Ye that fear the Lord, trust in the Lord:
He is their help and their shield.

The Lord hath been mindful of us: he will bless us;
He will bless the house of Israel;
He will bless the house of Aaron.

He will bless them that fear the Lord,
Both small and great.
The Lord shall increase you more and more,
You and your children.
Ye are blessed of the Lord
Which made heaven and earth.

The heaven, even the heavens, are the Lord's:
But the earth hath he given to the children of men.
The dead praise not the Lord,
Neither any that go down into silence.
But we will bless the Lord
From this time forth and for evermore,
Praise the Lord.

QUESTIONS. 1. What is the general sentiment intended to be inspired by this psalm? 2. What is the contrast made between the true God and the idols of the heathen?

SPELL AND DEFINE. 1. heathen   2. whatsoever   3. trusteth
4. increase 5. evermore

LESSON CII

The Fall of Babylon — Revelation 18:1–19:3

RULE. In reading anything solemn, a full, slow, and distinct manner should be preserved and particular attention paid to the stops.

Chapter 18

1 And after these things I saw another angel come down from heaven, having great power; and the earth was lightened with his glory.

2 And he cried mightily with a strong voice, saying, Babylon the great is fallen, is fallen, and is become the

habitation of devils, and the hold of every foul spirit, and a cage of every unclean and hateful bird.

3 For all nations have drunk of the wine of the wrath of her fornication, and the kings of the earth have committed fornication with her, and the merchants of the earth are waxed rich through the abundance of her delicacies.

4 And I heard another voice from heaven, saying, Come out of her, my people, that ye be not partakers of her sins, and that ye receive not of her plagues.

5 For her sins have reached unto heaven, and God hath remembered her iniquities.

6 Reward her even as she rewarded you, and double unto her double according to her works: in the cup which she hath filled, fill to her double.

7 How much she hath glorified herself, and lived deliciously, so much torment and sorrow give her: for she saith in her heart, I sit a queen, and am no widow, and shall see no sorrow.

8 Therefore shall her plagues come in one day, death, and mourning, and famine; and she shall be utterly burned with fire: for strong is the Lord God who judgeth her.

9 And the kings of the earth, who have committed fornication and lived deliciously with her, shall bewail her, and lament for her, when they shall see the smoke of her burning,

10 Standing afar off for the fear of her torment, saying, Alas, alas, that great city Babylon, that mighty city! for in one hour is thy judgment come.

11 And the merchants of the earth shall weep and mourn over her; for no man buyeth their merchandise any more:

12 The merchandise of gold, and silver, and precious stones, and of pearls, and fine linen, and purple, and silk, and scarlet, and all thyine wood, and all manner vessels of ivory, and all manner vessels of most precious wood, and of brass, and iron, and marble,

13 And cinnamon, and odors, and ointments, and frank-incense, and wine, and oil, and fine flour, and wheat, and

beasts, and sheep, and horses, and chariots, and slaves, and souls of men.

14 And the fruits that thy soul lusted after are departed from thee, and all things which were dainty and goodly are departed from thee, and thou shalt find them no more at all.

15 The merchants of these things, which were made rich by her, shall stand afar off for the fear of her torment, weeping and wailing,

16 And saying, Alas, alas, that great city, that was clothed in fine linen, and purple, and scarlet, and decked with gold, and precious stones, and pearls!

17 For in one hour so great riches is come to naught. And every shipmaster, and all the company in ships, and sailors, and as many as trade by sea, stood afar off

18 And cried when they saw the smoke of her burning, saying, What city is like unto this great city!

19 And they cast dust on their heads, and cried, weeping and wailing, saying, Alas, alas, that great city, wherein were made rich all that had ships in the sea by reason of her costliness! for in one hour is she made desolate.

20 Rejoice over her, thou heaven, and ye holy apostles and prophets; for God hath avenged you on her.

21 And a mighty angel took up a stone like a great millstone, and cast it into the sea, saying, Thus with violence shall that great city Babylon be thrown down, and shall be found no more at all.

22 And the voice of harpers, and musicians, and of pipers, and trumpeters, shall be heard no more at all in thee; and no craftsman, of whatsoever craft he be, shall be found any more in thee; and the sound of a millstone shall be heard no more at all in thee;

23 And the light of a candle shall shine no more at all in thee; and the voice of the bridegroom and of the bride shall be heard no more at all in thee: for thy merchants were the great men of the earth; for by thy sorceries were all nations deceived.

24 And in her was found the blood of prophets, and of saints, and of all that were slain upon the earth.

Chapter 19

1 And after these things I heard a great voice of much people in heaven, saying, Alleluia; Salvation, and glory, and honor, and power, unto the Lord our God:

2 For true and righteous are his judgments; for he hath judged the great whore, which did corrupt the earth with her fornication, and hath avenged the blood of his servants at her hand.

3 And again they said, Alleluia. And her smoke rose up for ever and ever.

QUESTIONS. 1. By whom was Revelation written? 2. Where? 3. What city is designated by the name "Babylon"? 4. Why is this supposed? 5. Are these prophecies yet accomplished?

SPELL AND DEFINE. 1. devils 2. hateful 3. merchants 4. iniquities 5. bewail 6. merchandise 7. cinnamon 8. frankincense 9. ointments 10. desolate 11. alleluia

LESSON CIII

Antony's Oration over Caesar's Dead Body — Shakespeare

RULE. When similar sounds come at the end of one word and at the beginning of the next word, they must not be blended into one.

EXERCISES. He sinks sorrowing to the tomb. Man loves society. Time flies swiftly. The birds sing.

Friends, Romans, countrymen, lend me your ears!
I come to bury Caesar, not to praise him.
The evil that men do lives after them,

The good is oft interred with their bones;
So let it be with Caesar. The noble Brutus
Hath told you Caesar was ambitious;
If it were so, it was a grievous fault,
And grievously hath Caesar answer'd it.
Here, under leave of Brutus and the rest
(For Brutus is an honorable man,
So are they all, all honorable men),
Come I to speak in Caesar's funeral.
He was my friend, faithful and just to me;
But Brutus says he was ambitious,
And Brutus is an honorable man.
He hath brought many captives home to Rome,
Whose ransoms did the general coffers fill;
Did this in Caesar seem ambitious?
When that the poor have cried, Caesar hath wept;
Ambition should be made of sterner stuff:
Yet Brutus says he was ambitious,
And Brutus is an honorable man.
You all did see that on the Lupercal
I thrice presented him a kingly crown,
Which he did thrice refuse. Was this ambition?
Yet Brutus says he was ambitious,
And sure he is an honorable man.
I speak not to disprove what Brutus spoke,
But here I am to speak what I do know.
You all did love him once, not without cause;
What cause withholds you then to mourn for him?
O judgment! thou art fled to brutish beasts,
And men have lost their reason. Bear with me,
My heart is in the coffin there with Caesar,
And I must pause till it come back to me.

But yesterday the word of Caesar might
Have stood against the world; now lies he there,
And none so poor to do him reverence.
O masters! if I were dispos'd to stir

Your hearts and minds to mutiny and rage,
I should do Brutus wrong, and Cassius wrong,
Who (you all know) are honorable men.
I will not do them wrong; I rather choose
To wrong the dead, to wrong myself and you,
Than I will wrong such honorable men.
But here's a parchment with the seal of Caesar.
I found it in his closet, 'tis his will.
Let but the commons hear this testament —
Which, pardon me, I do not mean to read —
And they would go and kiss dead Caesar's wounds,
And dip their napkins in his sacred blood;
Yea, beg a hair of him for memory,
And dying, mention it within their wills,
Bequeathing it as a rich legacy
Unto their issue.

. . . .

    If you have tears, prepare to shed them now.
You all do know this mantle. I remember
The first time ever Caesar put it on;
'Twas on a summer's evening, in his tent,
That day he overcame the Nervii.
Look, in this place ran Cassius' dagger through;
See what a rent the envious Casca made;
Through this the well-beloved Brutus stabb'd,
And as he pluck'd his cursed steel away,
Mark how the blood of Caesar followed it,
As rushing out of doors to be resolv'd
If Brutus so unkindly knock'd or no;
For Brutus, as you know, was Caesar's angel.
Judge, O you gods, how dearly Caesar lov'd him!
This was the most unkindest cut of all;
For when the noble Caesar saw him stab,
Ingratitude, more strong than traitors' arms,
Quite vanquish'd him. Then burst his mighty heart,
And in his mantle muffling up his face,
Even at the base of Pompey's statue

(Which all the while ran blood) great Caesar fell.
O, what a fall was there, my countrymen!
Then I, and you, and all of us fell down,
Whilst bloody treason flourish'd over us.
O now you weep, and I perceive you feel
The dint of pity. These are gracious drops.
Kind souls, what, weep you when you but behold
Our Caesar's vesture wounded? Look you here,
Here is himself, marr'd as you see with traitors.

Good friends, sweet friends, let me not stir you up
To such a sudden flood of mutiny.
They that have done this deed are honorable.
What private griefs they have, alas, I know not,
That made them do it. They are wise and honorable,
And will no doubt with reasons answer you.
I come not, friends, to steal away your hearts.
I am no orator, as Brutus is;
But (as you know me all) a plain blunt man
That love my friend, and that they know full well
That gave me public leave to speak of him.
For I have neither wit, nor words, nor worth,
Action, nor utterance, nor power of speech
To stir men's blood; I only speak right on.
I tell you that which you yourselves do know,
Show you sweet Caesar's wounds, poor, poor, dumb
    mouths,
And bid them speak for me. But were I Brutus,
And Brutus Antony, there were an Antony
Would ruffle up your spirits, and put a tongue
In every wound of Caesar, that should move
The stones of Rome to rise and mutiny.

QUESTIONS. 1. Who was Casca? 2. Where was Pompey's statue situated? 3. Was Antony sincere in disavowing an intention to stir the Romans up to mutiny? 4. Why does he express such respect for Brutus? 5. Relate the story of Caesar's death.

SPELL AND DEFINE. 1. interred   2. grievously   3. ambitious
4. captives   5. judgment   6. disposed   7. mutiny   8. parchment
9. testament   10. envious   11. vanquished   12. ingratitude   13. gracious
14. vesture   15. marred   16. utterance   17. ruffle

LESSON CIV

Egyptian Mummies, Tombs, and Manners — Belzoni

RULE. Pronounce the consonant sounds very distinctly.

EXAMPLE. Prolong the consonant sounds that are italicized: *b*-old,
d-eign, *f*-ather, *g*-ather, *j*-oy, *l*-ight, *m*-an, *n*-o, *q*-ueer, p-*r*-ay, *v*-ale, *w*-oe,
y-ours, *z*-one, *h*-ang.

Gournou is a tract of rocks, about two miles in length, at
the foot of the Libyan mountains on the west of Thebes, and
was the burial place of the great city of a hundred gates.
Every part of these rocks is cut out by art, in the form of
large and of small chambers, each of which has its separate
entrance. Though they are very close to each other, it is
seldom that there is any interior communication from one to
another. I can truly say, it is impossible to give any description sufficient to convey the smallest idea of those subterranean abodes and their inhabitants. There are no sepulchres in any part of the world like them, there are no
excavations or mines that can be compared to these truly
astonishing places. No exact description can be given of their
interior, owing to the difficulty of visiting these recesses.
The inconveniency of entering into them is such that it is not
everyone who can support the exertion.

A traveler is generally satisfied when he has seen the
large hall, the gallery, the staircase, and gone as far as he
can conveniently go. Besides, he is taken up with the strange
works he observes cut in various places and painted on each
side of the walls, so that when he comes to a narrow and

difficult passage or a descent to the bottom of a well or cavity, he declines taking such trouble. He naturally supposes that he cannot see in these abysses anything so magnificent as what he sees above, consequently deeming it useless to proceed any farther.

Of some of these tombs many persons could not withstand the suffocating air, which often causes fainting. A vast quantity of dust rises so fine that it enters into the throat and nostrils and chokes the nose and mouth to such a degree that it requires great power of lungs to resist it and the strong effluvia of the mummies. This is not all. The entry or passage where the bodies are is roughly cut in the rocks, and the falling of the sand from the upper part or ceiling of the passage causes it to be nearly filled up. In some places there is not more than a vacancy of a foot left, which you must contrive to pass through in a creeping posture like a snail, on pointed and keen stones that cut like glass.

After getting through these passages, some of them two or three hundred yards long, you generally find a more commodious place, perhaps high enough to sit. But what a place of rest! surrounded by bodies, by heaps of mummies in all directions which, previous to my being accustomed to the sight, impressed me with horror. The blackness of the wall, the faint light given by the candles or torches for want of air, the different objects that surrounded me, seeming to converse with each other, and the Arabs with the candles or torches in their hands, naked and covered with dust, themselves resembling living mummies, absolutely formed a scene that cannot be described. In such a situation I found myself several times. I often returned exhausted and fainting, until at last I became inured to it and indifferent to what I suffered, except from the dust, which never failed to choke my throat and nose. Though, fortunately, I am destitute of the sense of smell, I could taste that the mummies were rather unpleasant to swallow.

After the exertion of entering into such a place through a passage of fifty, a hundred, three hundred, or perhaps six hundred yards, nearly overcome, I sought a resting place, found one, and contrived to sit. But when my weight bore on the body of an Egyptian, it crushed like a bandbox. I naturally had recourse to my hands to sustain my weight, but they found no better support. So I sank altogether among the broken mummies with a crash of bones, rags, and wooden cases which raised such a dust as kept me motionless for a quarter of an hour, waiting till it subsided again. I could not remove from the place, however, without increasing it, and every step I took I crushed a mummy in some part or other.

Once I was conducted from such a place to another resembling it, through a passage of about twenty feet in length and no wider than what a body could be forced through. It was choked with mummies, and I could not pass without putting my face in contact with that of some decayed Egyptian. As the passage inclined downwards, my own weight helped me on. However, I could not avoid being covered with bones, legs, arms, and heads rolling from above. Thus I proceeded from one cave to another, all full of mummies piled up in various ways, some standing, some lying, and some on their heads.

The purpose of my research was to rob the Egyptians of their papyri, of which I found a few hidden in their breasts under their arms, in the space above the knees, or on the legs, and covered by the numerous folds of cloth that envelop the mummy. The people of Gournou, who make a trade of antiquities of this sort, are very jealous of strangers and keep the papyri as secret as possible, deceiving travelers by pretending that they have arrived at the end of the pits when they are scarcely at the entrance.

I must not omit that among these tombs we saw some which contained the mummies of animals intermixed with human bodies. There were bulls, cows, sheep, monkeys, foxes, bats, crocodiles, fishes, and birds in them. Idols often occur. One tomb was filled with nothing but cats, carefully folded in red and white linen, the head covered by a mask representing the cat and made of the same linen. I have opened all these sorts of animals. Of the bull, the calf, and the sheep, there is no part but the head which is covered with linen, and the horns project out of the cloth. The rest of the body is represented by two pieces of wood, eighteen inches wide and three feet long, in a horizontal direction, at the end of which was another placed perpendicularly, two feet high, to form the breast of the animal.

The calves and sheep are of the same structure and large in proportion to the bulls. The monkey is in its full form, in a sitting posture. The fox is squeezed up by the bandages, but in some measure the shape of the head is kept perfect. The crocodile is left in its own shape, and after being bound round with linen, the eyes and mouth are painted on this covering. The birds are squeezed together and lose their shape, except the ibis, which is found like a fowl ready to be cooked and bound round with linen like all the rest.

The next sort of mummy that drew my attention, I believe I may with reason conclude to have been appropriated to the priests. They are folded in a manner totally different from the others and so carefully executed as to show the great respect paid to those personages. The bandages are stripes of red and white linen intermixed, covering the whole body and producing a curious effect from the two colors. The arms and legs are not enclosed in the same envelope with the body, as in the common mode, but are bandaged separately, even the fingers and toes being preserved distinct. They have sandals of painted leather on their feet and bracelets on their arms and wrists. They are always found with the arms across the breast, but not pressing it. Though the body is bound with such a quantity of linen, the shape of the person is carefully preserved in every limb. The cases in which mummies of this sort are found are somewhat better executed, and I have seen one that had the eyes and eyebrows of enamel, beautifully executed in imitation of nature.

The dwelling place of the natives is generally in the passages between the first and second entrance into a tomb. The walls and the roof are as black as any chimney. The inner door is closed up with mud, except for a small aperture sufficient for a man to crawl through. Within this place the sheep are kept at night and occasionally accompany their masters in their vocal concert. Over the doorway there are always some half-broken Egyptian figures and the two foxes, the usual guardians of burial places. A small lamp, kept alive by fat from the sheep or rancid oil, is placed in a niche in the wall, and a mat is spread on the ground. This formed the grand divan wherever I was.

There the people assembled round me, their conversation turning wholly on antiquities. Such a one had found such a thing and another had discovered a tomb. Various articles were brought to sell to me, and sometimes I had reason to rejoice at having stayed there. I was sure of a supper of milk and bread served in a wooden bowl, but whenever they supposed I should stay all night, they always killed a couple of fowls for me. These were baked in a small oven heated with pieces of mummy cases and sometimes with the bones and rags of the mummies themselves. It is no uncommon thing to sit down near fragments of bones — hands, feet, or skulls are often in the way. These people are so accustomed to be among the mummies that they think no more of sitting on them than on the skins of their dear calves. I, also, became indifferent about them at last and would have slept in a mummy pit as readily as out of it.

Here they appear to be contented. The laborer comes home in the evening, seats himself near his cave, smokes his pipe with his companions, and talks of the last inundation of the Nile, its products, and what the ensuing season is likely to be. His old wife brings him the usual bowl of lentils and bread moistened with water and salt, and (when she can add a little butter) it is a feast. Knowing nothing beyond this, he is happy. The young man's chief business is to accumulate the amazing sum of a hundred piastres (eleven dollars and ten cents) to buy himself a wife and to make a feast on the wedding day.

If he have any children, they want no clothing. He leaves them to themselves till Mother Nature pleases to teach them to work, to gain money enough to buy a shirt or some other rag to cover themselves. While they are children, they are generally naked or covered with rags. The parents are roguishly cunning, and the children are schooled by their example, so that it becomes a matter of course to cheat strangers. Would anyone believe that, in such a state of life, luxury and ambition exist? If any woman be destitute of jewels, she is poor and looks with envy on one more fortunate than herself, who perhaps has the worth of half a crown round her neck. She who has a few glass beads or some sort of coarse coral, a couple of silver brooches or rings on her arms and legs is considered as truly rich and great. Some of them are as complete coquettes, in their way, as any to be seen in the capitals of Europe.

When a young man wants to marry, he goes to the father of the intended bride and agrees with him what he is to pay for her. This being settled, so much money is to be spent on the wedding-day feast. To set up housekeeping, nothing is requisite but two or three earthen pots, a stone to grind meal, and a mat which is the bed. The spouse has a gown and jewels of her own, and if the bridegroom presents her with a pair of bracelets of silver, ivory, or glass, she is happy and fortunate indeed.

The house is ready, without rent or taxes. No rain can pass through the roof, and there is no door, for there is no want of one, as there is nothing to lose. They make a kind of box of clay and straw which, after two or three days' exposure to the sun, becomes quite hard. It is fixed on a stand, an aperture is left to put all their precious things into it, and a piece of mummy case forms the door. If the house does not please them, they walk out and enter another, as there are several hundred at their command. I might say several thousand, but they are not all fit to receive inhabitants.

QUESTIONS. 1. Where are the Libyan mountains? 2. Do you know anything of the history of Thebes? 3. Why do so few travelers succeed in penetrating to the bottom of the tombs? 4. Mention some of the sources of annoyance in exploring them. 5. What was the result when Belzoni attempted to rest upon a mummy? 6. Are there any animals found embalmed? 7. What was Belzoni's object in exploring these tombs? 8. Why did he value the bits of papyrus? 9. Describe the furniture of the dwelling places of the natives.

SPELL AND DEFINE. 1. Libyan 2. subterranean 3. inconveniency 4. sepulchres 5. cavity 6. abysses 7. magnificent 8. suffocating 9. effluvia 10. commodious 11. torches 12. exhausted 13. contact 14. papyri 15. antiquities 16. horizontal 17. perpendicularly 18. appropriated 19. intermixed

LESSON CV

Address to the Mummy in Belzoni's Exhibition, London — New Monthly Mag.

RULE. Be careful to speak little words such as *a, in, at, on, to, by* very distinctly and yet not to dwell on them so long as on the more important words.

And thou hast walk'd about (how strange a story!)
    In Thebes' streets three thousand years ago,
When the Memnonium was in all its glory,
    And time had not begun to overthrow
Those temples, palaces, and piles stupendous,
Of which the very ruins are tremendous.

Speak! for thou long enough hast acted Dummy,
    Thou hast a tongue — come, let us hear its tune;
Thou'rt standing on thy legs, above ground, Mummy!

Revisiting the glimpses of the moon,
Not like thin ghosts or disembodied creatures,
But with thy bones and flesh, and limbs and features.

Tell us — for doubtless thou canst recollect,
    To whom should we assign the sphinx's fame?
Was Cheops or Khafre architect
    Of either pyramid that bears his name?
Is Pompey's pillar really a misnomer?
Had Thebes a hundred gates as sung by Homer?

Perhaps thou wert a Mason, and forbidden
    By oath to tell the mysteries of thy trade;
Then say what secret melody was hidden
    In Memnon's statue that at sunrise played?
Perhaps thou wert a priest — if so, my struggles
Are vain — Egyptian priests ne'er owned their jug-
        gles.

Perchance that very hand, now pinioned flat,
    Has hobb-a-nobb'd with Pharaoh glass to glass,
Or dropped a halfpenny in Homer's hat,
    Or doffed thine own to let Queen Dido pass,
Or held, by Solomon's own invitation,
A torch at the great Temple's dedication.

I need not ask thee if that hand, when armed,
    Has any Roman soldier mauled and knuckled,
For thou wert dead and buried and embalmed,
    Ere Romulus and Remus had been suckled —
Antiquity appears to have begun
Long after thy primeval race was run.

Since first thy form was in this box extended,
    We have, above ground, seen some strange muta-
        tions;
The Roman Empire has begun and ended;

New worlds have risen — we have lost old nations,
And countless kings have into dust been humbled,
While not a fragment of thy flesh has crumbled.

Didst thou not hear the pother o'er thy head,
　　When the great Persian conqueror, Cambyses,
March'd armies o'er thy tomb with thundering tread,
　　O'erthrew Osiris, Horus, Apis, Isis,
And shook the pyramids with fear and wonder,
When the gigantic Memnon fell asunder?

If the tomb's secrets may not be confessed,
　　The nature of thy private life unfold:
A heart has throbb'd beneath that leathern breast,
　　And tears adown that dusky cheek have rolled —
Have children climb'd those knees, and kissed that
　　face?
What was thy name and station, age and race?

Statue of flesh — immortal of the dead!
　　Imperishable type of evanescence!
Posthumous man, who quit'st thy narrow bed,
　　And standest undecayed within our presence,
Thou wilt hear nothing till the Judgment morning
When the great trump shall thrill thee with its warn-
　　ing.

Why should this worthless tegument endure,
　　If its undying guest be lost forever?
O let us keep the soul embalmed and pure
　　In living virtue; that when both must sever,
Although corruption may our frame consume,
Th' immortal spirit in the skies may bloom.

QUESTIONS. 1. What was the Memnonium?　2. Relate the fable of
Memnon's statue. 3. Who were Romulus and Remus? 4. Osiris? 5. Apis?
6. Isis? 7. What moral lesson is deduced?

SPELL AND DEFINE. 1. pother   2. stupendous   3. revisiting
4. pyramid 5. misnomer 6. mysteries 7. juggles 8. pinioned 9. mauled
10. primeval   11. mutations   12. evanescence   13. posthumous
14. tegument

LESSON CVI

Of Studies — Lord Bacon

RULE. When two or more consonants come together, let the pupil be
careful to sound every one distinctly.

EXERCISES UNDER THE RULE. He clenched his *fists*. He *lifts* his
awful form. He makes his *payments*. Thou *smoothed'st* his rugged path.
The *president's speech*.

Studies serve for delight, for ornament, and for ability.
Their chief use for delight is in privateness and retiring; for
ornament, is in discourse; and for ability, is in the judgment
and disposition of business. For expert men can execute, and
perhaps judge of particulars, one by one; but the general
counsels and the plots and marshaling of affairs come best
from those that are learned. To spend too much time in
studies is sloth; to use them too much for ornament is
affectation; to make judgment wholly by their rules is the
humor of a scholar. They perfect nature and are perfected by
experience, for natural abilities are like natural plants that
need pruning by study, and studies themselves do give forth
directions too much at large, except they be bounded in by
experience. Crafty men contemn studies, simple men admire
them, and wise men use them, for they teach not their own
use; but that is a wisdom without them, and above them,
won by observation. Read not to contradict and confute, nor
to believe and take for granted, nor to find talk and discourse, but to weigh and consider. Some books are to be
tasted, others to be swallowed, and some few to be chewed

and digested; that is, some books are to be read only in parts; others to be read, but not curiously; and some few to be read wholly and with diligence and attention. Some books also may be read by deputy and extracts made of them by others, but that would be only in the less important arguments and the meaner sort of books; else distilled books are like common distilled waters, flashy things. Reading maketh a full man, conference a ready man, and writing an exact man. And therefore, if a man write little, he had need have a great memory; if he confer little, he had need have a present wit; and if he read little, he had need have more cunning, to seem to know that he doth not. Histories make men wise; poets, witty; the mathematics, subtle; natural philosophy, deep; moral, grave; logic and rhetoric, able to contend. *Abeunt studia in mores.* Nay, there is no stond or impediment in the wit but what may be wrought out by fit studies, like as diseases of the body may have appropriate exercises. Bowling is good for the stone and reins; shooting for the lungs and breast, gentle walking for the stomach, riding for the head, and the like. So if a man's wit be wandering, let him study the mathematics; for in demonstrations, if his wit be called away ever so little, he must begin again. If his wit be not apt to distinguish or find differences, let him study the schoolmen, for they are *Cymini sectores.* If he be not apt to beat over matters and to call up one thing to prove and illustrate another, let him study the lawyer's cases. So every defect of the mind may have a special receipt.

QUESTIONS. 1. What is said of the influence of study upon the natural abilities? 2. For what purpose should we read? 3. Are all books to be read in the same manner? 4. What is said of abridgments? 5. What influence has the reading of history upon the mind? 6. Poetry? 7. Mathematics? 8. Logic and rhetoric? 9. Who are "the schoolmen"?

SPELL AND DEFINE. 1. ornament   2. ability   3. disposition 4. counsels   5. affectation   6. contemn   7. discourse   8. mathematics 9. demonstrations

LESSON CVII

Natural Ties among the Western States — Dr. Drake

RULE. Be careful to pronounce every syllable distinctly.

Let us leave the history and resume the physical and political geography of the West for the purpose of considering the relations of its different regions — not to the *Atlantic states,* but to *each other.* In reviewing their boundaries and connections, we find much to excite reflection and inspire us with deep emotion. The geography of the interior, in truth, admonishes us to live in harmony, cherish uniform plans of education, and found similar institutions. The relations between the upper and lower Mississippi states, established by the collective waters of the whole valley, must forever continue unchanged. What the towering oak is to our climbing winter grape, the "Father of Waters" must ever be to the communities along its trunk and countless tributary streams — an imperishable support, an exhaustless power of union. What is the composition of its lower coasts and alluvial plains but the soil of all the upper states and territories transported, commingled, and deposited by its waters?

Within her own limits, Louisiana has, indeed, the rich mold of ten sister states, which have thus contributed to the fertility of her plantations. It might almost be said that for ages this region has sent thither a portion of its soil where, in a milder climate, it might produce the cotton, oranges, and sugar which, through the same channel, we receive in exchange for the products of our corn fields, workshops, and mines. These facts prepare the way and invite perpetual union between the West and South.

The state of Tennessee, separated from Alabama and Mississippi on the south and Kentucky on the north by no natural barrier, has its southern fields overspread with floating cotton, wafted from the two former states by every autumnal breeze, while the shade of its northern woods lies for half the summer day on the borders of the latter state. The songs and uproar of a Kentucky husking are answered from Tennessee, and the midnight raccoon hunt that follows, beginning in one state, is concluded in the other.

The Cumberland, on whose rocky banks the capital of Tennessee rises in beauty, begins and terminates in Kentucky — thus bearing on its bosom at the same moment the products of the two states descending to a common market. Still further, the fine river Tennessee drains the eastern half of that state, dips into Alabama, recrosses the state in which it arose, and traverses Kentucky to reach the Ohio River, thus uniting the three into one natural and enduring commercial compact.

Further north, the cottonwood trees which fringe the borders of Missouri and Illinois throw their images toward each other in the waters of the Mississippi. The toiling emigrant's axe in the depths of the leafless woods and the crash of the falling rail tree on the frozen earth resound equally among the hills of both states. The clouds of smoke from their burning prairies mingle in the air above and crimson the setting sun of Kentucky, Indiana, and Ohio.

The pecan tree sheds its fruit at the same moment among the people of Indiana and Illinois, and the boys of the two states paddle their canoes and fish together in the Wabash or hail each other from opposite banks. Even villages belong equally to Indiana and Ohio, and the children of the two commonwealths trundle their hoops together in the same street.

But the Ohio River forms the most interesting boundary among the states of the West. For a thousand miles its fertile bottoms are cultivated by farmers who belong to the different states, while they visit each other as friends or neighbors. As the schoolboy trips or loiters along its shores, he greets his playmates across the stream, or they sport away an idle hour in its summer waters. These are to be among the future, perhaps the opposing statesmen of the different commonwealths.

When, at low water, we examine the rocks of the channel, we find them the same on both sides. The plants which grow above drop their seeds into the common current, which lodges them indiscriminately on either shore. Thus, the very trees and flowers emigrate from one state to another. When the bee tree sends out its swarms, they as often seek a habitation beyond the stream as in their woods.

Throughout its whole extent, the hills of western Virginia and Kentucky cast their morning shadows on the plains of Ohio, Indiana, Illinois, and Missouri. The thundercloud pours down its showers on different commonwealths, and the rainbow, resting its extremities on two sister states, presents a beautiful arch on which the spirits of peace may pass and repass in harmony and love.

Thus connected by nature in the great valley, we must live in the bonds of companionship or imbrue our hands in each other's blood. We have no middle destiny. To secure the former to our posterity, we should begin while society is still tender and pliable. The saplings of the woods, if intertwined, will adapt themselves to each other and grow together; the little bird may hang its nest on the twigs of different trees, and the dewdrops fall successively on leaves which are nourished by distinct trunks. The tornado strikes harmlessly on such a bower, for the various parts sustain each other, but the grown tree, sturdy and set in its way, will not bend to its fellow. When uprooted by the tempest, it is dashed with violence against all within its reach.

Communities, like forests, grow rigid by time. To be properly trained, they must be molded while young. Our duty, then, is quite obvious. All who have moral power should exert it in concert. The germs of harmony must be nourished and the roots of present contrariety or future discord torn up and cast into the fire. Measures should be taken to mold a uniform system of manners and customs out of the diversified elements which are scattered over the West.

Literary meetings should be held in the different states and occasional conventions in the central cities of the great valley be made to bring into friendly consultation our enlightened and zealous teachers, professors, lawyers, physicians, divines, and men of letters from its remotest sections. In their deliberations, the literary and moral wants of the various regions might be made known and the means of supplying them devised.

The whole should successively lend a helping hand to all the parts on the great subject of education, from the primary school to the university. Statistical facts bearing on this absorbing interest should be brought forward and collected. The systems of common school instruction should be compared and the merits of different schoolbooks, foreign and domestic, freely canvassed. Plans of education adapted to the natural, commercial, and social condition of the interior should be invented, a correspondence instituted among all our higher seminaries of learning, and an interchange established of all local publications on the subject of education. In short, we should foster western genius, encourage western writers, patronize western publishers, augment the number of western readers, and create a western heart.

When these great objects shall come seriously to occupy our minds, the Union will be secure, for its center will be sound and its attraction on the surrounding parts irresistible. Then will our state governments emulate each other in works for the common good, the people of remote places begin to feel as the members of one family, and our whole intelligent and virtuous population unite, heart and hand, in one long, concentrated, untiring effort to raise still higher the social character and perpetuate forever the political harmony of the green and growing West.

QUESTIONS. 1. What river establishes a commercial and social connection between Missouri and Louisiana? 2. What states are bound together by the Tennessee River? 3. What states does the Ohio River bind together? 4. In what manner will harmony among the western states perpetuate the Union?

SPELL AND DEFINE. 1. physical   2. connections   3. barrier
4. terminates 5. emigrants 6. cultivated 7. commonwealth 8. habitation
9. diversified 10. commercial 11. correspondence 12. concentrated

LESSON CVIII

The Better Land — Mrs. Hemans

RULE. In reading poetry, be careful not to join the final consonant of one word to the vowel of the next word.

EXAMPLE. Loud as His thunder shout His praise, and sound it lofty as His throne.

The following way of reading it shows the fault to be remedied by observing the rule: Lou das His thunder shout His praise, and soun dit lofty as His throne.

> "I hear thee speak of the better land;
> Thou call'st its children a happy band;
> Mother! oh, where is that radiant shore?
> Shall we not seek it, and weep no more?
> Is it where the flower of the orange blows,
> And the fireflies dance through the myrtle boughs?"
>   — "Not there, not there, my child!"

> "Is it where the feathery palm trees rise,
> And the date grows ripe under sunny skies?
> Or midst the green islands of glittering seas,
> Where fragrant forests perfume the breeze,
> And strange bright birds, on their starry wings,
> Bear the rich hues of all glorious things?"
>   — "Not there, not there, my child!"

"Is it far away, in some region old,
Where the rivers wander o'er sands of gold,
Where the burning rays of the ruby shine,
And the diamond lights up the secret mine,
And the pearl gleams forth from the coral strand?
Is it there, sweet mother! that better land?"
              — "Not there, not there, my child!"

"Eye hath not seen it, my gentle boy!
Ear hath not heard its deep sounds of joy;
Dreams cannot picture a world so fair;
Sorrow and death may not enter there;
Time doth not breathe on its fadeless bloom,
Beyond the clouds, and beyond the tomb;
              — It is there, it is there, my child!"

QUESTIONS. 1. What climate produces the myrtle, palm, and date? 2. Why is the palm tree called feathery?

SPELL AND DEFINE. 1. radiant 2. glittering 3. fragrant 4. gleams 5. diamond 6. coral 7. region

LESSON CIX

Benefits of Literature — Lord Lyttleton

RULE. When similar sounds come at the end of one word and at the beginning of the next word, they must not be blended into one.

EXERCISES. He sinks sorrowing to the tomb. Man loves society. Time flies swiftly. The birds sing.

Hercules. Do you pretend to sit as high on Olympus as Hercules? Did you kill the Nemaean lion, the Erymanthian boar, the Lernean serpent, and Stymphalian birds? Did you destroy tyrants and robbers? You value yourself greatly on subduing one serpent. I did as much as that while I lay in my cradle.

Cadmus. It is not on account of the serpent that I boast myself a greater benefactor to Greece than you. Actions should be valued by their utility rather than their splendor. I taught Greece the art of writing, to which laws owe their precision and permanency. You subdued monsters, I civilized men. It is from untamed passions, not from wild beasts, that the greatest evils arise to human society. By wisdom, by art, by the united strength of a civil community, men have been enabled to subdue the whole race of lions, bears, and serpents and, what is more, to bind by laws and wholesome regulation the ferocious violence and dangerous treachery of the human disposition. Had lions been destroyed only in single combat, men had had but a bad time of it. What, but laws, could awe the men who killed the lions? The genuine glory, the proper distinction of the rational species arises from the perfection of the mental powers. Courage is apt to be fierce, and strength is often exerted in acts of oppression, but wisdom is the assote of justice. It assists her to form equal laws, to pursue right measures, to correct power, protect weakness, and to unite individuals in a common interest and general welfare. Heroes may kill tyrants, but it is wisdom and laws that prevent tyranny and oppression. The operations of policy far surpass the labors of Hercules, preventing many evils which valor and might cannot even redress. You heroes regard nothing but glory and scarcely consider whether the conquests, which raise your fame, are really beneficial to your country. Unhappy are the people who are governed by valor not directed by prudence and not mitigated by the gentle arts!

Hercules. I do not expect to find an admirer of my strenuous life in the man who taught his countrymen to sit still and read and to lose the hours of youth and action in idle speculation and the sport of words.

Cadmus. An ambition to have a place in the registers of fame is the Eurystheus which imposes heroic labors on mankind. The Muses incite to action as well as entertain the hours of repose, and I think you should honor them for presenting to heroes so noble a recreation as may prevent their taking up the distaff when they lay down the club.

Hercules. Wits as well as heroes can take up the distaff. What think you of their thin-spun systems of philosophy or lascivious poems or Milesian fables? Nay, what is still worse, are there not panegyrics on tyrants and books that blaspheme the gods and perplex the natural sense of right and wrong? I believe if Eurystheus were to set me to work again, he would find me a worse task than any he imposed. He would make me read over a great library, and I would serve it as I did the Hydra, I would burn it as I went on, that one chimera might not rise from another to plague mankind. I should have valued myself more on clearing the library than on cleansing the Augean stables.

Cadmus. It is in those libraries only that the memory of your labor exists. The heroes of Marathon, the patriots of Thermopylae owe their fame to me. All the wise institutions of lawgivers and all the doctrines of sages had perished in the ear, like a dream related, if letters had not preserved them. O Hercules! it is not for the man who preferred Virtue to Pleasure to be an enemy to the Muses. Let Sardanapalus and the silken sons of luxury, who have wasted life in inglorious ease, despise the records of action which bear no honorable testimony to their lives. True merit, heroic virtue should respect the sacred source of lasting honor.

Hercules. Indeed, if writers employed themselves only in recording the acts of great men, much might be said in their favor. But why do they trouble people with their meditations? Can it be of any consequence to the world what an idle man has been thinking?

Cadmus. Yes it may. The most important and extensive advantages mankind enjoy are greatly owing to men who have never quitted their closets. To them mankind are obliged for the facility and security of navigation. The invention of the compass has opened to them new worlds. The knowledge of the mechanical powers has enabled them to construct such wonderful machines as perform what the united labor of millions, by the severest drudgery, could not accomplish. Agriculture, too, the most useful of arts, has received its share of improvement from the same source. Poetry, likewise, is of excellent use to enable the memory to retain with more ease and to imprint with more energy upon the heart precepts and examples of virtue. From the little root of a few letters, science has spread its branches over all nature and raised its head to the heavens. Some philosophers have entered so far into the counsels of divine wisdom as to explain much of the great operations of nature. The dimensions and distances of the planets, the cause of their revolutions, the paths of comets, and the ebbing and flowing of tides are understood and explained.

Can anything raise the glory of the human species more than to see a little creature, inhabiting a small spot amid innumerable worlds, taking a survey of the universe, comprehending its arrangement, and entering into the scheme of that wonderful connection and correspondence of things so remote and which it seems a great exertion of Omnipotence to have established? What volume of wisdom, what noble theology do these discoveries open to us? While some superior geniuses have soared to these sublime subjects, other sagacious and diligent minds have been inquiring into the most minute works of the Infinite Artificer. The same care, the same providence is exerted through the whole, and we should learn from it that, to true wisdom, utility and fitness appear perfection, and whatever is beneficial is noble.

Hercules. I approve of science as far as it is an assistant to action. I like the improvement of navigation and the discovery of the greater part of the globe, because it opens a wider field for the master spirits of the world to bustle in.

Cadmus. There spoke the soul of Hercules. But if learned men are to be esteemed for the assistance they give to active minds in their schemes, they are not less to be valued for their endeavors to give them a right direction and moderate their too great ardor. The study of history will teach the legislature by what means states have become powerful, and in the private citizen, it will inculcate the love of liberty and order. The writings of sages point out a private path of virtue and show that the best empire is self-government and that subduing our passions is the noblest of conquests.

Hercules. The true spirit of patriotism acts by a generous impulse and wants neither the experience of history nor the doctrines of philosophers to direct it. But do not arts and science render men effeminate, luxurious, and inactive? Can you deny that wit and learning are often made subservient to very bad purposes?

Cadmus. I will own that there are some natures so happily formed, they scarcely want the assistance of a master and the rules of art to give them force or grace in everything they do. But these favored geniuses are few. As learning flourishes only where ease, plenty, and mild government subsists, in so rich a soil and under so soft a climate the weeds of luxury will spring up among the flowers of art. But the spontaneous weeds would grow more rank if they were allowed the undisturbed possession of the field. Letters keep a frugal, temperate nation from growing ferocious, a rich one from becoming entirely sensual and debauched. Every gift of heaven is sometimes abused, but good sense and fine talents, by a natural law, gravitate towards virtue. Accidents may drive them out of their proper direction, but such accidents are an alarming omen and of dire portent to the times. For if Virtue cannot keep to her allegiance those men who in their hearts confess her divine right and know the value of her laws, on whose fideliand obedience can she depend? May such geniuses never descend to flatter vice, encourage folly, or propagate irreligion, but exert all their powers in the service of Virtue and celebrate the noble choice of those who, like Hercules, preferred her to Pleasure!

QUESTIONS. 1. Who was Hercules? 2. Can you enumerate some of the principal exploits of Hercules? 3. What is the difference between the character of the exploits of Hercules and those of Cadmus? 4. Who was Cadmus? 5. What did Cadmus do? 6. How should actions be valued? 7. From what must the genuine glory of rational beings arise? 8. To which of his labors does Hercules compare the reading of a modern library? The cleansing of it? 9. Since so much trash and folly is written, what is the use of writers? 10. What does Hercules think of science? 11. What is patriotism?

SPELL AND DEFINE. 1. Olympus   2. Stymphalian   3. wholesome 4. tyranny   5. strenuous   6. Eurystheus   7. panegyrics   8. Augean 9. Marathon 10. philosophers 11. omnipotence 12. infinite 13. ferocious

LESSON CX

Thalaba among the Ruins of Babylon — Southey

RULE. In reading poetry that does not rhyme, there should be no pause at the end of a line except when it terminates with an important word or the sense requires it.

The many-colored domes
Yet wore one dusky hue;
The cranes upon the mosque
Kept their night clatter still;

When through the gate the early traveler pass'd.
And when, at evening, o'er the swampy plain

The bittern's boom came far,
Distinct in darkness seen,
Above the low horizon's lingering light,
Rose the near ruins of old Babylon.

Once, from her lofty walls the charioteer
Look'd down on swarming myriads; once she flung
Her arches o'er Euphrates' conquered tide,
And, through her brazen portals when she poured
Her armies forth, the distant nations looked
As men who watch the thundercloud in fear,

Lest it should burst above them. She was fallen!
The queen of cities, Babylon was fallen!
Low lay her bulwarks; the black scorpion basked
In palace courts; within the sanctuary
        The she-wolf hid her whelps.

Is yonder huge and shapeless heap, what once
Hath been the aerial gardens, height on height
Rising, like Media's mountains, crowned with wood,
Work of imperial dotage? Where the fane
Of Belus? Where the golden image now,
Which, at the sound of dulcimer and lute,
Cornet and sackbut, harp and psaltery,
        The Assyrian slaves adored?
A labyrinth of ruins, Babylon
        Spreads o'er the blasted plain.
The wandering Arab never sets his tent
Within her walls. The shepherd eyes afar
Her evil towers, and devious drives his flock.
Alone unchanged, a free and bridgeless tide,
        Euphrates rolls along,
        Eternal nature's work.

        Through the broken portal,
        Over weedy fragments,
        Thalaba went his way.
        Cautious he trod, and felt
The dangerous ground before him with his bow.
        The jackal started at his steps;
        The stork, alarmed at sound of man,
From her broad nest upon the old pillar top,
        Affrighted fled on flapping wings.
        The adder, in her haunts disturbed,
Lanced at the intruding staff her arrowy tongue.

Twilight and moonshine, dimly mingling, gave
        An awful light obscure:

Evening not wholly closed —
The moon still pale and faint —
An awful light obscure,
Broken by many a mass of blackest shade;
Long columns stretching dark through weeds and
    moss;
Broad length of lofty wall,
Whose windows lay in light,
And of their former shape, low-arched or square,
Rude outline on the earth
Figured with long grass fringed.

Reclined against a column's broken shaft,
Unknowing whitherward to bend his way,
He stood and gazed around.
The ruins closed him in:
It seemed as if no foot of man
For ages had intruded there.
He stood and gazed awhile,
Musing on Babel's pride, and Babel's fall;
Then, through the ruined street,
And through the farther gate,
He passed in silence on.

QUESTIONS. 1. Where was Babylon situated and of what the capital? 2. How could a charioteer look down from the walls? 3. Describe the "aerial gardens." 4. What were the dimensions of the temple of Belus? 5. Do you know anything relative to the golden image mentioned in this lesson? 6. From what book do you learn this story?

SPELL AND DEFINE. 1. mosque   2. charioteer   3. myriads
4. bulwarks 5. imperial 6. dotage 7. dulcimer 8. psaltery 9. labyrinth
10. portal 11. haunts 12. column

LESSON CXI

William Tell — Knowles

RULE. Be careful not to join the last part of one word to the beginning of the next word.

SCENE 1. *A mountain with mist. Gessler seen descending with a hunting pole.*

Gessler. Alone — Alone! and every step the mist
Thickens around me! On these mountain tracks
To lose one's way, they say, is sometimes death.
What, ho! Holloa! No tongue replies to me.
What thunder hath the horror of this silence!
Cursed slaves, to let me wander from them! Ho — Holloa!
My voice sounds weaker to mine ear; I've not
The strength to call I had, and through my limbs
Cold tremor runs — and sickening faintness seizes
On my heart. O heaven, have mercy! Do not see
The color of the hands I lift to thee.
Look only on the strait wherein I stand,
And pity it! Let me not sink. Uphold!
Support me! Mercy! Mercy!
      [*He falls with faintness. Albert enters, almost breath
                less with the fury of the storm.*]
   Albert. I'll breathe upon this level, if the wind
Will let me. Ha! a rock to shelter me!
Thanks to it — a man! and fainting. Courage, friend!
Courage. A stranger that has lost his way.
Take heart, take heart — you are safe. How feel you now?
   Ges. Better.
   Alb. You have lost your way upon the hills?
   Ges. I have.
   Alb. And whither would you go?
   Ges. To Altorf.

Alb. I'll guide you thither.

Ges. You are a child.

Alb. I know the way; the track I've come
Is harder far to find.

Ges. The track you have come! What mean you? Surely
You have not been still farther in the mountains?

Alb. I have traveled from Mount Faigel.

Ges. No one with thee?

Alb. No one but Him.

Ges. Do you not fear these storms?

Alb. He's in the storm.

Ges. And there are torrents, too,
That must be crossed?

Alb. He's by the torrent too.

Ges. You are but a child.

Alb. He will be with a child.

Ges. You are sure you know the way?

Alb. 'Tis but to keep the side of yonder stream.

Ges. But guide me safely, I'll give thee gold.

Alb. I'll guide thee safely without.

Ges. Here's earnest for thee. Here — I'll double that,
Yea, treble it — but let me see the gate of Altorf.
Why do you refuse the gold? Take it.

Alb. No.

Ges. You shall.

Alb. I will not.

Ges. Why?

Alb. Because
I do not covet it — and though I did,
It would be wrong to take it as the price
Of doing one a kindness.

Ges. Ha! Who taught thee that?

Alb. My father.

Ges. Does he live in Altorf?

Alb. No, in the mountains.

Ges. How — a mountaineer?

He should become a tenant of the city.
He would gain by it.

 Alb. Not so much as he might lose by it.

 Ges. What might he lose by it?

 Alb. Liberty.

 Ges. Indeed! He also taught thee that?

 Alb. He did.

 Ges. His name?

 Alb. This is the way to Altorf, sir.

 Ges. I would know thy father's name.

 Alb. The day is wasting — we have far to go.

 Ges. Thy father's name, I say?

 Alb. I will not tell it thee.

 Ges. Not tell it me! Why?

 Alb. You may be an enemy of his.

 Ges. May be a friend.

 Alb. May be, but should you be
An enemy — although I would not tell you
My father's name — I would guide you safely to Altorf.
Will you follow me?

 Ges. Never mind thy father's name;
What would it profit me to know it? Thy hand;
We are not enemies.

 Alb. I never had an enemy.

 Ges. Lead on.

 Alb. Advance your staff
As you descend, and fix it well. Come on.

 Ges. What! must we take that steep?

 Alb. 'Tis nothing! Come,
I'll go before. Never fear — come on! come on!

SCENE 2. *The Gate of Altorf. Enter Gessler and Albert.*

Alb. You are at the gate of Altorf.

Ges. Tarry, boy!

Alb. I would be gone; I am waited for.

Ges. Come back!
Who waits for thee? Come, tell me; I am rich
And powerful, and can reward.

Alb. 'Tis close
On evening; I have far to go; I'm late.

Ges. Stay! I can punish, too.
Boy, do you know me?

Alb. No.

Ges. Why fear you, then,
To trust me with your father's name? Speak.

Alb. Why do you desire to know it?

Ges. You have served me,
And I would thank him, if I chanced to pass
His dwelling.

Alb. 'Twould not please him that a service
So trifling should be made so much of.

Ges. Trifling! You have saved my life.

Alb. Then do not question me,
But let me go.

Ges. When I have learned from thee
Thy father's name. What, ho! [*Knocks.*]

Sentinel. [*Within.*] Who's there?

Ges. Gessler. [*Soldiers enter.*]

Alb. Ha, Gessler!

Ges. [*To the soldiers.*] Seize him. Wilt thou tell me
Thy father's name?

Alb. No.

Ges. I can bid them cast thee
Into a dungeon! Wilt thou tell it now?

Alb. No.

Ges. I can bid them strangle thee! Wilt tell it?

Alb. Never.

Ges. Away with him! Send Sarnem to me.

[*Soldiers take Albert off.*]

Behind that boy I see the shadow of
A hand that must wear my fetters or 'twill try
To strip me of my power. How I loathed the free
And fearless air with which he trod the hills!
I wished some way
To find the parent nest of this fine eaglet,
And harrow it! I'd like to clip the broad
And full-grown wing that taught his tender pinion
So bold a flight. [*Enter Sarnem.*]
Ha, Sarnem! Have the slaves that
Attended me returned?

Sarnem. They have.

Ges. You'll see
That every one of them be laid in fetters.

Sar. I will.

Ges. Didst see that boy just now?

Sar. That passed me?

Ges. Yes.

Sar. A mountaineer.

Ges. You'd say so, saw you him
Upon the hills; he walks them like their lord!
I tell thee, Sarnem, looking on that boy,
I felt I was not master of those hills.
He has a father. Neither promises
Nor threats could draw from him his name — a father
Who talks to him of liberty. I fear that man.

Sar. He may be found.

Ges. He must — and soon
As found disposed of. I live
In danger till I find that man. Send parties
Into the mountains, to explore them far
And wide, and if they chance to light upon
A father who expects his child, command them
To drag him straight before us. Sarnem, see it done.

QUESTIONS. 1. Why does Gessler allude to the color of his hands in line 11? 2. To what purpose is a hunting pole applied? 3. What is meant by, "Here's earnest for thee"?

SPELL AND DEFINE. 1. tremor   2. breathe   3. mountaineer 4. dungeon 5. eaglet 6. threats 7. straight

LESSON CXII

William Tell — continued

RULE. Be careful to pronounce the little words like *a, the, and, in* distinctly and not to join them to the next word.

SCENE 3. *A chamber in the Castle. Enter Gessler, Officers, and Sarnem, with Tell in chains and guarded.*

Sar. Down, slave! Behold the governor.
Down! down! and beg for mercy.
　Ges. [*Seated.*] Does he hear?
　Sar. He does, but braves thy power.
　Officer. Why don't you smite him for that look?
　Ges. Can I believe
My eyes? — he smiles! Nay, grasps
His chains as he would make a weapon of them
To lay the smiter dead. [*To Tell.*]
Why speakest thou not?
　Tell. For wonder.
　Ges. Wonder?
　Tell. Yes, that thou shouldst seem a man.
　Ges. What should I seem?
　Tell. A monster!
　Ges. Ha! Beware — think on thy chains.
　Tell. Though they were doubled and did weigh me down
Prostrate to earth, methinks I could rise up —
Erect, with nothing but the honest pride

Of telling thee, usurper, to thy teeth,
Thou art a monster! Think upon my chains!
How came they on me?

 Ges. Darest thou question me?

 Tell. Darest thou not answer?

 Ges. Do I hear?

 Tell. Thou dost.

 Ges. Beware my vengeance.

 Tell. Can it more than kill?

 Ges. Enough — it can do that.

 Tell. No, not enough.

It cannot take away the grace of life,
Its comeliness of look that virtue gives,
Its port erect with consciousness of truth,
Its rich attire of honorable deeds,
Its fair report that's rife on good men's tongues.
It cannot lay its hands on these, no more
Than it can pluck the brightness from the sun,
Or with polluted finger tarnish it.

 Ges. But it can make thee writhe.

 Tell. It may.

 Ges. And groan.

 Tell. It may. And I may cry,

Go on, though it should make me groan again.

 Ges. Whence comest thou?

 Tell. From the mountains. Wouldst thou learn
What news from them?

 Ges. Canst tell me any?

 Tell. Aye. They watch no more the avalanche.

 Ges. Why so?

 Tell. Because they look for thee. The hurricane
Comes unawares upon them; from its bed,
The torrent breaks and finds them in its track.

 Ges. What do they then?

 Tell. Thank heaven it is not thou!

Thou hast perverted nature in them.
There's not a blessing heaven vouchsafes them, but

The thought of thee — doth wither to a curse.

Ges. That's right! I'd have them like their hills
That never smile, though wanton summer tempt
Them ever so much.

Tell. But they do sometimes smile.

Ges. Aye, when is that?

Tell. When they do talk of vengeance.

Ges. Vengeance! Dare they talk of that?

Tell. Aye, and expect it too.

Ges. From whence?

Tell. From heaven!

Ges. From heaven?

Tell. And their true hands
Are lifted up to it on every hill
For justice on thee.

Ges. Where's thy abode?

Tell. I told thee, on the mountains.

Ges. Art married?

Tell. Yes.

Ges. And hast a family?

Tell. A son.

Ges. A son! Sarnem!

Sar. My lord, the boy. [*Gessler signs to Sarnem to keep silence and, whispering, sends him off.*]

Tell. The boy! What boy?
Is't mine? Have they netted my young fledgling?
Now heaven support me, if they have! He'll own me,
And share his father's ruin! But a look
Would put him on his guard — yet how to give it!
Now, heart, thy nerve; forget thou art flesh, be rock.
They come — they come!
That step — that step — that little step, so light
Upon the ground, how heavy does it fall
Upon my heart! I feel my child!

[*Enter Sarnem with Albert, whose eyes are riveted on
Tell's bow, which Sarnem carries.*]

'Tis he! We can but perish.

    Sar. See!

    Alb. What?

    Sar. Look there!

    Alb. I do. What would you have me see?

    Sar. Thy father.

    Alb. Who? That — that my father?

    Tell. My boy, my boy! My own brave boy!
He's safe! [*Aside.*]

    Sar. [*Aside to Gessler.*] They're like each other.

    Ges. Yet I see no sign
Or recognition to betray the link
Unites a father and his child.

    Sar. My lord,
I am sure it is his father. Look at them.
It may be
A preconcerted thing 'gainst such a chance,
That they survey each other coldly thus.

    Ges. We shall try. Lead forth the caitiff.

    Sar. To a dungeon?

    Ges. No, into the court.

    Sar. The court, my lord?

    Ges. And send
To tell the headsman to make ready. Quickly!
The slave shall die! You marked the boy?

    Sar. I did. He started — 'tis his father.

    Ges. We shall see. Away with him!

    Tell. Stop! Stop!

    Ges. What would you?

    Tell. Time! A little time to call my thoughts together.

    Ges. Thou shalt not have a minute.

    Tell. Someone, then, to speak with.

    Ges. Hence with him!

    Tell. A moment! Stop!
Let me speak to the boy.

    Ges. Is he thy son?

Tell. And if
He were, art thou so lost to nature as
To send me forth to die before his face?

Ges. Well, speak with him.
Now, Sarnem, mark them well.

Tell. Thou dost not know me, boy, and well for thee
Thou dost not. I'm the father of a son
About thy age. Thou,
I see, wast born like him upon the hills.
If thou shouldst 'scape thy present thralldom, he
May chance to cross thee; if he should, I pray thee
Relate to him what has been passing here,
And say I laid my hand upon thy head
And said to thee — if he were here, as thou art,
Thus would I bless him. Mayest thou live, my boy!
To see thy country free, or die for her,
As I do! [*Albert weeps.*]

Sar. Mark! he weeps.

Tell. Were he my son,
He would not shed a tear! He would remember
The cliff where he was bred and learned to scan
A thousand fathoms' depth of nether air;
Where he was trained to hear the thunder talk
And meet the lightning eye to eye; where last
We spoke together, when I told him death
Bestowed the brightest gem that graces life —
Embraced for virtue's sake — he shed a tear!
Now were he by I'd talk to him, and his cheek
Should never blanch, nor moisture dim his eye ...
I'd talk to him ...

Sar. He falters!

Tell. 'Tis too much!
And yet it must be done! I'd talk to him —

Ges. Of what?

Tell. The mother, tyrant, thou dost make
A widow of! I'd talk to him of her.
I'd bid him tell her, next to liberty,

Her name was the last word my lips pronounced.
And I would charge him never to forget
To love and cherish her, as he would have
His father's dying blessing rest upon him!

    Sar. You see, as he doth prompt the other acts.

    Tell. So well he bears it, he doth vanquish me.
My boy, my boy! O for the hills, the hills,
To see him bound along their tops again,
With liberty.

    Sar. Was there not all the father in that look?

    Ges. Yet 'tis 'gainst nature.

    Sar. Not if he believes
To own the son would be to make him share
The father's death.

    Ges. I did not think of that! 'Tis well
The boy is not thy son — I've destined him
To die along with thee.

    Tell. To die? For what?

    Ges. For having braved my power, as thou hast. Lead
Them forth.

    Tell. He's but a child.

    Ges. Away with them!

    Tell. Perhaps an only child.

    Ges. No matter.

    Tell. He may have a mother.

    Ges. So the viper hath,
And yet, who spares it for the mother's sake?

    Tell. I talk to stone! I talk to it as though
'Twere flesh and know 'tis none. I'll talk to it
No more. Come, my boy,
I taught thee how to live — I'll show thee how to die.

    Ges. He is thy child?

    Tell. He is my child.

    Ges. I've wrung a tear from him! Thy name?

    Tell. My name?
It matters not to keep it from thee now;
My name is Tell.

Ges. Tell! William Tell?

Tell. The same.

Ges. What! he, so famed 'bove all his countrymen
For guiding o'er the stormy lake the boat?
And such a master of his bow, 'tis said
His arrows never miss! Indeed, I'll take
Exquisite vengeance! Mark! I'll spare thy life,
Thy boy's too — both of you are free — on one
Condition.

Tell. Name it.

Ges. I would see you make
A trial of your skill with that same bow
You shoot so well with.

Tell. Name the trial you
Would have me make.

Ges. You look upon your boy
As though instinctively you guessed it.

Tell. Look upon my boy! What mean you? Look upon
My boy as though I guessed it? Guessed the trial
You'd have me make! Guessed it
Instinctively! You do not mean — no — no —
You would not have me make a trial of
My skill upon my child! Impossible!
I do not guess your meaning.

Ges. I would see
Thee hit an apple at the distance of
A hundred paces.

Tell. Is my boy to hold it?

Ges. No.

Tell. No! I'll send the arrow through the core!

Ges. It is to rest upon his head.

Tell. Great heaven, you hear him!

Ges. Thou dost hear the choice I give —
Such trial of the skill thou art master of,
Or death to both of you, not otherwise
To be escaped.

Tell. O monster!

Ges. Wilt thou do it?

Alb. He will! he will!

Tell. Ferocious monster! Make
A father murder his own child.

Ges. Take off
His chains if he consent.

Tell. With his own hand!

Ges. Does he consent?

Alb. He does. [*Gessler signs to his officers, who proceed
    to take off Tell's chains. Tell is all the time uncon-
    scious of what they do.*]

Tell. With his own hand!
Murder his child with his own hand. This hand!
The hand I've led him, when an infant, by!
'Tis beyond horror — 'tis most horrible.
Amazement! [*His chains fall off.*] What's that you've done to
    me?
Villains! put on my chains again. My hands
Are free from blood and have no gust for it,
That they should drink my child's! Here! here! I'll not
Murder my boy for Gessler.

Alb. Father! Father!
You will not hit me, Father!

Tell. Hit thee! Send
The arrow through thy brain or, missing that,
Shoot out an eye — or, if thine eye escape,
Mangle the cheek I've seen thy mother's lips
Cover with kisses! Hit thee, hit a hair
Of thee, and cleave thy mother's heart —

Ges. Dost thou consent?

Tell. Give me my bow and quiver.

Ges. For what?

Tell. — To shoot my boy!

Alb. No, Father, no!
To save me! You'll be sure to hit the apple.
Will you not save me, Father?

Tell. Lead me forth —

I'll make the trial!

Alb. Thank you!

Tell. Thank me? Do
You know for what? I will not make the trial,
To take him to his mother in my arms
And lay him down a corpse before her!

Ges. Then he dies this moment — and you certainly
Do murder him whose life you have a chance
To save and will not use it.

Tell. Well — I'll do it. I'll make the trial.

Alb. Father —

Tell. Speak not to me.
Let me not hear thy voice. Thou must be dumb,
And so should all things be. Earth should be dumb,
And heaven — unless its thunders mutter at
The deed and send a bolt to stop it! Give me
My bow and quiver!

Ges. When all's ready.

Tell. Well — lead on!

QUESTIONS. 1. Why does Gessler express joy that his subjects are unhappy? 2. Why does Albert appear not to recognize his father? 3. Why does Tell at last acknowledge Albert?

SPELL AND DEFINE. 1. avalanche   2. hurricane   3. vouchsafe
4. fledgling   5. thralldom   6. instinctively   7. amazement   8. quiver
9. consciousness   10. rife   11. tarnish

LESSON CXIII

William Tell — continued

RULE. When two or more consonants come together, let the pupil be careful to sound every one distinctly.

SCENE 4. *Enter slowly, people in evident distress —
Officers, Sarnem, Gessler, Tell, Albert, and Soldiers — one
bearing Tell's bow and quiver, another with a basket of
apples.*

Ges. That is your ground. Now shall they measure thence
A hundred paces. Take the distance.

Tell. Is the line a true one?

Ges. True or not, what is't to thee?

Tell. What is't to me? A little thing,
A very little thing — a yard or two
Is nothing here or there — were it a wolf
I shot at! Never mind.

Ges. Be thankful, slave,
Our grace accords thee life on any terms.

Tell. I will be thankful, Gessler — Villain, stop!
You measure to the sun.

Ges. And what of that?
What matter whether to or from the sun?

Tell. I'd have it at my back. The sun should shine
Upon the mark and not on him that shoots.
I cannot see to shoot against the sun.
I will not shoot against the sun!

Ges. Give him his way! Thou hast cause to bless my
     mercy.

Tell. I shall remember it. I'd like to see
The apple I'm to shoot at.

Ges. Stay! Show me the basket! There —

Tell. You've picked the smallest one.

Ges. I know I have.

Tell. O do you? But you see
The color on't is dark. I'd have it light,
To see it better.

Ges. Take it as it is.
Thy skill will be the greater if thou hit'st it.

Tell. True, true! I did not think of that. I wonder
I did not think of that. Give me some chance

To save my boy! [*Throws away the apple with all his force.*]
                              I will not murder him,
If I can help it — for the honor of
The form thou wearest, if all the heart is gone.

 Ges. Well, choose thyself.

 Tell. Have I a friend among the lookers on?

 Verner. [*Rushing forward.*] Here, Tell!

 Tell. I thank thee, Verner!

He is a friend who runs out into a storm
To shake a hand with us. I must be brief.
When once the bow is bent, we cannot take
The shot too soon. Verner, whatever be
The issue of this hour, the common cause
Must not stand still. Let not tomorrow's sun
Set on the tyrant's banner! Verner! Verner!
The boy, the boy! Thinkest thou he hath the courage
To stand it?

 Ver. Yes.

 Tell. Does he tremble?

 Ver. No.

 Tell. Art sure?

 Ver. I am.

 Tell. How looks he?

 Ver. Clear and smilingly.

If you doubt it, look yourself.

 Tell. No — no — my friend;

To hear it is enough.

 Ver. He bears himself so much above his years —

 Tell. I know! I know.

 Ver. With constancy so modest.

 Tell. I was sure he would.

 Ver. And looks with such relying love

And reverence upon you —

 Tell. Man! Man! Man!

No more! Already I'm too much the father
To act the man. Verner, no more, my friend!
I would be flint — flint — flint. Don't make me feel

I'm not — do not mind me! Take the boy
And set him, Verner, with his back to me.
Set him upon his knees, and place this apple
Upon his head so that the stem may front me,
Thus, Verner. Charge him to keep steady. Tell him
I'll hit the apple. Verner, do all this
More briefly than I tell it thee.

    Ver. Come, Albert. [*Leading him out.*]
    Alb. May I not speak with him before I go?
    Ver. No.
    Alb. I would only kiss his hand.
    Ver. You must not.
    Alb. I must! I cannot go from him without.
    Ver. It is his will you should.
    Alb. His will is it?
I am content then — come.

    Tell. My boy! [*Holding out his arms to him.*]
    Alb. My father! [*Rushing into Tell's arms.*]
    Tell. If thou canst bear it, should not I? Go now,
My son, and keep in mind that I can shoot.
Go, boy. Be thou but steady, I will hit
The apple. Go! God bless thee — go. My bow!

                [*The bow is handed to him.*]
Thou wilt not fail thy master, wilt thou? Thou
Hast never failed him yet, old servant. No,
I'm sure of thee. I know thy honesty,
Thou art staunch — staunch. Let me see my quiver.

    Ges. Give him a single arrow.
    Tell. Do you shoot?
    Soldier. I do.
    Tell. Is it so you pick an arrow, friend?
The point you see is bent, the feather jagged. [*Breaks it.*]
That's all the use 'tis fit for.

    Ges. Let him have another.
    Tell. Why 'tis better than the first,
But yet not good enough for such an aim
As I'm to take. 'Tis heavy in the shaft;

I'll not shoot with it! [*Throws it away.*] Let me see my
      quiver.
Bring it! 'Tis not one arrow in a dozen
I'd take to shoot with at a dove, much less
A dove like that.

    Ges. It matters not.
Show him the quiver.

    Tell. See if the boy is ready.

                    [*Tell here hides an arrow under his vest.*]

    Ver. He is.

    Tell. I'm ready, too! Keep silent for
Heav'n's sake, and do not stir. And let me have
Your prayers — your prayers — and be my witnesses
That if his life's in peril from my hand,
'Tis only for the chance of saving it. [*To the people.*]

    Ges. Go on.

    Tell. I will.
O friends, for mercy's sake, keep motionless
And silent. [*Tell shoots — a shout of exultation bursts from
      the crowd. Tell's head drops on his bosom; he with
      difficulty supports himself upon his bow.*]

    Ver. [*Rushing in with Albert.*] Thy boy is safe, no hair of
      him is touched.

    Alb. Father, I'm safe. Your Albert's safe, dear Father.
Speak to me! Speak to me!

    Ver. He cannot, boy!

    Alb. You grant him life?

    Ges. I do.

    Alb. And we are free?

    Ges. You are. [*Crossing angrily behind.*]

    Alb. Thank heaven! Thank heaven!

    Ver. Open his vest,
And give him air. [*Albert opens his father's vest, and the ar-
      row drops. Tell starts — fixes his eye on Albert, and
      clasps him to his breast.*]

    Tell. My boy! My boy!

Ges. For what
Hid you that arrow in your breast? Speak, slave!
Tell. To kill thee, tyrant, had I slain my boy!

QUESTIONS. 1. In what kind of tone should you read, "True, I did not think of that," line 31? 2. Why? 3. Relate the whole story in your own language. 4. What was the fate of Gessler?

SPELL AND DEFINE. 1. reverence   2. staunch   3. briefly
4. constancy 5. vest 6. peril 7. issue 8. tyrant 9. banner 10. jagged
11. motionless

LESSON CXIV

The Vision of Mirza — Addison

RULE. When similar sounds come at the end of one word and at the beginning of the next word, they must not be blended into one.

EXAMPLE. Flowers soon fade. He addresse*th th*e understanding. Presumptuous sins. Time flies silently. A parent's sorrow.

On the fifth day of the moon, which according to the custom of my forefathers I always kept holy, after having washed myself and offered up my morning devotions, I ascended the high hills of Baghdad in order to pass the rest of the day in meditation and prayer. As I was here airing myself on the tops of the mountains, I fell into a profound contemplation on the vanity of human life. Passing from one thought to another, "Surely," said I, "man is but a shadow and life a dream."

While I was thus musing, I cast my eyes towards the summit of a rock that was not far from me, where I discovered one, in the habit of a shepherd, with a musical instrument in his hand. As I looked upon him he applied it to his lips and began to play upon it. The sound of it was exceedingly sweet and wrought into a variety of tunes that were inexpressibly melodious and altogether different from anything I had ever heard. They put me in mind of those heavenly airs that are played to the departed souls of good men upon their first arrival in paradise to wear out the impressions of the last agonies and qualify them for the pleasures of that happy place.

My heart melted away in secret raptures. I had been often told that the rock before me was the haunt of a Genius and that several who had passed by it had been entertained with music. But I never heard that the musician had before made himself visible. When he had raised my thoughts by those transporting airs which he played, to taste the pleasure of his conversation, as I looked upon him like one astonished, he beckoned to me and, by the waving of his hand, directed me to approach the place where he sat.

I drew near with that reverence which is due to a superior nature, and as my heart was entirely subdued by the captivating strains I had heard, I fell down at his feet and wept. The Genius smiled upon me with a look of compassion and affability that familiarized him to my imagination and, at once, dispelled all the fears and apprehensions with which I approached him. He lifted me from the ground and, taking me by the hand, said, "Mirza, I have heard thee in thy soliloquies. Follow me."

He then led me to the highest pinnacle of the rock and, placing me on the top of it, said, "Cast thy eyes eastward and tell me what thou seest." "I see," said I, "a huge valley and a prodigious tide of water rolling through it." "The valley that thou seest," said he, "is the valley of misery, and the tide of water that thou seest is part of the great tide of eternity." "What is the reason," said I, "that the tide I see rises out of a thick mist at one end and again loses itself in a thick mist at the other?"

"What thou seest," said he, "is that portion of eternity which is called time, measured out by the sun and reaching from the beginning of the world to its consummation. Examine now," said he, "this sea that is thus bounded with darkness at both ends, and tell me what thou discoverest in it." "I see a bridge," said I, "standing in the midst of the tide." "The bridge thou seest," said he, "is human life. Consider it attentively." Upon a more leisurely survey of it, I found that it consisted of threescore and ten entire arches, with several broken arches which, added to those that were entire, made up the number about a hundred.

As I was counting the arches, the Genius told me that the bridge consisted, at first, of a thousand arches but that a great flood swept away the rest and left the bridge in the ruinous condition I now beheld it. "But tell me further," said he, "what thou discoverest on it." "I see multitudes of people passing over it and a black cloud hanging on each end of it."

As I looked more attentively, I saw several of the passengers dropping through the bridge into the great tide that flowed underneath it. Upon further examination, I perceived there were innumerable trapdoors that lay concealed in the bridge. The passengers no sooner trod upon them but they fell through them into the tide and immediately disappeared. These hidden pitfalls were set very thick at the entrance of the bridge so that throngs of people no sooner broke through the cloud than many of them fell into them. They grew thinner towards the middle but multiplied and lay closer together towards the end of the arches that were entire.

There were indeed some persons — their number was very small — that continued a kind of hobbling march on the broken arches. They fell through, one after another, being quite tired and spent with so long a walk. I passed some time in the contemplation of this wonderful structure and the great variety of objects which it presented.

My heart was filled with a deep melancholy to see several dropping, unexpectedly, in the midst of mirth and jollity and catching by everything that stood by them to save themselves. Some were looking up towards the heavens in a thoughtful posture and, in the midst of a speculation, stumbled and fell out of sight. Multitudes were very busy in the pursuit of bubbles that glittered in their eyes and danced before them. Often, when they thought themselves within the reach of them, their footing failed and down they sank.

In this confusion of objects, I observed some with scimitars in their hands and others with lancets. They ran to and fro upon the bridge, thrusting several persons onto trapdoors which did not seem to lie in their way and which they might have escaped had they not been thus forced upon them.

The Genius, seeing me indulge myself in this melancholy prospect, told me I had dwelt long enough upon it. "Take thine eyes off the bridge," said he, "and tell me if thou yet seest anything thou dost not comprehend." Upon looking up, "What mean," said I, "those great flights of birds that are perpetually hovering about the bridge and settling upon it from time to time? I see vultures, Harpies, ravens, cormorants, and, among many other feathered creatures, several little winged boys that perch in great numbers upon the middle arches."

"These," said the Genius, "are Envy, Avarice, Superstition, Despair, and Love, with the like cares and passions that infest human life." I here fetched a deep sigh. "Alas!" said I, "man was made in vain! How he is given away to misery and mortality, tortured in life and swallowed up in death!" The Genius, being moved with compassion towards me, bid me quit so uncomfortable a prospect. "Look no more," said he, "on man in the first stage of his existence, in his setting out for eternity, but cast thine eye on that thick mist into which the tide bears the several generations of mortals that fall into it."

I directed my sight as I was ordered. Whether or not the good Genius strengthened my eyes with any supernatural force or simply dissipated part of the mist that was before too thick for the eye to penetrate, I cannot say. But I now saw the valley opening at the farther end and spreading forth into an immense ocean that had a huge rock of adamant running through the midst of it, dividing it into two equal parts. The clouds still rested on one half of it, insomuch that I could discover nothing in it, but the other appeared to me a vast ocean, planted with innumerable islands that were covered with fruits and flowers and interwoven with a thousand little shining seas that ran among them.

I could see persons dressed in glorious habits, with garlands upon their heads, passing among the trees, lying down by the sides of fountains, or resting on beds of flowers. I could hear a confused harmony of singing birds, falling waters, human voices, and musical instruments. Gladness grew in me upon the discovery of so delightful a scene. I wished for the wings of an eagle that I might fly away to those happy seats, but the Genius told me there was no passage to them except through the gates of death that I saw opening every moment upon the bridge.

"The islands," said he, "that lie so fresh and green before thee, with which the whole face of the ocean appears spotted as far as thou canst see, are more in number than the sands on the seashore. There are a myriad of islands behind those which thou here discoverest, reaching farther than thine eye or even thine imagination can extend itself. These are the mansions of good men after death who, according to the degrees and kinds of virtue in which they excelled, are distributed among these several islands, which abound with pleasures of different kinds and degrees suitable to the relishes and perfections of those who are settled in them. Every island is a paradise accommodated to its respective inhabitants.

"Are not these, O Mirza, habitations worth contending for? Does life appear miserable that gives thee opportunities of earning such a reward? Is death to be feared that will convey thee to so happy an existence? Think not man was made in vain, who has such an eternity reserved for him." I gazed with inexpressible pleasure on those happy islands. At length, said I, "Show me now, I beseech thee, the secrets that lie under those dark clouds that cover the ocean on the other side of the rock of adamant."

The Genius making me no answer, I turned about to address myself to him a second time, but I found that he had left me. I then turned again to the vision which I had been so long contemplating. Instead of the rolling tide, the arched bridge, and the happy islands, I saw nothing but the long, hollow valley of Baghdad with oxen, sheep, and camels grazing upon the sides of it.

QUESTIONS. 1. What is this kind of fiction called? 2. Why is the scene of almost all allegories laid in the East? 3. Why is instruction conveyed by parable or allegory more likely to be remembered than that communicated by any other method? 4. What is figured by the arches of the bridge? 5. What by the pitfalls? 6. Who are the persons with scimitars?

SPELL AND DEFINE. 1. ascended 2. contemplation 3. impressions 4. entertained   5. transporting   6. captivating   7. dispelled 8. apprehensions 9. pinnacle 10. consummation 11. arches 12. concealed 13. posture   14. strengthened   15. supernatural   16. interwoven 17. myriad 18. imagination 19. inexpressible

LESSON CXV

A Dirge — Croly

RULE. While each pupil reads, let the rest observe and then mention which syllables were pronounced wrong and which were omitted or indistinctly sounded.

"Earth to earth, and dust to dust!"
Here the evil and the just,
Here the youthful and the old,
Here the fearful and the bold,
Here the matron and the maid,
In one silent bed are laid;

Here the vassal and the king,
Side by side, lie withering;
Here the sword and scepter rust,
"Earth to earth, and dust to dust!"

Age on age shall roll along,
O'er this pale and mighty throng;
Those that wept them, those that weep,
All shall with these sleepers sleep.
Brothers, sisters of the worm,
Summer's sun, or winter's storm,
Song of peace, or battle's roar,
Ne'er shall break their slumbers more;
Death shall keep his sullen trust,
"Earth to earth, and dust to dust!"

But a day is coming fast,
Earth, thy mightiest and thy last!
It shall come in fear and wonder,
Heralded by trump and thunder;
It shall come in strife and toil;
It shall come in blood and spoil;
It shall come in empires' groans,
Burning temples, trampled thrones.
Then, ambition, rue thy lust!
"Earth to earth, and dust to dust!"

Then shall come the judgment sign;
In the east, the King shall shine;
Flashing from heav'n's golden gate,
Thousands, thousands round His state,
Spirits with the crown and plume;
Tremble, then, thou solemn tomb,
Heav'n shall open on our sight,
Earth be turned to living light,
Kingdom of the ransomed just!
"Earth to earth, and dust to dust!"

Then thy mount, Jerusalem,
Shall be gorgeous as a gem;
Then shall in the desert rise
Fruits of more than Paradise;
Earth by angel feet be trod,
One great garden of her God!
Till are dried the martyr's tears
Through a thousand glorious years.
Now in hope of Him we trust,
"Earth to earth, and dust to dust!"

QUESTIONS. 1. For what occasion is a dirge used?　2. What is inculcated in the first verse?　3. What is taught in the second verse? 4. What in the fourth?　5. What in the fifth?　6. What is the argument of the whole?

SPELL AND DEFINE. 1. vassal　2. heralded　3. ambition 4. ransomed　5. gorgeous　6. paradise　7. martyr

LESSON CXVI

Ladies' Headdresses — Spectator

RULE. Be careful and give a full sound to the vowels. Regard to this rule will correct the common flat, clipping, and uninteresting way in which many read.

EXERCISES. Prolong the italicized vowels: H*ai*l! h*o*ly l*i*ght. We pr*ai*se thee, *O* Lord God.

These names of the Deity are seldom pronounced with that full and solemn sound that is proper. *Lud* and *Law-ard* and *Gud* and *Gawd* are too frequently used instead of the proper sounds. If the pupil can learn to speak the three words *O Lord God* properly, it will be worth no little attention. Every pupil ought to be exercised on these words till he pronounces them properly and in a full and solemn tone.

There is not so variable a thing in nature as a lady's headdress. Within my own memory, I have known it rise and fall above thirty degrees. About ten years ago it shot up to a very great height, insomuch that the female part of our species were much taller than the men. The women were of such an enormous stature that we appeared as grasshoppers before them. At present the whole sex is in a manner dwarfed and shrunk into a race of beauties that seem almost another species.

I remember several ladies who were once very nearly seven feet high, that at present want some inches of five. How they came to be thus curtailed, I cannot learn. Whether the whole sex be at present under any penance which we know nothing of, or whether they have cast their head-dresses in order to surprise us with something of that kind which shall be entirely new, or whether some of the tallest of the sex, being too cunning for the rest, have contrived this method to make themselves appear sizeable, is still a secret. I find some are of the opinion that they are at present like trees newly lopped and pruned that will certainly sprout up and flourish with greater heads than before.

For my own part, as I do not love to be insulted by women who are taller than myself, I admire the sex much more in their present humiliation, which has reduced them to their natural dimensions, than when they had extended their persons and lengthened themselves out into formidable and gigantic figures. I am not for adding to the beautiful edifices of nature, not for raising any whimsical superstructure upon her plans. I must, therefore, repeat it, that I am highly pleased with the coiffure now in fashion and think it shows the good sense which at present very much reigns among the valuable part of the sex.

One may observe that women in all ages have taken more pains than men to adorn the outside of their heads. Indeed, I very much admire that those architects, who raise such wonderful structures out of ribbons, lace, and wire, have not been recorded for their respective inventions. It is certain that there have been as many orders in these kinds of buildings as in those which have been made of marble. Sometimes they rise in the shape of a pyramid, sometimes like a tower, and sometimes like a steeple.

In Juvenal's time, the building grew by several orders and stories, as he has very humorously described it.

> With curls on curls they build her head before,
> And mount it with a formidable tower.

But I do not remember, in any part of my reading, that the headdress aspired to such an extravagance as in the fourteenth century. It was built up in a couple of cones or spires which stood so excessively high on each side of the head that a woman who was but a pigmy without her headdress appeared like a colossus upon putting it on. Monsieur Paradin says "that these old-fashioned fontanges rose one ell above the head, that they were pointed like steeples and had long loose pieces of crepe fastened to the tops of them which were curiously fringed and hung down their backs like streamers."

The women might possibly have carried this Gothic building much higher had not a famous monk, Thomas Connecte, attacked it with great zeal and resolution. This holy man traveled from place to place to preach down this monstrous commode and succeeded so well in it that, as the magicians sacrificed their books to the flames upon the preaching of an apostle, many of the women threw down their headdresses in the middle of his sermon and made a bonfire of them within sight of the pulpit. He was so renowned as well for sanctity of his life as in his manner of preaching that he had often a congregation of twenty thousand people, the men placing themselves on the one side of the pulpit and the women on the other. They appeared, to use the similitude of an ingenious writer, like a forest of cedars with their heads reaching to the clouds.

He so warmed and animated the people against this

monstrous ornament that it lay under a kind of persecution. Whenever it appeared in public, it was pelted down by the rabble, who flung stones at the persons that wore it. Notwithstanding that this prodigy vanished while the preacher was among them, it began to appear again some months after his departure. To tell it in Monsieur Paradin's own words, "The women that, like snails in a fright, had drawn in their horns shot them out again as soon as the danger was over."

It is usually observed that a good reign is the only proper time for the making of laws against the exorbitance of power. In the same manner, an excessive headdress may be attacked the most effectually when the fashion is against it. I do, therefore, recommend this paper to my female readers by way of prevention.

I would desire the fair sex to consider how impossible it is for them to add anything that can be ornamental to what is already the masterpiece of nature. The head has the most beautiful appearance, as well as the highest station, in the human figure. Nature has laid out all her art in beautifying the face. She has touched it with vermilion, planted in it a double row of ivory, made it the seat of smiles and blushes, lighted it up and enlivened it with the brightness of the eyes, hung it on each side with curious organs of sense, given it airs and graces that cannot be described, and surrounded it with such a flowing shade of hair as sets all its beauties in the most agreeable light. In short, she seems to have designed the head as the cupola to the most glorious of her works, and when we load it with such a pile of supernumerary ornaments, we destroy the symmetry of the human figure and foolishly contrive to call off the eye from great and real beauties to childish gewgaws, ribbons, and bone lace.

QUESTIONS. 1. Do you know any of the authors who contributed to the *Spectator?*   2. In whose reign was it published?   3. May not the remarks in this lesson be with propriety applied to fashions in general? 4. Are we at liberty to disregard fashion entirely?

SPELL AND DEFINE.   1. degrees   2. enormous   3. curtailed 4. humiliation   5. edifices   6. coiffure   7. century   8. colossus   9. commode 10. similitude   11. masterpiece

LESSON CXVII

Childe Harold's Pilgrimage (Canto 4, Verses 178–79, 181–83) — Byron

RULE. Pronounce the consonant sounds very distinctly.

EXAMPLE. Prolong the consonant sounds that are italicized: *b*-old, *d*-eign, *f*-ather, *g*-ather, *j*-oy, *l*-ight, *m*-an, *n*-o, *q*-ueer, p-*r*-ay, *v*-ale, *w*-oe, *y*-ours, *z*-one, *h*-ang.

There is a pleasure in the pathless woods,
There is a rapture on the lonely shore,
There is society, where none intrudes,
By the deep Sea, and Music in its roar:
I love not Man the less, but Nature more,
From these our interviews, in which I steal
From all I may be, or have been before,
To mingle with the Universe, and feel
What I can ne'er express — yet can not all conceal.

Roll on, thou deep and dark blue Ocean — roll!
Ten thousand fleets sweep over thee in vain;
Man marks the earth with ruin — his control
Stops with the shore; — upon the watery plain
The wrecks are all thy deed, nor doth remain
A shadow of man's ravage, save his own,
When, for a moment, like a drop of rain,

He sinks into thy depths with bubbling groan —
Without a grave — unknelled, uncoffined, and unknown.
. . . .
The armaments which thunderstrike the walls
Of rock-built cities, bidding nations quake,
And Monarchs tremble in their Capitals,
The oak Leviathans, whose huge ribs make
Their clay creator the vain title take
Of Lord of thee, and Arbiter of War —
These are thy toys, and, as the snowy flake,
They melt into thy yeast of waves, which mar
Alike the Armada's pride, or spoils of Trafalgar.

Thy shores are empires, changed in all save thee —
Assyria — Greece — Rome — Carthage — what are
    they?
Thy waters washed them power while they were free,
And many a tyrant since; their shores obey
The stranger, slave, or savage; their decay
Has dried up realms to deserts: — not so thou,
Unchangeable save to thy wild waves' play;
Time writes no wrinkles on thine azure brow —
Such as Creation's dawn beheld, thou rollest now.

Thou glorious mirror, where the Almighty's form
Glasses itself in tempests; in all time,
Calm or convulsed — in breeze, or gale, or storm —
Icing the Pole, or in the torrid clime
Dark-heaving — boundless, endless, and sublime —
The image of Eternity — the throne
Of the Invisible; even from out thy slime
The monsters of the deep are made — each Zone
Obeys thee — thou goest forth, dread, fathomless, alone.

QUESTIONS. 1. What is the society which exists where none intrudes? 2. What is meant by "oak leviathans"? 3. How is the ocean the image of eternity?

SPELL AND DEFINE. 1. interviews   2. unknelled   3. thunderstrike
4. leviathans   5. arbiter   6. realms   7. azure

LESSON CXVIII

Reflections in Westminster Abbey — Addison

RULE. Be careful to speak little words such as *a, in, at, on, to, by* very distinctly and yet not to dwell on them so long as on the more important words.

When I am in a serious humor, I very often walk by myself in Westminster Abbey, where the gloominess of the place and the use to which it is applied, with the solemnity of the building and the condition of the people who lie in it, are apt to fill the mind with a kind of melancholy, or rather thoughtfulness, that is not disagreeable. I yesterday passed a whole afternoon in the churchyard, the cloisters, and the church amusing myself with the tombstones and inscriptions which I met with in those several regions of the dead.

Most of them recorded nothing else of the buried person but that he was born upon one day and died upon another, the whole history of his life being comprehended in these two circumstances that are common to all mankind. I could not but look upon those registers of existence, whether of brass or marble, as a kind of satire upon the departed persons, who had left no other memorial of themselves but that they were born and that they died.

Upon my going into the church, I entertained myself with the digging of a grave and saw, in every shovelful of it that was thrown up, the fragment of a bone or skull intermixed with a kind of fresh moldering earth that, sometime or other, had a place in the composition of a human body. Upon this, I began to consider what innumerable multitudes of people lay confused together under the pavements of that

ancient cathedral, how men and women, friends and enemies, priests and soldiers, monks and prebendaries were
crumbled among one another and blended together in the
same common mass — beauty, strength, and youth with old
age, weakness, and deformity lay undistinguished in the
same promiscuous heap of matter.

After having thus surveyed this great magazine of mortality as it was in the lump, I examined it more particularly
by the accounts which I found on several of the monuments
which are raised in every quarter of that ancient fabric.
Some of them were covered with such extravagant epitaphs
that, if it were possible for the dead person to be acquainted
with them, he would blush at the praises which his friends
have bestowed upon him. There are others so excessively
modest that they deliver the character of the person departed in Greek or Hebrew and by that means are not
understood once in a twelvemonth. In the poetical quarter, I
found that there were poets who had no monuments and
monuments which had no poets. I observed, indeed, that the
present war had filled the church with many of those unin-
habited monuments which had been erected to the memory
of persons whose bodies were perhaps buried in the plains of
Blenheim or in the bosom of the ocean.

I could not but be very much delighted with several
modern epitaphs, which are written with great elegance of
expression and justness of thought and which therefore do
honor to the living as well as the dead. As a foreigner is very
apt to conceive an idea of the ignorance or politeness of a
nation from the turn of their public monuments and inscriptions, they should be submitted to the perusal of men of
learning and genius before they are put into execution. Sir
Cloudesley Shovel's monument has very often given me
great offense. Instead of the brave rough English admiral
who was the distinguishing character of that plain gallant
man, he is represented on his tomb by the figure of a beau
dressed in a long periwig and reposing himself upon velvet
cushions under a canopy of state. The inscription is answer-

able to the monument, for instead of celebrating the many remarkable actions he had performed in the service of his country, it acquaints us only with the manner of his death, in which it was impossible for him to reap any honor.

The Dutch, whom we are apt to despise for want of genius, show an infinitely greater taste in their buildings and works of this nature than we meet with in those of our own country. The monuments of their admirals, which have been erected at the public expense, represent them like themselves and are adorned with rostral crowns and naval ornaments, with beautiful festoons of seaweed, shells, and coral.

I know that entertainments of this nature are apt to raise dark and dismal thoughts in timorous minds and gloomy imaginations, but for my own part, though I am always serious, I do not know what it is to be melancholy. I can, therefore, take a view of nature in her deep and solemn scenes with the same pleasure as in her most gay and delightful ones. By these means I can improve myself with objects which others consider with terror.

When I look upon the tombs of the great, every emotion of envy dies in me. When I read the epitaphs of the beautiful, every inordinate desire goes out. When I meet with the grief of parents upon a tombstone, my heart melts with compassion. When I see the tomb of parents themselves, I consider the vanity of grieving for those whom we must quickly follow. When I see kings lying by those who deposed them, when I consider rival wits placed side by side or the holy men that divided the world with their contests and disputes, I reflect with sorrow and astonishment on the little competitions, factions, and debates of mankind. When I read the several dates of the tombs, of some who died yesterday and some six hundred years ago, I consider that great day when we shall all of us be contemporaries and make our appearance together.

QUESTIONS. 1. To what use is Westminster Abbey applied? 2. What reflections are apt to arise in the mind on visiting such a place? 3. Are such reflections salutary?

SPELL AND DEFINE. 1. inscriptions   2. cloisters   3. fabric 4. epitaphs 5. genius 6. rostral 7. contemporaries

LESSON CXIX

The Journey of a Day: A Picture of Human Life — Dr. Johnson

RULE. Let the pupil stand at as great a distance from the teacher as possible and then try to read so loudly and distinctly that the teacher may hear each syllable.

Obidah, the son of Abensina, left the caravansary early in the morning and pursued his journey through the plains of Hindustan. He was fresh and vigorous with rest; he was animated with hope; he was incited by desire. He walked swiftly forward over the valleys and saw the hills gradually rising before him.

As he passed along, his ears were delighted with the morning song of the bird of paradise. He was fanned by the last flutters of the sinking breeze and sprinkled with dew by groves of spices. Sometimes he contemplated the towering height of the oak, monarch of the hills, and sometimes caught the gentle fragrance of the primrose, eldest daughter of the spring. All his senses were gratified and all care was banished from his heart.

Thus he went on till the sun approached its meridian and the increasing heat preyed upon his strength. He then looked round about him for some more commodious path. He saw, on his right hand, a grove that seemed to wave its shades as a sign of invitation. He entered it and found the coolness and verdure irresistibly pleasant. He did not, however, forget whither he was traveling but found a narrow way, bordered with flowers, which appeared to have the same direction with the main road. Thus he was pleased that, by this happy experiment, he had found means to unite pleasure with business and to gain the rewards of diligence without suffering its fatigues.

Therefore, he still continued to walk for a time without the least remission of his ardor, except that he was sometimes tempted to stop by the music of the birds, whom the heat had assembled in the shade, and sometimes amused himself with plucking the flowers that covered the banks on either side or the fruits that hung upon the branches. At last, the green path began to decline from its first tendency and to wind among the hills and thickets, cooled with fountains and murmuring with waterfalls.

Here Obidah paused for a time and began to consider whether it were any longer safe to forsake the known and common track. Remembering that the heat was now in its greatest violence and that the plain was dusty and uneven, he resolved to pursue the new path, which he supposed only to make a few meanders in compliance with the varieties of the ground and to end, at last, in the common road.

Having thus calmed his solicitude, he renewed his pace, though he suspected he was not gaining ground. This uneasiness of his mind inclined him to lay hold on every new object and give way to every sensation that might soothe or divert him. He listened to every echo, he mounted every hill for a fresh prospect, he turned aside to every cascade and pleased himself with tracing the course of a gentle river that rolled among the trees and watered a large region with innumerable caracoles.

In these amusements the hours passed away unaccounted. His deviations had perplexed his memory, and he knew not towards what point to travel. He stood pensive and confused, afraid to go forward lest he should go wrong, yet conscious that the time of loitering was now past. While he was thus tortured with uncertainty, the sky was overspread with clouds, the day vanished from before him, and a sudden tempest gathered round his head.

He was now roused by his danger to a quick and painful remembrance of his folly. He now saw how happiness is lost when ease is consulted. He lamented the unmanly impatience that prompted him to seek shelter in the grove and despised the petty curiosity that led him on from trifle to trifle. While he was thus reflecting, the air grew blacker and a clap of thunder broke his meditation.

He now resolved to do what remained yet in his power — to tread back the ground which he had passed and try to find some issue where the wood might open into the plain. He prostrated himself upon the ground and commended his life to the Lord of nature. He rose with confidence and tranquility and pressed on with his saber in his hand, for the beasts of the desert were in motion. On every hand were heard the mingled howls of rage, fear, ravage, and expiration. All the horrors of darkness and solitude surrounded him. The winds roared in the woods and the torrents tumbled from the hills.

Thus, forlorn and distressed, he wandered through the wild without knowing whither he was going or whether he was every moment drawing nearer to safety or to destruction. At length, not fear but labor began to overcome him. His breath grew short, his knees trembled, and he was on the point of lying down, in resignation to his fate, when he beheld, through the brambles, the glimmer of a taper. He advanced towards the light, and finding that it proceeded from the cottage of a hermit, he called humbly at the door and obtained admission. The old man set before him such provisions as he had collected for himself, on which Obidah fed with eagerness and gratitude.

When the repast was over, the hermit said, "Tell me by what chance thou hast been brought hither. I have been now twenty years an inhabitant of this wilderness, in which I never saw a man before." Obidah then related the occurrences of his journey without any concealment or palliation.

"Son," said the hermit, "let the errors and follies, the dangers and escapes of this day sink deep into thy heart. Remember, my son, that human life is the journey of a day. We rise in the morning of youth, full of vigor and full of expectation; we set forward with spirit and hope, with gaiety and with diligence, and travel on awhile in the straight road of piety towards the mansions of rest. In a short time we remit our fervor and endeavor to find some mitigation of our duty and some more easy means of obtaining the same end.

"We then relax our vigor and resolve no longer to be terrified with crimes at a distance but rely upon our own constancy and venture to approach what we resolve never to touch. We thus enter the bowers of ease and repose in the shades of security. Here the heart softens and vigilance subsides. We are then willing to inquire whether another advance cannot be made and whether we may not, at least, turn our eyes upon the gardens of pleasure. We approach them with scruple and hesitation. We enter them, but enter timorous and trembling and always hope to pass through them without losing the road of virtue which we, for awhile, keep in our sight and to which we propose to return.

"But temptation succeeds temptation and one compliance prepares us for another. We, in time, lose the happiness of innocence and solace our disquiet with sensual gratifications. By degrees we let fall the remembrance of our original intention and quit the only adequate object of rational desire. We entangle ourselves in business, immerge ourselves in luxury, and rove through the labyrinths of inconstancy until the darkness of old age begins to invade us and disease and anxiety obstruct our way. We then look back upon our lives with horror, with sorrow, and with repentance. We wish, but too often vainly wish, that we had not forsaken the paths of virtue.

"Happy are they, my son, who shall learn from thy example not to despair but shall remember that, though the day is past and their strength is wasted, there yet remains one effort to be made — that reformation is never hopeless nor sincere endeavors ever unassisted, that the wanderer may at length return after all his errors, and that he who implores strength and courage from above shall find danger and difficulty give way before him. Go now, my son, to thy repose, commit thyself to the care of Omnipotence, and when the morning calls again to toil, begin anew thy journey and thy life."

QUESTIONS. 1. What type of composition is this lesson? 2. Repeat the chief incidents of the story, with their appropriate moral. 3. Is it because we have but few men who are capable of becoming great that so few distinguish themselves?

SPELL AND DEFINE. 1. caravansary   2. animated   3. deviations
4. loitering   5. tranquility   6. resignation   7. timorous   8. labyrinths
9. gratifications

LESSON CXX

Morning — Anonymous

RULE. In reading poetry that does not rhyme, there need be no pause at the end of lines terminating with unimportant words, except when the sense requires it.

How lovely is the morn!
Earth wakes like a young maiden from her sleep,
And smiles. The playful breeze, that all night long
Has sported with thy flowers, and sipped at will
Their balmy breath, shakes freshness from its wings,
And greets alike the fevered brow of care,
Roused from his broken slumbers, and the cheek
Of cherub youth, which, sleeping, smiles as though
It dreamed of paradise. It visits e'en
The crowded city and breaks in upon
The miser, gloating o'er his thrice-told heap

Of dross, a visitor unwelcome, for
Its purity reproves his heart *impure*.
Then perchance it greets the fading cheek
And wasted form of one whose step was once
As light and joyous as the fairies' trip
In moonlit dance. In her ear it whispers
Hopes of happier days, and as it leaves her,
Sighs in sorrow for her fate, whose hopes
Before its next return, may all decay,
And nought be left behind but the sad wreck
Of all that once was lovely.

                      Now the sun
Appears, and with his golden beams illumes
The mountain's brow with hues of heaven, and wakes
The bustling earth from dull inaction. Now
The haunts of men once more are seen teeming
With life, and birds and beasts once more rejoice
In their renewed existence. *These* again
With joyous twitter, seem to chirp their praise;
Those, in their various ways, their gratitude
Express, while thankless man, with eye scarce turned
To heaven, once more renews his toil, nor thinks
Of Him to whom he owes his life renewed,
His health preserved, his friends still true, and all
The countless blessings which have made this earth
A paradise.

QUESTIONS. 1. What is the character of a miser?   2. What does "told" signify, in line 11? 3. Who were the "fairies"? 4. What does "these" refer to in line 29? 5. "Those," in line 31?

SPELL AND DEFINE. 1. paradise   2. gloating   3. perchance
4. illumes 5. teeming 6. twitter

LESSON CXXI

Woe to Ariel — Isaiah 29:1–14

Woe to Ariel, to Ariel,
The city where David dwelt!
Add ye year to year;
Let them kill sacrifices.
Yet I will distress Ariel,
And there shall be heaviness and sorrow:
And it shall be unto me as Ariel.
And I will camp against thee round about,
And will lay siege against thee with a mount,
And I will raise forts against thee.
And thou shalt be brought down, and shalt speak out of
   the ground,
And thy speech shall be low out of the dust,
And thy voice shall be, as of one that hath a familiar
   spirit, out of the ground,
And thy speech shall whisper out of the dust.
Moreover the multitude of thy strangers shall be like
   small dust,
And the multitude of the terrible ones shall be as chaff
   that passeth away:
Yea, it shall be at an instant suddenly.
Thou shalt be visited of the Lord of hosts
With thunder, and with earthquake, and great noise,
With storm and tempest,
And the flame of devouring fire.
And the multitude of all the nations
That fight against Ariel,
Even all that fight against her and her munition, and
   that distress her,
Shall be as a dream of a night vision.
It shall even be

As when an hungry man dreameth, and, behold, he
    eateth;
But he awaketh, and his soul is empty:
Or as when a thirsty man dreameth, and, behold, he
    drinketh;
But he awaketh, and, behold, he is faint, and his soul
    hath appetite:
So shall the multitude of all the nations be,
That fight against mount Zion.

Stay yourselves, and wonder;
Cry ye out, and cry:
They are drunken, but not with wine;
They stagger, but not with strong drink.
For the Lord hath poured out upon you the spirit of deep
    sleep,
And hath closed your eyes:
The prophets and your rulers, the seers hath he covered.
And the vision of all is become unto you
As the words of a book that is sealed,
Which men deliver to one that is learned,
Saying, Read this, I pray thee:
And he saith, I cannot; for it is sealed:
And the book is delivered to him that is not learned,
Saying, Read this, I pray thee:
And he saith, I am not learned.
    Wherefore the Lord said,
Forasmuch as this people draw near me with their
    mouth,
And with their lips do honor me,
But have removed their heart far from me,
And their fear toward me is taught by the precept of
    men:
Therefore, behold, I will proceed to do a marvelous work
    among this people,
Even a marvelous work and a wonder:
For the wisdom of their wise men shall perish,

And the understanding of their prudent men shall be
hid.

LESSON CXXII

The Proverbs of Solomon — Proverbs 10

1 The Proverbs of Solomon. A wise son maketh a glad
father: but a foolish son is the heaviness of his mother.

2 Treasures of wickedness profit nothing: but righteousness delivereth from death.

3 The Lord will not suffer the soul of the righteous to
famish: but he casteth away the substance of the wicked.

4 He becometh poor that dealeth with a slack hand: but
the hand of the diligent maketh rich.

5 He that gathereth in summer is a wise son: but he that
sleepeth in harvest is a son that causeth shame.

6 Blessings are upon the head of the just: but violence
covereth the mouth of the wicked.

7 The memory of the just is blessed: but the name of the
wicked shall rot.

8 The wise in heart will receive commandments: but a
prating fool shall fall.

9 He that walketh uprightly walketh surely: but he that
perverteth his ways shall be known.

10 He that winketh with the eye causeth sorrow: but a
prating fool shall fall.

11 The mouth of a righteous man is a well of life: but
violence covereth the mouth of the wicked.

12 Hatred stirreth up strifes: but love covereth all sins.

13 In the lips of him that hath understanding wisdom is
found: but a rod is for the back of him that is void of
understanding.

14 Wise men lay up knowledge: but the mouth of the foolish is near destruction.

15 The rich man's wealth is his strong city: the destruction of the poor is their poverty.

16 The labor of the righteous tendeth to life: the fruit of the wicked to sin.

17 He is in the way of life that keepeth instruction: but he that refuseth reproof erreth.

18 He that hideth hatred with lying lips, and he that uttereth a slander, is a fool.

19 In the multitude of words there wanteth not sin: but he that refraineth his lips is wise.

20 The tongue of the just is as choice silver: the heart of the wicked is little worth.

21 The lips of the righteous feed many: but fools die for want of wisdom.

22 The blessing of the Lord, it maketh rich, and he addeth no sorrow with it.

23 It is as sport to a fool to do mischief: but a man of understanding hath wisdom.

24 The fear of the wicked, it shall come upon him: but the desire of the righteous shall be granted.

25 As the whirlwind passeth, so is the wicked no more: but the righteous is an everlasting foundation.

26 As vinegar to the teeth, and as smoke to the eyes, so is the sluggard to them that send him.

27 The fear of the Lord prolongeth days: but the years of the wicked shall be shortened.

28 The hope of the righteous shall be gladness: but the expectation of the wicked shall perish.

29 The way of the Lord is strength to the upright: but destruction shall be to the workers of iniquity.

30 The righteous shall never be removed: but the wicked shall not inhabit the earth.

31 The mouth of the just bringeth forth wisdom: but the froward tongue shall be cut out.

32 The lips of the righteous know what is acceptable: but the mouth of the wicked speaketh frowardness.

LESSON CXXIII

Comfort Ye My People — Isaiah 40

Comfort ye, comfort ye my people,
Saith your God.
Speak ye comfortably to Jerusalem, and cry unto her,
That her warfare is accomplished,
That her iniquity is pardoned:
For she hath received of her Lord's hand
Double for all her sins.

The voice of him that crieth in the wilderness,
    Prepare ye the way of the Lord,
    Make straight in the desert a highway for our God.
    Every valley shall be exalted,
    And every mountain and hill shall be made low:
    And the crooked shall be made straight,
    And the rough places plain:
    And the glory of the Lord shall be revealed,
    And all flesh shall see it together:
    For the mouth of the Lord hath spoken it.
The voice said, Cry. And he said, What shall I cry?
    All flesh is grass,
    And all the goodliness thereof is as the flower of the field:
    The grass withereth, the flower fadeth;
    Because the spirit of the Lord bloweth upon it:
    Surely the people is grass.
    The grass withereth, the flower fadeth:
    But the word of our God shall stand for ever.
        O Zion, that bringest good tidings, get thee up into
            the high mountain;

O Jerusalem, that bringest good tidings,
Lift up thy voice with strength;
Lift it up, be not afraid;
Say unto the cities of Judah, Behold your God!
Behold, the Lord God will come with strong hand,
And his arm shall rule for him:
Behold, his reward is with him,
And his work before him.
He shall feed his flock like a shepherd:
He shall gather the lambs with his arm,
And carry them in his bosom,
And shall gently lead those that are with young.
Who hath measured the waters in the hollow of his hand,
And meted out heaven with the span,
And comprehended the dust of the earth in a measure,
And weighed the mountains in scales,
And the hills in a balance?
Who hath directed the Spirit of the Lord,
Or being his counselor hath taught him?
With whom took He counsel, and who instructed him,
And taught him in the path of judgment,
And taught him knowledge,
And showed to him the way of understanding?
Behold, the nations are as a drop of a bucket,
And are counted as the small dust of the balance:
Behold, he taketh up the isles as a very little thing.
And Lebanon is not sufficient to burn,
Nor the beasts thereof sufficient for a burnt offering.
All nations before him are as nothing;
And they are counted to him less than nothing, and vanity.
    To whom then will ye liken God?
Or what likeness will ye compare unto him?
The workman melteth a graven image
And the goldsmith spreadeth it over with gold,
And casteth silver chains.
He that is so impoverished that he hath no oblation
Chooseth a tree that will not rot;

He seeketh unto him a cunning workman to prepare a
    graven image, that shall not be moved.
Have ye not known? have ye not heard?
Hath it not been told you from the beginning?
Have ye not understood from the foundations of the
    earth?
It is he that sitteth upon the circle of the earth,
And the inhabitants thereof are as grasshoppers;
That stretcheth out the heavens as a curtain,
And spreadeth them out as a tent to dwell in:
That bringeth the princes to nothing;
He maketh the judges of the earth as vanity.
Yea, they shall not be planted;
Yea, they shall not be sown;
Yea, their stock shall not take root in the earth:
And He shall also blow upon them, and they shall
    wither,
And the whirlwind shall take them away as stubble.
    To whom then will ye liken me,
Or shall I be equal?
Saith the Holy One.
Lift up your eyes on high, and behold
Who hath created these things,
That bringeth out their host by number:
He calleth them all by names by the greatness of his
    might, for that he is strong in power;
Not one faileth.
    Why sayest thou, O Jacob, and speakest, O Israel,
My way is hid from the Lord,
And my judgment is passed over from my God?
Hast thou not known? hast thou not heard,
That the everlasting God, the Lord,
The Creator of the ends of the earth,
Fainteth not, neither is weary?
There is no searching of his understanding.
He giveth power to the faint;
And to them that have no might he increaseth strength.

Even the youths shall faint and be weary,
And the young men shall utterly fall:
But they that wait upon the Lord shall renew their
    strength;
They shall mount up with wings as eagles;
They shall run, and not be weary;
And they shall walk, and not faint.

LESSON CXXIV

The Celestial City — Revelation 19:11–22:5

And I saw heaven opened, and behold a white horse; and he that sat upon him was called Faithful and True, and in righteousness he doth judge and make war. His eyes were as a flame of fire, and on his head were many crowns; and he had a name written, that no man knew, but he himself. And he was clothed with a vesture dipped in blood: and his name is called The Word of God. And the armies which were in heaven followed him upon white horses, clothed in fine linen, white and clean. And out of his mouth goeth a sharp sword, that with it he should smite the nations; and he shall rule them with a rod of iron: and he treadeth the winepress of the fierceness and wrath of Almighty God. He hath on his vesture and on his thigh a name written, KING OF KINGS, AND LORD OF LORDS.

And I saw an angel standing in the sun; and he cried with a loud voice, saying to all the fowls that fly in the midst of heaven, Come and gather yourselves together unto the supper of the great God; that ye may eat the flesh of kings, and the flesh of captains, and the flesh of mighty men, and the flesh of horses, and of them that sit on them, and the flesh of all men, both free and bond, both small and great.

And I saw the beast, and the kings of the earth, and their armies, gathered together to make war against him that sat on the horse, and against his army. And the beast was taken, and with him the false prophet that wrought miracles before him, with which he deceived them that had received the mark of the beast, and them that worshipped his image. These both were cast alive into a lake of fire burning with brimstone. And the remnant were slain by the sword of him that sat upon the horse, which sword proceeded out of his mouth: and all the fowls were filled with their flesh.

And I saw an angel come down from heaven, having the key of the bottomless pit and a great chain in his hand. And he laid hold on the dragon, that old serpent, which is the Devil, and Satan, and bound him a thousand years, and cast him into the bottomless pit, and shut him up, and set a seal upon him, that he should deceive the nations no more, till the thousand years should be fulfilled: and after that he must be loosed a little season.

And I saw thrones, and they that sat upon them, and judgment was given unto them: and I saw the souls of them that were beheaded for the witness of Jesus, and for the word of God, and which had not worshipped the beast, neither his image, neither had received his mark upon their foreheads, or in their hands; and they lived and reigned with Christ a thousand years. But the rest of the dead lived not again until the thousand years were finished. This is the first resurrection. Blessed and holy is he that hath part in the first resurrection: on such the second death hath no power, but they shall be priests of God and of Christ, and shall reign with him a thousand years.

And when the thousand years are expired, Satan shall be loosed out of his prison, and shall go out to deceive the nations which are in the four quarters of the earth, Gog and Magog, to gather them together to battle: the number of whom is as the sand of the sea. And they went up on the breadth of the earth, and compassed the camp of the saints about, and the beloved city: and fire came down from God out of heaven, and devoured them. And the devil that deceived them was cast into the lake of fire and brimstone, where the beast and the false prophet are, and shall be tormented day and night for ever and ever.

And I saw a great white throne, and him that sat on it, from whose face the earth and the heaven fled away; and there was found no place for them. And I saw the dead, small and great, stand before God; and the books were opened: and another book was opened, which is the book of life: and the dead were judged out of those things which were written in the books, according to their works. And the sea gave up the dead which were in it; and death and hell delivered up the dead which were in them: and they were judged every man according to their works. And death and hell were cast into the lake of fire. This is the second death. And whosoever was not found written in the book of life was cast into the lake of fire.

And I saw a new heaven and a new earth: for the first heaven and the first earth were passed away; and there was no more sea. I John saw the holy city, new Jerusalem, coming down from God out of heaven, prepared as a bride adorned for her husband. And I heard a great voice out of heaven saying, Behold, the tabernacle of God is with men, and he will dwell with them, and they shall be his people, and God himself shall be with them, and be their God. And God shall wipe away all tears from their eyes; and there shall be no more death, neither sorrow, nor crying, neither shall there be any more pain: for the former things are passed away.

And he that sat upon the throne said, Behold, I make all things new. He said unto me, Write: for these words are true and faithful. And he said unto me, It is done. I am Alpha and Omega, the beginning and the end. I will give unto him that is athirst of the fountain of the water of life freely. He that overcometh shall inherit all things; and I will be his God, and he shall be my son. But the fearful, and unbelieving, and the abominable, and murderers, and whoremongers, and sorcerers, and idolaters, and all liars, shall have their part in the lake which burneth with fire and brimstone: which is the second death.

And there came unto me one of the seven angels which had the seven vials full of the seven last plagues, and talked with me, saying, Come hither, I will show thee the bride, the Lamb's wife. And he carried me away in the spirit to a great and high mountain, and showed me that great city, the holy Jerusalem, descending out of heaven from God, having the glory of God: and her light was like unto a stone most precious, even like a jasper stone, clear as crystal; and had a wall great and high, and had twelve gates, and at the gates twelve angels, and names written thereon, which are the names of the twelve tribes of the children of Israel: on the east three gates; on the north three gates; on the south three gates; and on the west three gates. And the wall of the city had twelve foundations, and in them the names of the twelve apostles of the Lamb.

And he that talked with me had a golden reed to measure the city, and the gates thereof, and the wall thereof. And the city lieth foursquare, and the length is as large as the breadth: and he measured the city with the reed, twelve thousand furlongs. The length and the breadth and the height of it are equal. And he measured the wall thereof, a hundred and forty and four cubits, according to the measure of a man, that is, of the angel. And the building of the wall of it was of jasper: and the city was pure gold, like unto clear glass. And the foundations of the wall of the city were garnished with all manner of precious stones. The first foundation was jasper; the second, sapphire; the third, a chalcedony; the fourth, an emerald; the fifth, sardonyx; the sixth, sardius; the seventh, chrysolite; the eighth, beryl; the ninth, a topaz; the tenth, a chrysoprasus; the eleventh, a jacinth; the twelfth, an amethyst. And the twelve gates were twelve pearls; every several gate was of one pearl: and the street of the city was pure gold, as it were transparent glass.

I saw no temple therein: for the Lord God Almighty and

the Lamb are the temple of it. And the city had no need of the sun, neither of the moon, to shine in it: for the glory of God did lighten it, and the Lamb is the light thereof. And the nations of them which are saved shall walk in the light of it: and the kings of the earth do bring their glory and honor into it. And the gates of it shall not be shut at all by day: for there shall be no night there. And they shall bring the glory and honor of the nations into it. There shall in no wise enter into it any thing that defileth, neither whatsoever worketh abomination, or maketh a lie: but they which are written in the Lamb's book of life.

And he showed me a pure river of water of life, clear as crystal, proceeding out of the throne of God and of the Lamb. In the midst of the street of it, and on either side of the river, was there the tree of life, which bare twelve manner of fruits, and yielded her fruit every month: and the leaves of the tree were for the healing of the nations. And there shall be no more curse: but the throne of God and of the Lamb shall be in it; and his servants shall serve him: and they shall see his face; and his name shall be in their foreheads. And there shall be no night there; and they need no candle, neither light of the sun; for the Lord giveth them light: and they shall reign for ever and ever.

LESSON CXXV

America — National Hymn — Mason's Sacred Harp

(This beautiful lesson is found, set to music, in *Mason's Sacred Harp,* a new collection of hymn tunes, sacred songs, and anthems.)

My country, 'tis of thee,
Sweet land of liberty,
    Of thee I sing;
Land where my fathers died,

Land of the pilgrims' pride,
From every mountain side
   Let freedom ring.

My native country, thee,
Land of the noble free,
   Thy name I love;
I love thy rocks and rills,
Thy woods and templed hills;
My heart with rapture thrills
   Like that above.

Let music swell the breeze,
And ring from all the trees
   Sweet Freedom's song;
Let mortal tongues awake,
Let all that breathe partake,
Let rocks their silence break,
   The sound prolong.

Our fathers' God, to Thee,
Author of liberty,
   To Thee we sing;
Long may our land be bright
With Freedom's holy light;
Protect us by Thy might,
   Great God, our King.